ETHICAL
STANDARDS

of the
AMERICAN
EDUCATIONAL
RESEARCH
ASSOCIATION
Cases and Commentary

ETHICAL STANDARDS

of the

AMERICAN
EDUCATIONAL
RESEARCH
ASSOCIATION

Cases and Commentary

Kenneth A. Strike, Chair
University of Maryland

Melissa S. Anderson
University of Minnesota

Randall Curren
University of Rochester

Tyll van Geel
University of Rochester

Ivor Pritchard
U.S. Department of Education

Emily Robertson
Syracuse University

AMERICAN EDUCATIONAL RESEARCH ASSOCIATION
WASHINGTON, D.C.

Published by
American Educational Research Association
1230 17th Street, NW
Washington, D.C. 20036-3078

Printed in the United States of America

ISBN: 0-935302-28-X

CONTENTS

PREFACE

The American Educational Research Association's (AERA) code of ethics, **Ethical Standards of the American Educational Research Association**, *was written by an ad hoc committee, appointed by AERA President Phil Jackson and chaired by Professor Nel Noddings of Stanford University. Other ad hoc committee members were Ron Glass, Egon Guba, Valerie Janesick, Betty Sichel, Ken Strike, and Merlin Wittrock. Legal consultant was Louis Fischer. The Code was adopted by AERA in June 1992.*

One issue discussed by the "Noddings Committee" was that of implementation of the standards. It became apparent that it was both impossible and inappropriate for AERA to enforce its standards through any quasi-judicial mechanism. AERA lacks the means to investigate and adjudicate the complex issues of fact and interpretation that might arise. It has no credible penalties. Moreover, to attempt enforcement would bring AERA into jurisdictional conflict with universities, government agencies, and other professional societies. Thus, the Noddings Committee recommended that AERA take an educational approach to implement the standards.

AERA has accepted this approach. Its publication of the **Standards** contains a note that claims that the standards were developed and adopted as *an educational document, to stimulate collegial debate, and to evoke voluntary compliance by moral persuasion.**

In the spring of 1994, then-president Ann Brown appointed another committee, chaired by Professor Kenneth Strike of Cornell University, to develop strategy to further these objectives. This committee recommended that AERA publish a book that would facilitate the educational approach that AERA had decided to take in implementing the standards. This volume is the result of that decision.

An educational approach to the standards requires at least three things. First, it requires the communication and clarification of the central intentions of the standards. This is especially important for new scholars who may lack experience with the ethical norms and ethical problems that can arise in the research process. Their need is for reasonably clear characterizations of the point of the standards and for exemplars of cases to which they paradigmatically apply.

Second, since any set of ethical standards produces tensions and conflicts between its provisions as well as cases where the application of its provisions are unclear or problematic, there should be an opportunity to explore and discuss the complexities and ambiguities in the standards.

Finally, there are larger issues that are raised by codes of ethics. Writing a code of ethics assumes that ethical obligations are amenable to codification. It must be, to a degree, possible to describe obligations and responsibilities abstractly and generally apart from a detailed knowledge of the circumstances in which the code is applied. The view that ethical obligations and responsibilities can be asserted without a context is a view that some would deny. A code of ethics assumes that some ethical claims are reasonable and objective and also assumes the possibility of ethical knowledge. This is also controversial. While a code of ethics is a means to promote a form of professional accountability, codes may have other uses. Codes may reduce ethical expectations to the lowest common standard to which people can agree; or they may be used to argue that, since the members of a profession have a mechanism for policing their ethics, they are not accountable to people outside of the guild. Thus, codes are not uncontroversial, and some opportunity to discuss the broader role of codes is needed.

These three tasks are reflected in the organization of this book. After this introductory discussion, we take up the six major parts of the code. In each of these sections, we describe a rationale for the code's provisions and illustrate, through cases, how the code might be applied. Here the purposes are to seek understanding and to assist interpretation through explanation and illustration.

While we include illustrations of how the standards might be applied where misunderstanding is possible or even likely and explore some complexities and problem areas, we also try to avoid highly complicated or controversial assertions or illustrations. This is not always possible.

---

* All *italicized* passages are quotations from **Ethical Standards of the American Educational Research Association**.

In ethics, little is ever quite so obvious that reasonable people cannot disagree. Moreover, there are places in the standards that seem to us ambiguous or that have issues that are not resolved by the language. Where this is the case, we usually point it out. Nevertheless, in these discussions, our main purpose is to explain and illustrate by emphasizing central principles and clear application to cases.

We follow each exposition of the standards with several hard cases. Ethical claims expressed in AERA's **Standards** may conflict. When this happens, a balance is needed between competing moral responsibilities or duties. Furthermore, while there may be clear cases of how the standards are applied, there will also be borderline or ambiguous cases. Resolving such cases requires the capacity for discernment in moral complexity. These are cases where reasonable people may certainly disagree. Such cases, especially, require discussion, dialogue, and openness to a diversity of views. Dialogue is a way of getting the argument out on the table, refining it, criticizing it, listening to different perspectives on issues, and struggling to a consensus or resolution, where possible, about difficult issues.

Participation in such discussions serves an educational purpose. It helps develop a more refined understanding of what is at stake in the standards, and it helps develop the argumentative skills and moral sensitivities needed to develop wisdom and judgment in the face of complexity. Thus, we develop a number of hard cases with some questions and comments designed to facilitate their discussion. While we provide some discussion of these cases, we do not always attempt an authoritative resolution of them.

The final section of this volume, an essay by Martha McCarthy, a lawyer, and Barry Bull, a philosopher, raises issues about the interpretation of codes, their legitimate use and their interaction with the law. This essay is intended to illuminate the role of the codes of ethics in the life of professional societies. It is intended to promote understanding and discussion of the issues the codes raise and of their legitimate and illegitimate uses.

We need finally to comment on the "voice" that speaks in our work. Although the material was written by a committee, we regard ourselves as speaking with different voices in different parts of this volume. The voice in the interpretive sections is, in one sense, largely the voice of AERA. Here we were doing our best to faithfully and carefully explain and interpret AERA's standards. Moreover, we have submitted this document to review by AERA according to an agreed-upon plan and have made revisions where appropriate. This is a consensual document. Its voice is that of AERA saying as well and as clearly as it can, "This is what we mean."

However, it is also the case that the voice of the authors remains to a degree that will likely be quite noticeable to the reader. In drafting this material, the "Strike Committee" began by agreeing to the rough shape of a format, and then, after working through some examples to achieve a sense of common purpose, the Committee divided the parts of the **Standards** among its members.

This strategy produced less commonality of style and approach than we had intended. The consequence is that you will find case material written with different styles and approaches. Some of us honed in on what seemed overarching issues and produced cases that were not always tightly linked to the language of particular standards. We tried to find and illustrate the main ideas in a standard. Others worked through each standard idea by idea and sometimes line by line. We tried to exegete the text. Sometimes these different approaches reflect differences between the standards themselves. Some of the standards seem to express broad ideals (**Standard 1** of **Part I** is an example.) Others contain language that is similar to current law. (**Standard 11** of **Part I** is an example.) The standards of **Part VI** emphasize the nurturance of students. Here the code begins to add a concern for care to its concern for duties and prescriptions. The varied content of these different standards seems to require different expository approaches.

In other cases, however, differences in approach seem to reflect the initial drafters' sense of how to do the task. Here we have reviewed each other's material and have discussed and resolved matters about which we disagree. (Surprisingly, there has been little substantive disagreement about the meaning and substance of the standards.) We have also agreed to have at least one case per standard and that our discussions of cases should appeal to the language of the standards. However, we have also decided, after a little soul searching, that some diversity of style and approach is as much of a virtue as a vice.

While our intent is to interpret the standards, this task is not analogous to the role that case law has in interpreting the Constitution or that regulations play in making statutes clearer and more detailed. AERA's standards are viewed by AERA as an educational device and a means to promote discussion. They neither carry the force of law nor are they meant to be enforced.

Thus, our task does not require the uniformity of style that might be needed for an exposition that carries some formal authority with it. Our work is rather to convey a sense of the standards' point, display some paradigmatic cases of how they should be understood, point out some issues that are raised but not resolved, and suggest how these more complex issues might be thought about.

This is an educational, not a legal, task. Its intent is to initiate novices into a discourse. This aim is consistent with some diversity of style and approach. Moreover, we think these different styles have their own virtues because readers might profit from seeing that different people can think about these matters conscientiously and usefully in different ways.

Indeed, the standards themselves provide some warrant for this diversity of approach. The **Preamble** to **Part I** says that *educational researchers should warrant their research conclusions adequately in a way consistent with the standards of their own theoretical and methodological perspectives.* Since the standards seem to approve of some measure of "epistemic pluralism," we thought it would be more reasonable to permit the expression of different styles and analytic strategies than to seek to impose a uniformity of approach. After all, the Strike Committee contains lawyers, philosophers, teachers of administration, and a government agency employee. These roles are associated with different, but equally legitimate, intellectual styles and approaches to ethical issues. Thus, while we have employed a common format, we have not thought it essential to try to remove differences of style and approach.

Where we present hard cases, the voice is more that of the Strike Committee than that of AERA. While we do voice the occasional opinion, we also recognize that these cases raise difficult issues about which reasonable people can disagree. Thus, we do not seek to speak with an authoritative voice. We have not sought agreement on the views and interpretations asserted. Nevertheless, the cases we present and the questions we pose about them do assume views about what is controversial or ambiguous. Such assumptions are largely those of the Strike Committee. Readers should not only seek to answer the questions we ask and resolve the dilemmas we pose, but should also ask what assumptions enter into these questions and dilemmas and what other questions and dilemmas might have been posed.

The voice in the essay "Professional Codes, Morality, and the Law" is that of the authors, Martha McCarthy and Barry Bull. While the Strike Committee has obviously exercised its judgment about topics and authors, we have not attempted to influence or restrain the views and arguments presented. These belong to the authors and need not express the views either of AERA or of the committee.

Interpreting Codes and Reading Cases:
The Importance of Context

The provisions of any code of ethics are usually intended to address a particular problem or problems that are well known to the drafters of the code. Often, however, the problem to be solved by a given provision of a code is not clearly announced. The discussions that lead to a given standard commonly begin with the experience of members of the committee that wrote the standards. "Here's what happened, and here is some language for a standard that prohibits doing this" is the form of a discussion leading to a standard.

Rebuttals or modifications of such suggestions can result from questions like, "But imagine if the facts were these," or "Wouldn't your language also require this?" There is an exchange of examples and counter examples leading to refinement of the language of a standard. Typically, however, the problems to be solved and the examples and counter examples that lead to the language of various standards are not specified in the provision of the code.

Unfortunately, the interpretation of a standard may assume knowledge about the kind of context to which the provision is appropriate. Some professional socialization may be necessary to have this largely tacit knowledge. Consider, for example, **Standard 1a** of **Part III** of AERA's **Standards**. It says that all those who have made a substantial creative contribution to the generation of an intellectual product are entitled to authorship of that product. One problem area that this provision is intended to deal with is the relationship between researchers and their subordinates on research teams. If a researcher hires an assistant to help with a research product and the assistant makes a creative contribution to the research product, the assistant is entitled to authorship. The fact that the researcher employs the assistant is not a reason to deny authorship.

Another problem the provision is intended to solve is one of misunderstanding. Suppose that an assistant contributes a great deal of work to a project, but that this work consists of such tasks as routine data entry or text editing. Here **Standard 1a** says that mere effort apart from creative contribution does not warrant authorship. Hence the paradigmatic problems that this standard seems intended to deal with are exploitation and misunderstanding in relationships between researchers and subordinates. People who have worked in research universities for very long will all have stories about the exploitation of graduate assistants or misunderstandings about when authorship is appropriate. If one keeps the intended problem space in mind, **Standard 1a** makes perfectly good sense.

Suppose that we change our picture of the problem space. Suppose that we imagine a relationship between a journal editor and an author of a paper. The author has submitted a paper to a journal whose editor asks for revisions and makes a number of valuable suggestions about how to improve the paper. The author uses these suggestions and the paper is subsequently published. Suppose further that these suggestions are sufficient to count as a creative contribution. In this case, a demand for authorship on the part of the editor would normally be inappropriate. Typically, authors would be expected to acknowledge the assistance of an editor in a note. Here, too, this is tacit knowledge that most experienced researchers would possess.

If we ignore the problem that **Standard 1a** is intended to deal with, its language seems to require that the journal editor be listed as an author. Should we be concerned about this problem? Probably not. Most readers of AERA's **Standards** would quickly understand that **Standard 1a** is intended to govern the relationships between individuals on research teams and is not intended to govern the relationships between researchers and journal editors. What this illustration does suggest is that reading a code of ethics requires us to have a view of the problem being solved. If we substitute a different problem than the one intended, we can produce odd results. One of the roles cases serve is to suggest the paradigmatic problems that the standards are intended to solve. Our cases often serve to make explicit or to illustrate the tacit knowledge that experienced researchers employ to think about these issues.

Standard 1a also suggests that it is difficult to provide enough precision in a code of ethics to provide clear interpretations of all cases. It assumes that we can make a distinction between a creative contribution and a contribution that is not creative. Of course, one can give clear examples of these categories as we do; however, the boundary between creative and noncreative contributions is not a sharp one, and many instances are likely to be contentious. Here our examples and their discussions function as an imaginary case law. However, no finite set of examples is likely to cure the inherent vagueness of the concept; nor will additional language in the standard.

Something like this is also true of reading cases. The author of any given case must assume some context. Often sharing the assumptions of the author is important to the interpretation of the cases. Consider, for example, the very first case. There we imagine a researcher who has a history of public drunkenness at academic conferences. Our discussion of this case concludes that the researcher's conduct is regrettable but is a private (not job-related) matter. Furthermore, it would be inappropriate to take notice of this conduct in any way that jeopardized the researcher's professional standing. We argued that the researcher's history of drunkenness is not a reason for rejecting his papers, threatening his employment, or otherwise using such authority as other researchers might have over him to damage his professional standing. The concern behind our reasoning is that **Standard 1** of **Part I** generates a responsibility on the part of researchers to act in an appropriate manner, so as not to jeopardize the public standing of the field. We worry that a failure to restrict this provision to professional misconduct might be thought to warrant broad interference in or censorship of the private lives of researchers. Such interference or censorship might be enacted, if not by AERA, which has elected not to seek enforcement of its standards, then by some other agent that has power over the researcher, such as, for example, his university. The question we asked is this: "Is this researcher's offensive conduct a reason for sanctioning him with respect to his professional activities?" We concluded that it is not.

As one reviewer of this volume has commented, however, it is not clear that a decision on the part of the organizers of some conference not to invite this researcher to give an address because of his offensive behavior would be unwarranted. We agree, and we have modified the case to express this agreement. The duties of conference organizers go beyond providing an intellectually rewarding experience. They include some concern for the social environment at the conference. Hence, a decision made by conference organizers not to extend an invitation to this particular researcher, to avoid subjecting conference attendees to potentially offensive behavior, does not seem unreasonable.

Is there a difference of opinion here? Probably not. The difference in response is elicited by a difference in the imagined actions that might be taken against this researcher. Again, the facts we imagine in a case enter into its interpretation.

Should we not, then, provide all of the relevant facts? One rule of thumb for a good case is that it should include sufficient facts to allow a decision on the case. It is not clear, however, that this is possible. The assumption that it is possible may involve an inaccurate view of how rules or standards apply to cases. The assumption may involve the belief that rules determine what we should believe about a case that is largely independent of context. Consider the rule "Don't lie." No doubt we all think that telling the truth is important. If "Don't lie" applies to all cases of lying apart from context, then all we need to know to judge whether some act is wrong is if it is a case of lying. Yet most of us probably believe that it is not wrong to lie in order to prevent harm, and many of us think this extends to telling white lies such as "Don't you look nice today?" to someone who does not look nice. If so, to decide what we think about a lie, we need to know the context in which it occurred.

Consider this simple case: A researcher misrepresented his data to a colleague in discussing his research. This case says little more than that a researcher did what **Standard 1** of **Part I** forbids. Is this clearly wrong, and do we have enough information to know that it is wrong? Here we might say that, other things being equal, we know that misrepresenting data is wrong. However, "other things being equal" covers a multitude of potential complexities. Suppose that a researcher was abbreviating her results in a hallway conversation and omitted only minor details to avoid a protracted discussion. Suppose the researcher was trying to prevent someone from stealing her results, or suppose the researcher was a research assistant under unreasonable pressure from her supervisor to finish a task, or she had misread a number in her data set. Some of these additional facts suggest that the misrepresentation was not a lie. Some suggest it may be an excusable lie or even a justifiable lie.

Some other facts might mitigate our feelings about the severity of the offense or the nature of an appropriate penalty. No doubt the reader can create another possible context that will generate other interpretations. So, if we have a case that is as simple as this one, do we have enough information to decide the case? We do have enough information to render an "other things being equal" judgment. How much more information would we need to make a firm determination? Probably there is no right answer to this question. More information will answer some questions and raise further problems. It is likely that no matter how little information is provided, an "other things being equal" judgment will be possible, and no matter how much information is provided, it will be possible to imagine another fact that might change our minds. The amount of detail required of a good case is indeterminant.

Two additional observations are required for clarity. First, the claim that moral judgments are context dependent as suggested previously should not be viewed as denying the objectivity of moral judgments, or as asserting some form of moral relativism or skepticism. Moral skepticism claims that moral principles and judgments are arbitrary and cannot be justified rationally. Relativism claims that moral judgments are relative to the moral outlook brought to bear in making such judgments and that reasons cannot be given for preferring one moral outlook to another.

We have made neither of these claims. What we have said is that the moral judgment reached in a given situation depends on what the facts of the case are and that sometimes in reading cases we envision the facts differently. Moral theories sometimes differ about what facts are important or needed and assign different interpretations to them. But all moral theories rely on the characterization of the facts of a case as a factor in determining the best conclusion. The claim that judgments are relative to facts assumes the objectivity of moral judgments and does not assert either skepticism or relativism.

Second, our purpose in this discussion is to note one source of potential disagreement about cases and to suggest a response to it. We do not mean to suggest that all cases are so ambiguous that we cannot have any confidence in a moral judgment until we know everything. If Professor Jones murders Professor Smith because he coveted an academic prize that Smith won, we are entitled to make a judgment that this was wrong. Adding that we believe it wrong, "other things being equal" does no useful work in this case. We believe the reader will find that most of our cases contain sufficient information to resolve the issue and that the "other things being equal" caveat will not be necessary or will function as an invitation to envision improbable circumstances. Our exploration of complex cases should not obscure the fact that there are many cases in which the moral judgment reached is perfectly clear.

The main point of these observations is to suggest some points about how readers should read these cases and should respond to disagreement when it occurs. First, if you disagree with our discussion of the cases we provide, you might begin to probe this disagreement by asking if you and we have imagined a different context. Could you change the interpretation of the imagined context so that you would agree with us? What do you think is our paradigm case? Second, ask how either your judgment or ours might change if either the imagined context or the facts provided were different.

Here are some questions the reader might bring to any of our cases and to the ensuing discussions:

1. What are the problems being solved? How do the assumptions made about paradigmatic problems affect the interpretation of the standard at issue?

2. Are there situations or problems that might technically fall under the language of a provision in the standards, but which are not intended to be dealt with by its provisions? How is the meaning of the standards distorted if we select the wrong problems?

3. What concepts in a given standard are vague or ambiguous? Are there ways to make the meaning of these concepts clearer?

4. What are the imagined facts that seem to provide a context for the judgment reached? How does the judgment reached depend on these facts?

5. How would the judgment reached change if the context changed?

INTERPRETATION
OF THE CODE

Foreword

Educational researchers come from many disciplines, embrace several competing theoretical frameworks, and use a variety of research methodologies. AERA recognizes that its members are already guided by codes in the various disciplines and, also, by organizations such as institutional review boards. AERA's code of ethics incorporates a set of standards designed specifically to guide the work of researchers in education. Education, by its very nature, is aimed at the improvement of individual lives and societies. Further, research in education is often directed at children and other vulnerable populations. A main objective of this code is to remind us, as educational researchers, that we should strive to protect these populations, and to maintain the integrity of our research, of our research community, and of all those with whom we have professional relations. We should pledge ourselves to do this by maintaining our own competence and that of people we induct into the field, by continually evaluating our research for its ethical and scientific adequacy, and by conducting our internal and external relations according to the highest ethical standards.

The standards that follow remind us that we are involved not only in research but in education. It is, therefore, essential that we continually reflect on our research to be sure that it is not only sound scientifically but that it makes a positive contribution to the educational enterprise.

1

Rationale

The **Foreword** to the **Ethical Standards of the American Educational Research Association** states that, *AERA's code of ethics incorporates a set of standards designed specifically to guide the work of researchers in education*. We begin by asking three connected questions:

1. To whom is the code addressed?

2. What is the nature of the claim that AERA's standards have on those to whom they are addressed?

3. What exactly is a standard?

The code addresses AERA members. It might also address research employees of educational organizations, whose profession is educational research, or an even larger group, including consultants, freelance authors writing books about education, government lawyers researching a question of whether there has been compliance with a regulation, or even investigative reporters working on a story for the local newspaper.

There are several reasons for thinking that the code is addressed largely to AERA's membership. The title of the code states that these are the ethical standards of the American Educational Research Association. This is underscored by another sentence in the **Foreword**, which begins as follows: *A main objective of this code is to remind us . . . .* The code appears to be a means whereby AERA addresses its members about research ethics. Although all researchers should honor many standards within the code because it reflects broadly applicable norms, the standards that AERA has adopted have special force within its community.

This view of the code's audience suggests a tempting way to answer the question, "Why should I follow these standards?" One answer might be that by joining AERA, you have consented to them. Here the obvious rejoinder is that, "Merely joining AERA does not mean I consented to the standards; membership in AERA has never been conditioned on consent to the standards." We agree that mere membership in AERA does not entail consent to its standards. However, we also believe that AERA, by formally promulgating these standards, is speaking to its members and urging that we place these standards under serious consideration in our work. This view suggests that the standards have special force for AERA members. However, it also suggests that the standards are an attempt to provide a particular expression of broader ethical norms that often apply to all those who do educational research, regardless of their affiliation.

It is important to note that the code refers to the standards as "ethical" standards. Use of the terms "ethics" and "ethical" probably connotes that these are not mere ordinary standards of prudence, or sound policy. These are standards that embody prima facie duties and obligations. There is a presumption that a given standard is to be followed unless those who are subject to it have a countervailing ethical standard that takes precedence in the situation, or an excuse or a justification which itself meets ethical standards. Reasons of expediency, efficiency, or convenience do not warrant a departure from ethical standards.

But identifying these standards as "ethical," not prudential, does not answer the question of the ethical foundation for the standards. Why do we, the membership of AERA, say to ourselves that we really should consider that we have an ethical duty according to **Standard 5** of **Part I** to report our findings to all relevant stakeholders? The reasons for particular standards are addressed in the commentary that follows them. Our approach is rooted in the assumption that AERA's standards are specifications of broader norms that have reasoned justification and have a claim to our attention because they express justifiable moral norms.

In what we have said so far, we have presumed that there is a distinction to be made between standards and the ethical principles that underlie them. It will also be useful to distinguish standards from rules. In common parlance, designating a command as a "rule" might suggest that compliance is required. There are no acceptable justifications or excuses for noncompliance. That the term "rule" was not used might suggest that AERA did not intend to provide detailed prescriptions. In contrast, the term "principle" connotes that the prescriptions are reasonably general and do not require specific or directed behaviors. An example is the principle of "do no harm." The term "standards" also suggests a prescription that is both less vague and ambiguous than a guideline, and a prescription that one is less free to disregard. To legitimately depart from standards requires meeting a heavier burden of proof than is required to refuse to acknowledge the guidance of a guideline. Therefore, unlike rules that are followed without question, standards are abandoned but only for extremely good reasons, such as that another standard takes precedence in the situation. Who counts as an ethical researcher is measured against the minimum requirements established in this code. We are not counted as an ethical researcher if we depart from the standards for insufficient reason.

The fact that standards fall between principles and rules also suggests something about their justification and interpretation. That standards are less specific and more flexible than rules suggests that judgment is required in their application. It is possible for reasonable people to disagree in some cases. As we have suggested, departures from the standards may be justified for good and sufficient reasons. Even the best creator of standards cannot foresee how they will work out in each case.

Here two points about interpretation may be useful. First, as previously noted, often the standards presuppose a view of the kind of case to which they apply. Applications to nonparadigmatic cases may produce puzzling interpretations.

Second, standards get some of their force from the more general ethical principles that are appealed to in justifying them. In applying standards to cases, it is helpful to see them in the context of their justification. The meaning of a standard cannot be separated from the reasons for accepting it.

The **Foreword's** concluding paragraph begins with the statement, *The standards that follow remind us that we are involved not only in research but in education.* We are also told that the standards were *designed specifically to guide the work of researchers in education.*

Two important points are embodied in these sentences. First, the standards are not intended merely to reflect general ethical or moral standards that any person is obligated to follow. They are focused on the activity of research and the behavior of people doing research. Of course, when AERA promulgated these standards, it did not intend to say that they, the members of AERA, were not also citizens and human beings who are obligated to follow more generally applicable duties and obligations. In fact, as we shall see, a number of the standards in the code are specific versions of general ethical standards. For example, **Standard 2** of **Part I** holds that: *Educational researchers must not fabricate, falsify, or misrepresent authorship, evidence, data, findings, or conclusions.* This standard is an instantiation of the more general duty not to lie. Because these standards were designed for a specific audience engaged in a specific practice, the possibility is open, as is true with other codes of ethics, of a conflict between what AERA standards require and what general moral or ethical obligations require. This is a problem that also arises with other codes.

Lawyers, for example, have an obligation to keep confidential the information their clients tell them confidentially, an obligation that can conflict with the more general obligations of citizens to report or turn over evidence of crimes. Similarly, the conflict between our citizen obligations and our obligations as educational researchers can arise. A parallel conflict is theoretically possible regarding the requirements of AERA code and our obligations as teachers, or perhaps conflict arises between the code and obligations to employers. In other words, educational researchers take on many roles, and individual researchers living out multiple roles could find themselves being confronted with conflicting obligations.

So far, we have raised the possibility of these standards conflicting with other obligations derived from other sources. The second point emerging from the sentences quoted previously raises the possibility of a different kind of conflict—a conflict internal to the standards. The possibility of this internal conflict arises because the standards embody a dual set of obligations—obligations AERA members have as scientists and as people involved in education. This double duty is captured in the last sentence of the **Foreword**: *It is, therefore, essential that we continually reflect on our research to be sure that it is not only sound scientifically but that it makes a positive contribution to the educational enterprise.*

The first of these themes, the obligation to produce scientifically sound research, is reflected in various sentences of the **Foreword**. We are informed that a main objective of the code is to *remind us, as educational researchers, that we should strive . . . to maintain the integrity of our research . . . . We should pledge ourselves to do this by maintaining our own competence and that of people we induct into the field, by continually evaluating our research for its ethical and scientific adequacy . . . .*

The **Foreword** also addresses the second set of obligations. It does this by briefly taking a stand on the nature of education. *Education, by its every nature, is aimed at the improvement of individual lives and societies.* The plausible implication of this sentence is that AERA membership, in fulfilling its obligation to make *a positive contribution to the educational enterprise,* must be involved in seeking to improve individual lives and societies.

Thus, the **Foreword** conceives of the educational researcher as shouldering a dual obligation as scientist and as a person engaged in ameliorating individual lives and society. Needless to say, the systematic working out of this dual obligation is a difficult undertaking. Are the two roles compatible? Can we always be true to science and true to the role of social and individual improvement? If there comes a time that researchers perceive a conflict between the two obligations, which takes precedence? To answer many of these questions, we must also answer such additional questions as "What are the criteria used to determine if research is scientifically sound? What is to count as 'positive' versus 'negative' contributions to the educational enterprise?"

Without attempting to answer these questions, we can add that the **Foreword**, by implication, takes a position on the educational researcher's role that may be controversial. The **Foreword** seems to say that these standards avoid the notion that educational researchers may perform science for science's sake, producing knowledge for knowledge's sake, despite the individual or social consequences of the work. This is not to say that the **Foreword** makes applied research the ethical obligation of all educational researchers. The **Foreword** takes no explicit stand on this issue and makes no implication of this sort. Yet the **Foreword** indicates that even researchers who develop or test theory should know that educational research is a social as well as a scientific activity and that it has a dual scientific–educational role for educational researchers.

The **Foreword** also indicates another fact about educational research today: *Educational researchers come from many disciplines, embrace several competing theoretical frameworks, and use a variety of research methodologies.* The **Foreword** also states that *AERA recognizes that its members are already guided by codes in the various disciplines.* By recognizing what might be called the "epistemic pluralism" as well as the multiple affiliations of AERA membership, the

Foreword takes the first step in developing a theme that receives a fuller voice in the specific standards—the value of integrity. As will be shown, the code deals with the reality of epistemic pluralism by urging the heterogeneous AERA membership to have the ethic of being true to our own perspective.

Epistemological or methodological pluralism makes it far more complicated to achieve an understanding of the proper relationship between scientific soundness and social reform. Although it may, other things being equal, be a good thing for researchers to be true to their own perspective, it is less clear that this is an adequate guarantee that every perspective is defensible or that it serves the good of education. Moreover, often perspectives that differ about research methodology also differ about the nature of a good education. These turn out not to be entirely separate matters. Arguably, the answer to what this relationship should be between methodological soundness and good education varies from perspective to perspective. These difficult matters are not explicitly addressed in the **Foreword**.

A final important theme in the **Foreword** is the reminder to educational researchers that they are embedded in many relationships with specific people and other research enterprises. Each of these relationships has its own obligations and responsibilities. First, there are children and other vulnerable populations who frequently function as the objects of research for educational researchers. The **Foreword** simply notes that educational researchers should strive to protect these populations.

Another relationship in which individual researchers find themselves is with the research community. With regard to this community, the **Foreword** notes that the obligation of researchers is to maintain the integrity of that community, the integrity of *all those with whom we have professional relations,* and to conduct their internal relations with the community *according to the highest ethical standards.* These generally phrased obligations are developed and made specific by the numbered standards.

Here we note that, just as the code states that the integrity of research depends significantly on the competence with which it is conducted, it also states that the integrity of the community significantly depends on maintaining the climate of free and open debate. The frequency with which the code defends the marketplace of ideas suggests that AERA believes vigorous debate is central to vital research. The code also views the role of researchers more as independent scholars than as servants of educational or policy agendas achieved by government or by advocacy groups. Thus, while AERA believes that educational research should serve the public good, it also encourages its members to independently determine what the public good is and what educational practices should be employed to meet that good.

The **Foreword** also makes one reference to *external relations,* which it says must also be conducted *according to the highest ethical standards.* This noncontroversial exhortation can be read in connection with the **Foreword's** other admonition that educational researchers should strive to maintain the *integrity . . . of our research community.* An implication from these two injunctions is that the educational researcher, while obliged to defend the educational research community from external interference, should use only ethical means.

The **Foreword** states that: *AERA recognizes that its members are already guided by codes in the various disciplines and, also, by organizations such as institutional review boards.* Nothing more is said about these other codes, but the implication is that AERA membership is sensitive to the codes' requirements and that the codes were written with awareness of the complex context in which these standards are to be carried out.

In summary, the **Foreword** informs us that the standards of the code are addressed by the membership of AERA to itself. We also learn that the prescriptive statements that compose the code are more specific than principles and are expected to garner adherence to a greater extent than mere guidelines, but they are less absolute than rules. The **Foreword** informs us that these standards were specifically designed to guide the work of educational researchers. The **Foreword** also broadly sketches the content of the standards and, in doing so, alerts us to the dual role that educational researchers have as scientists and social reformers. It also reminds us that educational researchers conduct their work within a complex set of personal and institutional relationships, which entail their own obligations and duties.

We believe that the practice of sound ethics is best achieved in communities in which ethical responsibilities are regularly discussed and debated. This is how the art of judgment required to apply principles and standards to real issues is learned, how disagreements are resolved, how new members are initiated into the standards of the community, and how the community creates a sense of commitment to its ethical standards. The cases and discussions of the codes that follow are intended to accomplish these purposes.

RESPONSIBILITIES TO THE FIELD

The Preamble, the Standards, and Their Rationale

Preamble

To maintain the integrity of research, educational researchers should warrant their research conclusions adequately in a way consistent with the standards of their own theoretical and methodological perspectives. They should keep themselves well informed in both their own and competing paradigms where those are relevant to their research, and they should continually evaluate the criteria of adequacy by which research is judged.

STANDARDS

1 *Educational researchers should conduct their professional lives in such a way that they do not jeopardize future research, the public standing of the field, or the discipline's research results.*

2 *Educational researchers must not fabricate, falsify, or misrepresent authorship, evidence, data, findings, or conclusions.*

3 *Educational researchers must not knowingly or negligently use their professional roles for fraudulent purposes.*

4 *Educational researchers should honestly and fully disclose their qualifications and limitations when providing professional opinions to the public, to government agencies, and others who may avail themselves of the expertise possessed by members of AERA.*

5 *Educational researchers should attempt to report their findings to all relevant stakeholders, and should refrain from keeping secret or selectively communicating their findings.*

6 *Educational researchers should report research conceptions, procedures, results, and analyses accurately and sufficiently in detail to allow knowledgeable, trained researchers to understand and interpret them.*

7 *Educational researchers' reports to the public should be written straightforwardly to communicate the practical significance for policy, including limits in effectiveness and in generalizability to situations, problems, and contexts. In writing for or communicating with non-researchers, educational researchers must take care not to misrepresent the practical or policy implications of their research or the research of others.*

8 *When educational researchers participate in actions related to hiring, retention, and advancement, they should not discriminate on the basis of gender, sexual orientation, physical disability, marital status, color, social class, religion, ethnic background, national origin, or other attributes not relevant to the evaluation of academic or research competence.*

9 *Educational researchers have a responsibility to make candid, forthright personnel recommendations and not to recommend those who are manifestly unfit.*

10 *Educational researchers should decline requests to review the work of others where strong conflicts of interest are involved, or when such requests cannot be conscientiously fulfilled on time. Materials sent for review should be read in their entirety and considered carefully, with evaluative comments justified with explicit reasons.*

11 *Educational researchers should avoid all forms of harassment, not merely those overt actions or threats that are due cause for legal action. They must not use their professional positions or rank to coerce personal or sexual favors or economic or professional advantages from students, research assistants, clerical staff, colleagues, or any others.*

12 *Educational researchers should not be penalized for reporting in good faith violations of these or other professional standards.*

RATIONALE

The **Preamble** of **Part I** emphasizes the importance of the intellectual integrity of research by requiring researchers to warrant their conclusion adequately and to maintain their capacity to do good research. Its language is focused on the integrity of research, not of researchers. It views the integrity of research as principally a matter of the epistemological warrant for its conclusions and of the competence with which it is conducted.

The 12 standards of **Part I**, however, deal with issues that go well beyond this understanding of research integrity. They include provisions for nondiscriminatory hiring, proscribe harassment, demand forthrightness in recommendations and openness and honesty in dealing with the public. It may be that the idea of the integrity of research can be expanded to include such notions. We might argue, for example, that fair hiring not only avoids discrimination, but it also recruits the most qualified researchers—people who will do the best work. Thus, the integrity of research is maintained.

However, it may also be that we can understand the connection of the **Preamble** with the standards that fall under it better if we see the **Preamble** as concerned not only with the integrity of research, but also with its credibility. **Standard 1** seems to emphasize the connection between the ethical behavior of researchers in their professional lives and the credibility of their work.

Credibility concerns the general public's respect for research. It is a more utilitarian notion than integrity. The work of researchers is not likely to serve its public function if it lacks credibility. Moreover, while the credibility of research is enhanced by its integrity, credibility may require that researchers behave responsibly in their professional lives. Researchers may, not only in the way they conduct their research but also by how they represent themselves to others (**Standard 4**) and how they treat their colleagues or subordinates (**Standards 8** and **11**), bring discredit to or disrepute on their own work and that of other researchers. Hence, in the **Preamble** and the 12 standards that develop it, educational researchers are exhorted to maintain integrity in their own work, in the field, and in their relationships with subordinates. They are to do this not only to do research that meets appropriate intellectual standards but also to ensure that their work has the credibility required to perform its public function.

Note the following four points. First, because the idea of maintaining credibility applies not just to issues of professional competence but also to any actions that bring credit or discredit on the field, the requirement to maintain credibility should encompass all of the AERA code. Any form of professional misconduct may bring research and researchers into disrepute.

Second, while it is important to not bring the profession into disrepute, this is not the primary reason why the provisions of **Part I** or the rest of the AERA code have force. Engaging in conduct that the AERA code seeks to enjoin brings discredit on the field because this conduct is wrong; it is not wrong because it brings discredit on the field. We should avoid harassment or discrimination, not just because these activities bring research into disrepute, but because such activities are inherently wrong.

Third, unethical actions that bring research or researchers into disrepute need not undermine the epistemological integrity of research. Unethical researchers may produce good arguments. Hence, we should not uncritically dismiss the work of researchers if they prove unethical in those areas of their professional lives that are unrelated to the validity of their work. Some of the standards of **Part I** affect the integrity of research. Falsification of data (**Standard 2**) is inconsistent with the integrity of research. However, the arguments of researchers do not inevitably become invalid if researchers are guilty of harassment or discrimination.

Finally, the idea that researchers have a duty not only to do their research with integrity, but also to preserve the credibility of the research community potentially invites the scrutiny of the ethical conduct of researchers outside of their professional lives. As an empirical matter, it may be that unethical conduct that is unrelated to any professional matter is as likely to bring disrepute on the research community as is professional misconduct (although, as an empirical matter, it is unlikely that we have genuine knowledge about the consequences of unethical behavior on the credibility of research or researchers.) Nevertheless, as we argue in the exposition of **Case 1**, we believe that the scope of AERA's code is limited to professional behavior.

The **Preamble** to **Part I** and the standards that follow suggest that maintaining the integrity and credibility of research requires the following qualities from researchers.

First, research must be intellectually competent. Although researchers often disagree about the nature of intellectual standards, they have a responsibility to argue their conclusions by employing theories, methods, and intellectual standards they regard as appropriate and by giving fair recognition to alternative views. Researchers must also maintain their competence and currency in their fields and uphold high standards of honesty in dealing with data, interpreting evidence, representing their qualifications, and reporting results.

Second, the integrity and credibility of research are enhanced when research is subjected to examination and criticism. More than self-examination by researchers is required. Ideas and arguments must be subjected to the critical examination of others. Thus, researchers are responsible for the robustness and sophistication of the marketplace of ideas in which research claims are assessed and refined. Secrecy or partial reporting is inconsistent with the marketplace of ideas if it leads to presenting research results in a way that renders them incapable of critical examination.

Moreover, the marketplace of ideas works best when people with diverse perspectives examine the research. Researchers must take responsibility for producing, disseminating, and effectively communicating their work so as to facilitate its accessibility and reasoned evaluation.

These two points are concerned with what might be called "methodological or epistemological integrity." However, the standards also suggest that the credibility of educational researchers' work depends on the researchers exhibiting integrity in broader areas of their work. The credibility of research is influenced to the extent that professional relationships among researchers exhibit integrity.

Hence, judgments about people or their work must be made on professionally appropriate criteria, conflicts of interest should be avoided, and a responsible work environment must be maintained. While discrimination and harassment are wrong for reasons independent of, and more important than the effects of such conduct on the credibility of research, nevertheless, it may undermine that credibility.

Finally, a sense of collective responsibility for the integrity of the research community is important in order to maintain the credibility of the communities' work. It is appropriate for researchers to report violations of professional integrity and to be protected from retribution.

The **Preamble** suggests two issues that are especially important to interpreting some of the 12 standards under **Part I**. First, as we have noted, the **Preamble** emphasizes the methodological or epistemological aspects of research integrity. The 12 standards that follow, especially the first, expand the scope of the integrity expected of researchers to include their relations to "subordinates" and note that researchers have a sweeping obligation not to jeopardize future research, the public standing of the field, or research results. Perhaps these obligations are too sweeping. Are these obligations understood so the profession can scrutinize a researcher's personal life? Here we argue that the standards should not be understood in this way.

Second, the suggestion that researchers must warrant their conclusions in a way that is consistent with their chosen methodology might be understood in at least two ways. (See the discussion of these issues in the **Rationale** of **Part IV**.) One reading might imply that the researcher's obligation is limited to the consistent application of a self-chosen methodology. A second reading might add the stronger obligation to employ an appropriate methodology. In both cases, the **Preamble** intends to warrant methodological pluralism. Both here and in **Part IV** where the issue recurs, the question of whether there is a duty to choose a suitable or justifiable methodology, as well as a duty to conscientiously follow a self-chosen methodology, is not resolved by the code's text. This is not surprising. The epistemological issues involved are notoriously difficult and contentious. However, it seems reasonable to hold that the **Preamble** intends to affirm at least two ideas.

First, since the **Preamble** asks us to continually reassess our paradigms and stances and be aware of others, it cannot presuppose any thorough going relativism. If one paradigm is as good as another, then there would be little sense in appraising our paradigm or being aware of others. Thus, while intellectual integrity may involve conscientiously applying a self-chosen paradigm, it also seems to require that our paradigm be chosen for appropriate and good reasons.

Second, the **Preamble** may state that in educational research reasonable and competent people often disagree about the appropriate approach to studying educational phenomena in ways that have yet to be resolved by evidence and argument. Hence, the philosophy within the **Preamble** not only tells us that we should select the methodology that is appropriate to the questions we ask. It also warrants reasonable disagreement about what approach to take.

Note also that the **Preamble** employs two different phrases to refer to the idea of epistemological pluralism. It talks about the researcher's *own theoretical and methodological perspectives,* and it talks about *competing paradigms.* We assume that these phrases are meant to be equivalent. The term "paradigm" was popularized by Thomas Kuhn in his book *The Structure of Scientific Revolutions.*[1] There is much discussion about what exactly Kuhn meant; however, the term seems to have become widely employed in education in a way that seems to refer to a perspective that organizes one's research. The use of this term suggests that the standards assume that there is no one right way to do educational research. Kuhn also suggested that different paradigms might be incommensurable or that it was difficult to judge or even understand one paradigm from the perspective of another. In addition, there is not a more general place to stand from which all paradigms can be rationally assessed. If so, then the choice of paradigms seems to depend more on taste than argument. While the standards do not resolve many issues about epistemological pluralism, they do not assume that paradigms are incommensurable.

The standards of **Part I** appear in a numbered list that has no clear internal organization. They can, however, be conveniently grouped into four general categories, reflecting different dimensions of educational research practice:

(a) Responsibilities of principal investigators and their associates regarding the integrity of their research project: **Standards 1, 2, 3, 4.**

(b) Responsibilities of principal investigators regarding dissemination of research: **Standards 5, 6, 7.**

(c) Responsibilities of principal investigators regarding their working relationship with "subordinates": **Standards 8, 11**.

(d) Responsibilities of researchers "in the field" regarding other researchers doing research and research-related activities: **Standards 9, 10, 12**.

Because these groupings reflect significantly different issues, we will divide our discussion of the standards into four corresponding sections.

Interpretation of the Standards: Issues, Cases, and Discussions

Integrity of the Research Project

ISSUE

Standard 1 notes that there is an interest in protecting future research opportunities, the public standing of the field, and the field's research results. The reasoning behind this interest might be this: Educational research is of social value because it contributes to the appropriateness and effectiveness of education. If so, then researchers must conduct their professional lives in such a way as to produce a public climate of respect for research and researchers so that research cooperation is forthcoming and the research product is respected, valued, and employed in decisions. One concern with this standard is that it may be overbroad because it invites scrutiny of researchers' personal lives or personal aspects of their professional lives. The scope of what counts as one's professional life is far from clear. Note, however, that the character of researchers' professional responsibilities is implicitly defined by the standards of **Part I** and in the rest of the code.

Case 1

Professor Jones is a leading researcher on moral development. He is frequently invited to conferences to speak on his research. Professor Jones meets his obligations as a conference speaker with excellence. However, Professor Jones is also a heavy drinker. He has often been visibly, loudly, and obnoxiously drunk in the hotel lobby in front of large numbers of conference participants.

> *Discussion:* Does Professor Jones's behavior jeopardize the public standing of his work or the research community? Because his behavior is rude, tactless, or offensive to colleagues or other conference attendees, we believe that it could be reasonably characterized as unethical. However, as long as such behavior does not affect his performance in the professional role he has agreed to perform, it seems reasonable to view it as personal and not professional misconduct. The boundaries between what is personal and what is professional must be distinguished from the boundaries between what is ethical and not ethical. When we view something as professional misconduct, we are not only saying that it is misconduct by a professional, but we are also saying that this misconduct warrants official attention, notice, or censure by the researcher's colleagues or professional associations. To warrant such attention, the conduct must be done in the performance of recognized professional duties. In this case, Professor Jones confines his offensive behavior to nonprofessional duties. This distinction is vital because if we fail to make it, AERA might take notice of any aspects of researchers' lives that draw negative attention to their research and cause others to not respect researchers or their work. Instead, the standards should be understood to forbid *professional* unethical conduct. And the standards, in their totality, implicitly define (at least in

part) what that professionally related conduct is. **Standard 1** must therefore be understood in the context of the other standards. For example, **Standard 4** informs us that it is unethical to misrepresent one's credentials, and it also informs us that doing so is *professional* misconduct. Although the fact that Professor Jones's drunken behavior occurred at a conference might be viewed as professionally related, the connections between his behavior and his professional responsibilities are too remote. His behavior has not invalidated or misrepresented his work.

Moreover, he has not been drunk at any conference session in which he had professional responsibilities, and he has performed his responsibilities competently. Finally, nothing in the code views alcohol abuse, as unfortunate as it may be, as professional misconduct. Thus, while the distinction between what is professional and what is personal is not always clear, we believe that Professor Jones's behavior, even if it leads some to a lowered view of educational researchers, is not professional misconduct.

At the same time, there are some occasions when the personal misconduct of an individual may be noticed by a professional group. It might plausibly be argued that organizers of a conference have an obligation to respect and ensure the comfort of attendees. This might extend to not inviting speakers who have a history of obnoxious behavior toward other attendees. Hence, we would not view it as beyond reason were a conference committee to consider Professor Jones's history of offensive behavior as a factor relevant to not inviting him to speak. We would distinguish this from a professional society's attempt to sanction Jones for such behavior. Indeed, if Jones had submitted a paper to this conference and had been selected on the basis of merit, we would not reject his presentation because of his offensive behavior.

ISSUE

Standard 2 prohibits researchers from such misconduct as fabricating data or misrepresenting results. It prohibits lying or misleading in the conduct of research. This goes to the heart of the research enterprise. If researchers were to routinely, or even occasionally, lie, their results would lose credibility. But there are also common justifications for lying. Sometimes lying serves a good cause. Sometimes it seems to do no harm. Might it be reasonable to misrepresent data or other features of a research effort if some benefit results and no real harm is done?

Case 2

Harry Standish recently completed a study of the effects of a new math curriculum on student learning. He also did the preliminary analysis of his data and drew some tentative conclusions. Before he was able to complete the more thorough analysis that he intended, he had a computer crash. The data for one of the classrooms he studied was lost. Because he had reasonable confidence in his preliminary analysis and he thought his conclusions were valuable to the field, he decided to create a new data set for this one class that would support his preliminary analysis.

Case 3

Professor Sheila Janeway was testifying before a committee of her state legislature. She was presenting evidence on the results of the state's recent school reform initiatives. At one point, Mr. Hobart, a legislator who was hostile to these reforms, was grilling her. His question was, "Are you sure of these results, or is this just another piece of ivory tower speculation at the cost of our children's education?" Her results were subject to several interpretations. While she was far from certain that the conclusions she had drawn were correct, she also believed that they were supported by the evidence and were the most reasonable interpretation that she could provide without more research. She also knew that if she said this, Representative Brown would use her tentativeness to undermine the reform. Thus, she said, "Mr. Brown, the conclusions of my research are as certain as they can be." She added to herself the caveat "which is not very," but what everyone else heard was that her results were secure.

Discussion: These are cases of professional misconduct. In both cases, the conduct is professionally related. In both cases, **Standard 2** forbids the conduct. In the first case, Harry Standish has fabricated data. In the second, Professor Janeway has misrepresented her conclusions. Here, note that it is possible to misrepresent our conclusions both by misleading characterizations of their content and by misleading representations of their warrant. In both cases, it is possible to sympathize with the researcher. Both individuals can point to extenuating circumstances. Neither seems motivated to lie merely for personal gain. Nevertheless, each case is an instance of professional misconduct because both are lies and harm the marketplace of ideas. Harry Standish does not know that his preliminary conclusions are true. He must do an analysis on the data he has lost in order to be confident. Professor Janeway is not entitled to a high level of security in her research conclusions. Thus, both have introduced their results into debate in a way that is calculated to enhance its argumentative effect beyond what the evidence warrants. The reasonableness of the argument that results can only suffer as a consequence.

ISSUE

The arguments of accomplished scholars are often not capable of assessment by those who lack training. Often, what persuades non-experts of the merits of researchers' conclusions is their expertise and reputation. That a conclusion was reached by someone in a knowledgeable position is reasonably viewed as an argument to support this conclusion. Such arguments presuppose trust on the part of consumers of research and integrity on the part of researchers. Trust and integrity are undermined when researchers lend their credentials, expertise, or reputations to enterprises that are unworthy or fraudulent as proscribed by **Standard 3** or when they claim expertise that they do not have as proscribed by **Standard 4**. What enterprises can researchers lend their expertise to, and how may they represent themselves?

Case 4

Professor Halder was a young scholar of cooperative learning. He published a set of well-received papers emphasizing how cooperative learning might be structured to avoid the situation in which some students exploit their more conscientious peers. While he favored cooperative learning, his work was geared to fine-tuning it rather than showing its superiority. Professor Halder was pleased when he was invited to attend a seminar put on by Creative Pedagogy Inc. (CPI), an educational consulting firm dealing with cooperative learning. He was asked to talk only informally with the conference participants and was offered $5,000 for his services. He sent CPI a file photograph and a professional biography, and he cashed the check.

When Dr. Halder got the conference brochure, he noticed that he was featured as "the world's foremost advocate of cooperative learning." He was also listed as a conference participant, and it was not apparent that he was not a conference speaker. Also, CPI was described as the "major pedagogical innovation of the 20th century" and "the most important piece of a comprehensive school reform package." Finally, cooperative learning was characterized as "the only teaching method proven to improve race relations." Dr. Halder regarded these characterizations as gross exaggerations. The fee for attending the conference was $2,000.

Discussion: Dr. Halder was used to legitimate a costly seminar that was fraudulently described. This violates **Standard 3**. Dr. Halder's role in the conference was misleadingly described, and his credentials were exaggerated. The latter violates **Standard 4**. On the other hand, Dr. Halder was not responsible for, nor initially aware of, these misrepresentations. Note, however, that **Standard 3** precludes either knowingly or negligently being used for fraudulent purposes. It is plausible to believe that Professor Halder was negligent. One is negligent when one fails to take reasonable precautions or make reasonable inquiries about a project to which one lends one's name.

Dr. Halder did not investigate CPI's reputation, and he was offered an unusually high fee for limited services. He should have checked out CPI before accepting their offer. At best, he was naive. A continuation of his relationship with CPI would be clearly a case of negligence and possibly a case of fraud on Dr. Halder's part once he became aware of CPI's misrepresentations. Moreover, Dr. Halder may have a responsibility to protest these abuses. If he is able, Dr. Halder should set the record straight by returning the check, withdrawing from the conference, and having participants be told that he would not attend the conference.

Dissemination of Research

ISSUE

Three connected values are paramount in research dissemination. The first value is honesty. Researchers should not lie or mislead. Hence, **Standard 6** requires reports of research to be accurate and adequate.

The second value in research dissemination is the marketplace of ideas. Research should be reported so as to promote reasoned discussion and criticism. This requires reporting in sufficient detail and clarity to permit reasoned debate. Hence, **Standard 5** requires full reporting and forbids keeping information secret. **Standard 6** requires that research be reported to permit adequate assessment and criticism by other scholars.

Effective and appropriate communication to the public as well as the research community is important. In a democracy, research should be meaningfully available to the public. Meaningful communication requires that research findings be presented in a useful form to audiences with diverse capacities to consume, understand, and apply such research. Furthermore, because research may be included in public debate on important policy issues, it is especially important, as required by **Standard 7** that research reports be forthcoming about the limits and generalizability of research.

The third value in research dissemination is representational appropriateness. Research results may impact significantly on various groups. Researchers need to inform stakeholders in the research outcome since they have a right to know. Hence **Standard 5** requires that research be reported to relevant stakeholders.

Each of these criteria for research dissemination requires some judgment on the part of the researcher who must decide who should be informed and what information is suitable for the audience. Sometimes these goals are conflicting.

For example, policymakers may wish that research results be stated in a brief and summary form more suitable for action than reflection. Often the general public is not likely to be willing or able to follow a detailed statistical analysis, nor is the researcher likely to have the opportunity to provide one by the local newspaper. Thus, effective communication may require simplification. But such simplification reduces the ability of the research recipient to assess its merits. Sometimes simplification can amount to misrepresentation. When does simplification amount to misrepresentation? How can researchers inform the public in a way that serves the marketplace of ideas? How can they decide who needs to know? Who are the stakeholders, and when should stakeholders be notified of what research?

Case 5

Dr. Rosemore did some work on desegregation in a recently desegregated small school district in the northeastern United States. His work was funded by a conservative think tank, the Hobbs Foundation, that opposed desegregation. While he was clear about the views of the Foundation, he prided himself on his objectivity and was careful that the Hobbs Foundation had no control over the substance of his work. His results, while far from certain, suggested that in the first years of the desegregation plan, there had been little effect on minority achievement. Dr. Rosemore provided his report, together with a summary of his results, to the Hobbs Foundation. He also sent his report to several other think tanks and advocacy groups since he wanted funding for the next phase of his work. However, no group favoring desegregation was included on this list.

Discussion: Stakeholders are individuals or groups with legitimate interests in the results of research. One way in which a group gains an interest in work is by paying for it. Thus, sponsors are stakeholders. However, the primary meaning of stakeholder is that stakeholders are individuals or groups that have a legitimate interest in the issue under discussion. One might possess such an interest in virtue of representing a group that is affected by the decisions or by having a history of advocacy about the issue.

Hence, the National Association for the Advancement of Colored People (NAACP) is a stakeholder on issues about desegregation. **Standard 5** requires that all relevant stakeholders be notified and prohibits secrecy. Here again we may usefully view **Standard 5** as serving the marketplace of ideas. It seeks to guarantee a reasoned debate by ensuring that interested parties are fully informed of relevant evidence. Typically, this communication is satisfied by publishing one's work in scholarly journals or other publicly available sources. Apart from public publication, it is impossible to notify all stakeholders concerning specific research. Sometimes, as in the case under discussion, however, research is reported through non-public channels. Here **Standard 5** is especially important. It serves the marketplace of ideas by prohibiting privileged access to research that would give one party in a debate an unfair advantage over others. This also suggests that there is a principle of equity assumed by **Standard 5**. Moreover, **Standard 5** implicitly recognizes that truth seeking in educational debates is sometimes an adversarial process.

Standard 5 might be satisfied by informing appropriate representatives of a suitable range of opinion on a research issue. If so, then Dr. Rosemore violated **Standard 5**. By making his research available only to potential sponsors, he selectively made his work available to one side of a debate, but not the other. **Standard 5** suggests that he should have ensured that his work was available to groups that might advance other views.

Case 6

Professor Gail Norris often performed program evaluation for the Westtown schools. Westtown had a large grant from a computer software company, Educational Systems, Ltd. (ESYL), to develop a computer math-teaching program. There had been considerable unevenness in implementation. Professor Norris did the evaluation of Phase I. The results showed that even when the program was fully implemented with a high investment of funds and staff time, groups using the new program did only slightly better than groups using the old math program. The computer-based program was not cost-effective. Professor Norris explained this to the teachers and administrators who were in charge of the project who were reluctant for Professor Norris to report her results in their current form to ESYL.

One member of the team put it this way. "Look, if you say this to ESYL or go public with it, there will be no Phase II. That means no more money for new computers, and certainly no more money to evaluate the program. Even if this program doesn't help, it doesn't hurt, and when we're done with Phase II, we'll have a lot of new equipment to use for other purposes." In the executive summary of Professor Norris's report, the key phrase read, "Positive results were obtained in all cases where the program was fully implemented." Details were buried in the statistical tables in the appendixes of the 75-page report, which Professor Norris expected no one to read.

Discussion: Professor Norris has communicated one message to Westtown and another to EYSL. This seems to violate the prohibition against selective communication in **Standard 5**. Moreover, she has sought to mislead EYSL and the public. The Executive Summary omits crucial facts and presents the study's results in a way that is calculated to mislead. The whole truth is given only in the appendixes and is available only to parties with the will and ability to unravel the data. Thus, there has been a deliberate attempt to mislead the sponsor of the project. Even if Professor Norris desires only to secure more computer equipment for Westtown, she has lied. Her report fails to meet the full disclosure and appropriateness requirements of **Standard 6** and **Standard 7**.

Case 7

Professor Consuela Rodriguez did a complicated analysis of a large state data set in which she found a weak but statistically significant relationship between the number of courses teachers took in their subject areas and the achievement of their students. This relationship disappeared after the number of courses reached five. Moreover, Professor Rodriguez explored this relationships using different models. This relationship appeared only when certain plausible, but far from certain, assumptions were made. These facts were reported in the article Professor Rodriguez published. However, a year later Professor Rodriguez picked up a publication, aimed at a broad readership, in which her research was cited and summarized. One sentence claimed that Professor Rodriguez had shown that there is a significant relationship between teacher knowledge and student achievement. The article went on to argue for spending more money on teacher education.

Discussion: This summation of Professor Rodriguez's work violates **Standard 7** and probably **Standard 2**. The article on Professor Rodriguez's work has two problems. First, it uses the word "shown," which substantially misrepresents the degree of security that should be attached to Professor Rodriguez's work, even in her own estimation. Second, it appears to use the word "significant" in a way that seems calculated to mislead the article's readers. While Professor Rodriguez found a statistically significant relationship, the word in the article suggests that the relationship was large or important. Neither interpretation is accurate.

Responsibilities Toward Subordinates and Others

ISSUE

Standard 8 imposes a duty not to discriminate in hiring, retention, and advancement decisions on the basis of *attributes* that are *not relevant to the evaluation of academic or research competence.* The standard offers its own suggested list of (presumptively) irrelevant attributes: gender, sexual orientation, physical disabilities, marital status, color, social class, religion, ethnic background, and national origin. This list is not intended to be exhaustive of the impermissible grounds for decision making as indicated by the phrase *or other attributes not relevant.*

Standard 8 also implies that it is the irrelevance of these attributes to job performance that makes employing them in decision making discriminatory. However, it should also be noted that the list of "irrelevant attributes" provided in **Standard 8** is more than a list of characteristics that are typically not associated with job performance. If that were all that were involved, the list of attributes might have included hair color or whether one can wiggle one's ears.

The list contains attributes that have historically been the basis of invidious discrimination in our society. Moreover, these attributes have one or more of these features: they are easily identified, not easily changed, and may be central to an individual's life and identity. This suggests that the grounds for not using these features for decision making are more than that they are usually not associated with job performance. It may also be that attributes such as race, religion, or disability should not be the basis for employment decisions, even if they are connected with job performance. For example, law or policy sometimes requires that we accommodate religious belief or disability even if doing so adds expense or inefficiency to the employment situation. Hence irrelevance to job performance is not the sole concern.

Standard 11 requires researchers to avoid improper harassment or coercion of those over whom they have power. One way to understand standards 8 and **11** is to say that they embody the content of those federal and state statutes that prohibit discrimination, harassment, or coercion in employment. There are, however, many clues in the text of the standards to suggest this is not a proper approach. **Standard 8** is broader than many antidiscrimination statutes, most of which do not address discrimination on the basis of sexual orientation. **Standard 11** explicitly notes that researchers have a duty to avoid *all forms of harassment, not merely those overt actions or threats that are due cause for legal action.* In short, there are sufficient differences between the standards and the law that suggest they were not written to replicate legal requirements. It is legally permissible for the standards to place a higher or stronger set of obligations on AERA membership, e.g., obligations that are more stringent regarding avoiding sexual harassment. To the extent the standards impose a lesser duty than the law does, it should be obvious that AERA members are held to the more demanding standards of the law.

Case 8

Professor Hyde recalls with nostalgia the days when his department was a comfortable club of White Anglo-Saxon Protestants. While he considers himself to be free of bias, he generally uses his power to ensure that no one disturbs his peace and tranquility. Because he fears that women and minorities are sources of uncomfortable debate and strange new conceptions, he generally hires white males as his new colleagues.

Discussion: This seems a clear case of what **Standard 8** forbids. **Standard 8**, whatever its complexities, expresses a broadly shared commitment that such egregious discrimination is wrong. We should note that the case has several confusing aspects. Professor Hyde views himself as not really prejudiced. It is not that he is hostile to women or minorities. It is rather that they introduce tension and discord into his life when he values peace and tranquility. However, such feelings do not constitute relevant grounds for personnel judgments. Acting on them is discrimination. Moreover, finding someone uncomfortable merely because they introduce new and controversial ideas into our life, apart from any serious appraisal of these ideas, is especially offensive in a university, where diversity is a goal of the marketplace of ideas.

ISSUE

In prohibiting discrimination on the basis of irrelevant attributes, **Standard 8** also implicitly permits judgments based on "attributes" that are judged "relevant," with "relevant" always being "relevant to." In **Standard 8** permissible grounds for decisions must be relevant to *academic or research competence*. Yet it is not always clear what we should count as relevant to academic or research competence, and it may be that there are cases in which we should not discriminate on the basis of an attribute even if it is relevant. For example, if we were researching Catholic schools, it may be impermissible to prefer Catholic research assistants even if they understand such schools better than non-Catholics. What counts as relevant, and when does relevance count?

Case 9

Professor Jennifer Avoronti is editing the papers of a famous educator and is recruiting a research assistant with appropriate editorial skills. Professor Paul Clemens is involved in a project on statistical analysis of a large database and is recruiting a research assistant with appropriate statistical skills.

>*Discussion:* These are easy cases. The attributes considered are relevant to the position, and the irrelevant attributes listed in **Standard 8** are unlikely to be relevant in evaluating a person's competence in these tasks. These are situations in which **Standard 8** provides clear guidance.

Case 10

Peter Jenkins, who researches urban school systems, is involved in a project involving interviewing African-American research subjects. He is recruiting a research assistant with appropriate interviewing skills. He wonders if an African-American interviewer would gain the confidence of interviewees more easily.

>*Discussion:* **Standard 8** may not provide clear guidance in this situation. Is the race of interviewers relevant to the assessment of their competence? Non-African-American interviewers might have all the technical skills needed to be competent interviewers, and yet their race may arguably make it less likely that the subjects will be open and frank. Are interviewers evaluated as less competent because their race has a bearing on the subjects' reaction? This is not a question to which **Standard 8** offers a quick answer.

>Note also that this case is distinguishable from cases dealing with affirmative action. In this instance, there is a plausible case made that race and culture are job related. The question of whether we should ignore such attributes in hiring, even when they may be performance related, is raised. In our **Rationale** to the **Preamble** of **Part I**, we noted that the list of characteristics that may not be used to discriminate is justified for reasons other than that such characteristics are normally irrelevant to qualifications for employment. Hence we may not wish to consider such characteristics even if they are job related.

This may be a matter of judgment. (Obviously, for example, we would wish to take gender into account in hiring someone to model women's clothing, although there are few such analogous instances in educational research.) Here it might also be useful to consider whether it would be similarly appropriate to hire white candidates to interview white subjects if we believed that they were more comfortable with white interviewers.

ISSUE

Standard 8 prohibits discrimination on the basis of physical disability. It does not, however, discuss non-physical disabilities, and it does not note whether, when, or to what degree, disabilities must be accommodated.

Case 11

Professor Wong is seeking an assistant to help with the literature review for her project. One applicant, Sara Clemens, is very qualified in Professor Wong's research area and is the best-qualified candidate. However, Sara is partially deaf and mildly dyslexic. Professor Wong reasons that because this assistantship requires duties that include taking some instructions over the phone, reading and digesting material, and writing up summaries of research, Sara Clemens's disabilities are job-related. Hence, she does not hire Sara.

> *Discussion*: While AERA's standards are not meant to mirror the law and may permissibly set a more demanding standard, they should not be interpreted to make them inconsistent with current law. The law requires that we not discriminate on both physical and non-physical disabilities.
>
> Hence, if disabilities such as dyslexia are viewed as non-physical, they should be precluded as bases of discrimination by **Standard 8**. Moreover, the law requires reasonable accommodation for disabilities. The law here is complex, and it is not our purpose to discuss its provisions in detail. However, the law requires that disabilities not be considered if the candidate can perform the essential job tasks and that reasonable steps be taken to allow disabled people to do their work.
>
> Here, as in the previous case, we should ask whether other considerations beyond mere job relevance are important in understanding the grounds for prohibiting discrimination. In this case, although there is the need to treat disabled people humanely, the law does not require researchers to hire people who cannot do the work for which they are hired. It does, however, require them to provide reasonable accommodation. In this case, Professor Wong might provide Sara with a special phone or provide instructions in writing and allow more time for her to read and digest research.

ISSUE

Educational researchers are informed that they should not discriminate on the basis of irrelevant attributes. Suppose, however, that bias is only one factor in a decision. How might that affect our understanding of **Standard 8**?

Case 12

Professor Lynn has a deep hostility toward Asians. In one instance he decides not to retain an Asian, Thomas Lee, as a research assistant associate because of this antipathy. In another instance he decides not to retain an Asian employee, Sarah Chen, who has a history of poor job performance. However, Professor Lynn is happy to reach this conclusion because of his prejudice regarding Asians.

> *Discussion:* The dismissal of Mr. Lee is the standard example of a violation of the principle of nondiscrimination. **Standard 8**, if it does nothing else, makes it a duty not to discriminate. The second example is a more difficult problem. **Standard 8** is not clear on whether it would be violated if an irrelevant attribute played a role in the decision making but was not the sole or even determinative criterion. We are not sure that this case represents a violation of **Standard 8**. While Professor Lynn's prejudice is regrettable, it appears that it is not the determinative reason for the dismissal. Since Sarah Chen is incompetent, this is sufficient reason for dismissing her. Perhaps the crucial question is whether it is clear that Chen would have been discharged apart from Professor Lynn's prejudice. The case assumes Chen's incompetence. However, since it is Professor Lynn who made this judgment, there are grounds for concern about its objectivity. Perhaps this judgment should not be fully in Professor Lynn's hands. Appeals mechanisms may provide a check on such prejudice.

ISSUE

Standard 8 applies to educational researchers who *participate in actions related to hiring, retention, and advancement.* The term "participate" is a broad term. The use of such a broad term suggests that **Standard 8** does not apply merely to researchers who are the final decision makers regarding the listed employment decisions but also to other forms of participation in decision making.

Case 13

Andrew Jones was accused of writing a racially biased letter of reference and providing a negative performance review of an employee. He was also involved in discussions leading to not allowing this employee to take a day of personal leave and in a decision regarding the research space allocation. When challenged, Jones claims that since he was not the final decision maker in any of these cases, he cannot be judged as a participant under **Standard 8**. Jones also notes that **Standard 8** does not mention employment relations beyond hiring, retention, or advancement.

> *Discussion:* The term "participate" is sufficiently broad to cover these situations. An AERA member asked to write a letter of recommendation must evaluate the academic and research competence of the subject without reliance on such irrelevant attributes as the person's gender, sexual orientation, etc. While **Standard 8** does not explicitly indicate that it is relevant to all employment-related decisions, it seems implausible that **Standard 8** should be limited only to hiring, retention, and advancement decisions.

ISSUE

The first sentence of **Standard 11** requires researchers to *avoid all forms of harassment* and explicitly notes that this standard is expected to exceed what is required by law. Yet even the legal definition of harassment is complex. Thus, the boundaries or limits to the responsibility embodied in this broadly phrased standard are hard to specify.

Case 14

Professor Norton has, at one time or another, done all of the following: He made giving sexual favors a condition to receive wage increases; persistently touched the breasts and buttocks of a research assistant without consent; and persistently made comments that, as researchers, women are not as competent or dedicated as men.

Discussion: These are primary examples of the behavior that is forbidden by **Standard 11**. The first is an example of what is termed "quid pro quo" sexual harassment. The second and third are examples of "environmental" harassment. We can begin to explore the many difficulties in understanding **Standard 11** by considering the following examples.

Case 15

- Professor Sally Hitchcock gives special employment advantages to someone she is sleeping with without making it a requirement to receive the employment advantages.
- John Stewart had an affair with a junior colleague that has ended unpleasantly, and then he wrote an unfavorable letter about her work to their department chair.
- Carl Anderson asked a female colleague for a date after she clearly said she did not want to date him.
- Paul Smith is genuinely affectionate and hugs his female employees at holiday parties to express gratitude for well-done jobs and also to express sympathy. Smith also keeps a picture of his wife clad in a bikini on his desk in view of anybody who comes to his office.
- Professor Andreas Constantine frequently tells his female co-workers that they look good in a tone of sexual appraisal. He told one co-worker that she gained weight, and his conversation is frequently laced with vulgarities.

Discussion: The probabilities are low that any of these examples would be the basis for successful legal action, yet they may be covered by **Standard 11**. One court, for example, viewed a case like that of John Stewart as a failed friendship, and the adverse employment actions could be viewed neither as quid pro quo nor environmental harassment. Regardless of whether the court was correct in its legal judgment, it is plausible that **Standard 11** covers this situation. The behavior of Carl Anderson and Paul Smith raises the question of how the standard determines harassment. Perhaps the average person would not view these examples as harassment. Yet it is possible that some women would feel offended and uncomfortable by the behaviors.

Hence the question arises whether **Standard 11**'s conception of harassment should mean that educational researchers have a duty not to engage in any behavior that others experience as sexual, racial, religious, or some other form of harassment. This is an exacting standard because it can be both subjective and capricious. An alternative standard is to believe that such conduct is harassment only if a hypothetical reasonable person would find it so, but that is not always a clear standard either. Regardless of the answer, it may be that morally sensitive people ought to keep a standard beyond what the law or a code of ethics requires.

Thus, we might assume that Paul Smith should not be required to remove the picture of his wife from public display since neither the law or AERA's code of ethics clearly requires him to do so, but we might also assume that it might be good for him to respect the sensitivities of his students and co-workers about the picture since they are not unreasonable.

The law tends to view harassment as illegal because it is discriminatory. Harassment tends to exclude or deny equal access to employment or educational opportunities. Harassment may, however, be morally wrong for other reasons. It may demean or threaten the person harassed. It may unfairly assert power or control over the harassed person. That harassment is wrong for such reasons may be a reason for **Standard 11** to set a more demanding standard than that set by the law. Moreover, since AERA's standards are not enforceable, some of the difficulties involved in a more demanding, yet ambiguous, standard may not be so problematic.

The example of Andreas Constantine may become a standard case of sexual harassment if the comments are part of a campaign to obtain a date or sexual favors or if they are persistently vulgar. Standing by themselves, they may simply be annoying and not represent a classic case of sexual harassment. Yet some might argue that annoyance is harassment, and this example would also be covered by **Standard 11**.

ISSUE

Whatever the scope of the harassment concept, a related question needs to be addressed. What are the types of harassment covered by **Standard 11**?

Case 16

- Professor Jonas Violas posts an anti-gay note directed to a specific gay person on a departmental bulletin board.
- Professor Anita Casper, a strongly pro-life educational researcher, makes frequent and critical anti-abortion comments to a colleague who has recently had an abortion.
- Dr. Kenneth Griffiths conducts a campaign to get his co-workers who continue to smoke to break the habit. He frequently follows people outside their building during their coffee break and, if he finds them smoking, lectures them about it.

Discussion: It seems safe to say that harassment on the basis of sex, race, religion, sexual orientation, physical disability, marital status, social class, ethnic background, and national origin are covered by **Standard 11**. Recall that these are the specifically listed grounds in **Standard 8** of its prohibited discrimination. Thus, the behavior of Professor Violas is certainly an example of behavior prohibited by **Standard 11**.

The other examples are more difficult cases. One thing that makes them complex is the possibility that the speech involved is protected by the First Amendment. (We take this up in **Hard Case 9**) It may also be important here to distinguish between legitimate comments that are tactless or annoying and those that are harassing. In making such judgments, context is important. In the cases of Professor Casper and Griffiths, there is some evidence that they are both persistent and intrusive in communicating their views. It is these elements of the case, rather than the fact that the messages are unpopular with those to whom they are addressed, that make them harassing. Here, as above, it is important to recall that AERA's code of ethics is not enforceable. Given this, its provisions may be taken as advice to morally sensitive people who may permissibly go beyond what would appropriately be enforced.

ISSUE

The second sentence of **Standard 11** states: *They* [educational researchers] *must not use their professional positions or rank to coerce personal or sexual favors or economic or professional advantages from students, research assistants, clerical staff, colleagues, or any others.* Part of this sentence repeats in a more specific way an aspect of the more generally phrased duty contained in the first sentence of the standard.

As noted above, the first sentence imposes a duty to avoid sexual harassment, which includes the duty not to engage in quid pro quo sexual harassment. This second sentence repeats that duty but goes on to cover a broader range of cases. Educational researchers are told they should not engage in coercion by using their *professional positions or rank to coerce personal or sexual favors or economic or professional advantages from students, research assistants, clerical staff, colleagues, or any others.*

Case 17

Professor Johnson has offered the following exchanges to his students:

- He has threatened Saundra, a student in his class, with a bad grade unless she rakes his lawn;
- He has offered his advisee, Haseem, an opportunity to be a second author of a paper if Haseem will do some unpaid research and a few home chores for him;
- He later offered Haseem the opportunity to be his paid research assistant but expected Haseem to help him put up a new fence as part of his duties.
- Professor Johnson is also a highly respected expert on school district budgeting. For presentations before school boards, he asks an honorarium of $5,000, a figure far higher than most educational researchers can command—one that school boards that are dependent on his advice for important budget decisions find unreasonable.

Discussion: The first example represents a clear example of coercion. A conditional threat was made to Saundra—the threat states that unless she rakes Professor Johnson's lawn, she will get a bad grade. **Standard 11** certainly forbids this.

The final example is clearly distinguishable from the others because Professor Johnson stands in a different relationship with the school board than he does with Saundra or Haseem. He has no power to coerce the school board. The only retribution he can take if his demand is refused is not to deliver his presentation, and this refusal makes the school board no worse off than before the bargaining process began. Thus, in this case, there is a fair bargaining position for Professor Johnson's services.

The second and third examples are more complex. In these cases, Professor Johnson obtains a personal or economic advantage by making various offers to Haseem. Under one interpretation of these cases, Professor Johnson has made offers that he need not have made. If Haseem accepts the offer, he will have acted of his own volition and a deal will have been struck in which both parties will see themselves as better off than if the offer had not been made and accepted. A voluntary contract will have been struck between researcher and student. Under a different interpretation of the cases, once certain background factors have been taken into account, these offers are interpreted as coercive offers. Professor Johnson stands in a power relationship with Haseem; Haseem may fear retaliation and recriminations, even in the absence of any explicit threat, if he refuses the offer. He may fear that he will not get a favorable letter of recommendation. The reasonableness of this fear on the part of Haseem would be enhanced if there were a history of Professor Johnson engaging in recriminations when similar offers were made to other students. Moreover, the fact that it is clearly inappropriate for Professor Johnson to make authorship contingent on nonacademic work (see **Part III, Standard 1**) or to pay for this work with his research funds, may heighten the sense of threat.

One might credit less reasonableness to Haseem's fear if he were not a student of Professor Johnson's (e.g., if Haseem were not a student in Professor Johnson's department). But what if Haseem and Professor Johnson were in the same department, but otherwise had no ongoing relationship?

Service to the Research Field

ISSUE

Standard 9 requires researchers to make candid personnel recommendations. What exactly is required?

Case 18

Professor Porter is often asked to write recommendations for his graduate students who apply for research positions. In the last year he has done all of the following in writing recommendations: he has written a favorable recommendation for a weak student, Allen Klees, on the grounds that Allen had a family to support; he has failed to note that an otherwise competent student, Paula Torres, is notoriously unreliable in completing assigned tasks, reasoning that it is only his responsibility to comment on students' intellectual responsibility and not on their reliability; and he has failed to note that a student, Ken Spare, was accused of plagiarism early in his student career.

> *Discussion:* The point of **Standard 9** is to create a meritocratic system of employment. One assumption underlying such a system is that human resources are most effectively used when people are matched to positions because they possess relevant qualifications or possess them to a degree that exceeds other applicants.
>
> The first instance above clearly violates **Standard 9**. Professor Porter has lied about the qualifications of Klees out of sympathy. It is also reasonably clear that he has violated **Standard 9** in the case of Paula Torres. The purpose of a candid job recommendation is to discuss the candidate's suitability for a position. Reliability is a relevant job qualification, and Professor Porter should mention it.
>
> The issue of Ken Spare is harder. Certainly a propensity to plagiarize is a relevant consideration in hiring a researcher. However, Spare's transgression is not recent, he has been suitably punished, and he has shown no tendency to repeat the offense. If Professor Porter believes that Spare has learned his lesson, he might reason that there is no longer a concern about plagiarism and it need not be mentioned. Perhaps he also reasons that in a tight job market even a hint of plagiarism will absolutely and unfairly exclude Spare from the field, and it is too severe a penalty for a single, repented offense. However, it might be most reasonable for Porter to acknowledge the issue and clearly state that he believes Spare has learned his lesson.

ISSUE

The first sentence of **Standard 10**, addresses all situations in which one person is asked to review the work of another person. Examples are promotion reviews, hiring reviews, grant application reviews, fellowship reviews, book and article reviews, and reviews of presentation proposals at the annual AERA meeting. It requires that researchers recuse themselves from rendering judgments in cases where they have strong conflicts of interest. A key issue is, what counts as a strong conflict of interest?

One reason why **Standard 10** did not seek to prohibit all conflicts of interest is that researchers often are in a position to advance their careers by criticizing those who hold contrary views. To view such cases as strong conflicts of interest would diminish the marketplace of ideas by preventing those who may be among the most knowledgeable on a topic from criticizing the views of their intellectual rivals. An example of the core problem the first sentence of this standard addresses is illustrated in the following cases:

Case 19

Professors Webster and Frenck are vying for the same job at a prestigious university. Professor Webster is deeply familiar with Professor Frenck's work and, despite the fact that they are rivals for the position, is asked to write a letter of reference regarding Professor Frenck.

Discussion: **Standard 10** requires Professor Webster to decline the invitation to write the letter. It may, however, be in Professor Frenck's interest for Professor Webster to write a letter, and Frenck may have confidence in Webster's integrity. He may, therefore, wish to waive his protection under **Standard 10**. Whether or not waivers by those whom the standard protects are appropriate is a complex topic. The reasonableness of such waivers is affected by the following questions. Is the standard solely designed to protect specific persons from the harm that may occur when others who have something to gain judge their work? Or, is the standard also designed to promote accuracy and truth generally, to protect the interests of all people who may want to rely on reviewers' comments?

Case 20

- Professors Blake and Watts have argued over a financial loan. Professor Blake is now asked to review an article of Professor Watts' for publication in a journal.
- Professor Jefferson is asked to review an essay titled "The Federal Role in Education" by his friend Professor Madison.

Discussion: Professor Blake does not have something to gain in the same sense that Professor Webster did in the previous case. Nevertheless, these are situations in which most people would doubt the impartiality of Professor Blake's judgment. A broad reading of **Standard 10** suggests that Professor Blake should decline the invitation to review Professor Watts' work. Personal animosity for Professor Watts would seem to disqualify Professor Blake as a reviewer.

The example of Professor Madison raises a different problem. Impartiality may be compromised here for a different reason. As much as Professor Jefferson may disagree with Professor Madison's views on the power of the federal government, he may ignore that difference and emphasize the points he and Madison agree on in his comments. Does **Standard 10** require Professor Jefferson to decline review of the essays because he knows he may disagree with some of Professor Madison's views but wants to remain friends? The answer may be "yes."

Yet, if the standard is read in this way, intellectual dialogue can be diminished. In some cases, it may be that all of the most qualified people available to review a work will know its author well. This is often the case in small, specialized fields. In such cases, it may be permissible to go ahead with the review, but the reviewer should disclose any possible conflict of interest to the editor.

Case 21

Professors Gunther and Kazin do not know each other personally but have a long history of being on opposite sides of an issue. A journal asks Professor Gunther to review the latest book by Professor Kazin that deals with that issue.

Discussion: One possible interpretation of **Standard 10** suggests that Professor Gunther must decline because she has much to gain by offering a damaging review of Professor Kazin's work. Yet such an interpretation seems to restrain the marketplace of ideas that may be served, even by vigorous criticism. Reading **Standard 10** as preventing Professor Gunther from offering her views would severely damage the intellectual enterprise in which AERA is engaged. The better course would be not to read **Standard 10** as barring Professor Gunther from commenting. More broadly, the marketplace of ideas is harmed if we construe disagreement, even strong disagreement over a long period, as a conflict of interest.

ISSUE

The first sentence of **Standard 10** is concerned not just with conflicts of interest but also with delivering promised reviews on time. What counts as on time?

Case 22

Professor Knight agrees to review a book manuscript for a publisher by a certain date knowing full well that a trip out of the country will mean that his review will be submitted to the publisher three weeks after that date.

Discussion: This case represents a clear violation of the standard. Professor Knight has deceived the publisher. The question is more difficult if Professor Knight accepted a review without being sure he could meet the deadline. If Professor Knight acted recklessly, without consideration of whether or not he could make the deadline, he would have violated the standard. But this also might be a case in which Professor Knight could be excused from his duty if he informed the publisher of his uncertainty of meeting the deadline when the original review request was made, and the publisher agreed to the possible delay.

ISSUE

We now turn to the second sentence of **Standard 10**, which addresses the quality of the reviewing process and the review provided: *Materials sent for review should be read in their entirety and considered carefully, with evaluative comments justified with explicit reasons.* What is required?

Case 23

Professor Davidson receives a journal article for review. He reads the first five pages of the article, and, deciding the article is poor, recommends that the journal reject the article.

Discussion: This seems a clear case of what is forbidden by **Standard 10**. Reviewers have at least two obligations to those whose work they review. The first is to provide a conscientious judgment. The second is to provide useful feedback. Neither obligation can be met on the basis of a partial reading of an article.

Case 24

Professor Grove agrees to write a letter of reference on a promotion review case of a faculty member whom he does not personally know. Professor Grove receives a package of 12 articles written by the candidate and reads only three of these articles before writing his letter.

Discussion: Professor Grove's approach to the reviewing process appears to be a blatant violation of **Standard 10**. Yet would Professor Grove be justified in reading only three articles if these were the only three published in a peer-reviewed journal, with the other materials being speeches, items for a professional newsletter, etc.? The answer is probably "no." Professor Grove's selection of only the three items for careful consideration may do the candidate a disservice as well as the institution that is considering the candidate for promotion. Because all of these materials were sent indicated that they were considered relevant to the promotion decision by the institution.

However, there might be other circumstances that would justify Professor Grove in reading only some of the articles. It might be that only these articles fall in his area of expertise. Or it might be that Professor Grove lacks the time to read lengthy articles and must choose between reading a subset or not writing the recommendation at all. In such cases, Professor Grove should be clear to those to whom the letter is written what he has read and not generalize beyond these articles. He should also discuss his procedure in his response and it would be best if this were agreed to in advance. **Standard 10** should not be understood to preclude the common practice of requesting that reviewers in promotion cases respond to a sample of articles.

Case 25

The heart of Professor Grove's letter is in the following paragraph: "Assistant Professor Elgar's publishing record is a bit meager. Yet his three published articles have appeared in respected scholarly journals. The topics he has addressed in these articles should be of interest to professionals in the field and are well researched and documented. I recommend him for promotion, but not with great enthusiasm."

Discussion: Under one interpretation, this review fully complies with **Standard 10**. Professor Grove has backed up his recommendation for promotion with reasons. However, one might question whether they are adequately explicit reasons. Many would say that this review is superficial. For example, Professor Grove provided no supporting analysis of his conclusion that the articles were well researched. He did not situate the writing of Professor Elgar in a larger scholarly context nor comment on the contribution Professor Elgar has made to that body of literature. **Standard 10** seems to require not only that reviewers achieve a conscientious judgment, but also that they develop an adequate justification for it.

ISSUE

Standard 12 states that *educational researchers should not be penalized for reporting in good faith violations of these or other professional standards.* However, in a note at the end of the **Standards**, it is added that AERA views its **Standards** as *an educational document, to stimulate collegial debate, and to evoke voluntary compliance by moral persuasion.* Hence the standards specifically disavow any intent to *monitor adherence to the standards or to investigate allegations of violations to the Code.* Moreover, there is no duty imposed on AERA members by the standards to report violations of them, except for **Part V, Standard 4**. Indeed, the standards do not provide a means to report violations. The standards do not address whether, by whom, or to what degree a researcher should be penalized for a violation of the standards. It could be argued, however, that the very existence of the standards carries with it an implicit duty on AERA members to enforce the standards when this is appropriate and there are means available.

Moreover, membership in other professional institutions may carry with it a duty to report violations. AERA members normally will be members of other organizations that will have ethical expectations that intersect with the standards as well as the means to enforce them. In other cases, the seriousness of the violations carries with it a duty to report violations, and violations of the standards may also be reported to those who are harmed by them or to other interested parties. **Standard 12** seems to envision this in a reference to *other professional standards*. Hence it makes sense to include **Standard 12**, which protects AERA members from retribution for good faith "whistle-blowing."

Many of the cases already discussed provide opportunities for whistle-blowing. When Professor Johnson (see **Case 17**) coerced Haseem to do his housework, or paid him to do it with grant money, the violations might be reported to the dean of the school in which Professor Johnson is employed or to the agency that is funding Professor Johnson's research.

Case 26

Professor Snyder discovers that his colleague, Professor Bender, has been using his teaching assistant to help with his research and yard work at home. Snyder views this as a misuse of university funds, and he reports this violation to the dean of their college. The dean regards this as a minor matter and unworthy of his time. He tells Snyder to mind his own business, suggesting that if he does not, his pay raises may suffer.

> *Discussion:* This seems a clear case of what **Standard 12** was intended to protect against. **Standard 12** requires that Professor Snyder not be penalized.

ISSUE

A key phrase in **Standard 12** is the term "good faith." What does good faith mean?

Case 27

Professor Thomas has correctly observed that Professor Brennan hired his research team employing an affirmative action policy. Thus, Professor Brennan chose to hire a Hispanic female in preference to a more qualified Anglo female. Professor Thomas reports to the dean that Professor Brennan has violated **Standard 8**.

> *Discussion:* Professor Thomas has acted based on his interpretation of **Standard 8**. If he was not sure that **Standard 8** prohibited affirmative action policies, did Professor Thomas act in good faith? Perhaps the best interpretation of **Standard 12's** good-faith requirement is that Professor Thomas can act in bad faith only if his interpretation of **Standard 8** is wholly unreasonable (i.e., no reasonable person would have interpreted the standard as he did). Thus, in this case, Professor Thomas did not act in bad faith. (Some complexities of "good faith" are discussed in **Hard Case 10**.)

Hard Cases

ISSUE

The **Preamble** of **Part I** requires respect for diverse methodologies and approaches. What are the limits on such diversity?

Case 1

Dr. Daniel McGruder was a professor of music education at Callison State. He was asked to do a needs assessment concerning the music education program at the Mozart High School (Mozart). His report included the following conclusions and recommendations:

1. There is too much emphasis on classical music at Mozart, and this emphasis alienates most students.
2. Students prefer listening over performing.
3. The school should pay more attention to "authentic" adolescent art forms.

Thus, Mozart should place less emphasis on band, orchestra, and choir in its music program and should shift instruction into a music appreciation class with the emphasis on listening to the music that the students want to listen to, chiefly rap and rock.

Mozart's music department staff was appalled. At the outset, they made several objections. First, they claimed, students could listen to their music whenever they wanted outside of school. Second, it was the staff's responsibility to develop their students' taste in music, not to concede to current adolescent fads. Third, the appreciation of music was much enhanced by performance. Even if most students did not continue to perform after graduation, it was band, orchestra, and choir that really developed their ability to appreciate all kinds of music.

The music department became even more irate when they looked at how Dr. McGruder had done his research. It was based on a simple interview format. Students were asked how they would like to study music in school. Moreover, he had nothing resembling a random sample of Mozart students. In fact, he had focused his interviews on those students who were enrolled in Mozart's nonacademic curriculum.

When confronted with this, McGruder provided the following defense. "Classical music is oppressive. It's a form of cultural capital that serves to separate elites from the working class. Moreover, it is culturally inappropriate. It speaks to the experience of the ruling classes of a bygone age. It's working class kids who are the people. We need to emphasize music that speaks to them and comes out of their experience. My research procedures were exactly what was needed to discover the real music of our age."

Needless to say, this produced considerable debate. At a minimum, the Music Department staff wanted to affirm the value of classical music for every age and to insist that they also taught the better forms of contemporary music. After all, Mozart's jazz band regularly won state competitions. The staff also insisted that if interviews were used, it was absolutely necessary to have a random sample that represented all of Mozart's students.

Dr. McGruder's reply to this was simple: "You are just working out of a different paradigm, that's all. My procedures are perfectly justified given my assumptions. Of course, if you begin with bourgeois values, you'll do it differently. Progressive people will understand."

QUESTIONS

1. Does the **Preamble** to **Part I** of the code warrant Dr. McGruder's response? Could it be argued that even if McGruder's methodology is his own, it is inappropriate?

2. Is the disagreement here about research methods or values? Is the distinction between values and methods itself clear? To what extent do research methods presuppose values?

3. If the disagreement is about values, does it follow that there are no facts that could show McGruder's values as the right or wrong ones? Is there evidence that counts for or against values?

4. Is it likely that most disagreements about "paradigms" in research result from different values? What exactly is a paradigm?

5. Sometimes it is claimed that all research presupposes the values of the researcher. What does this mean? Is it true?

6. Sometimes, the best researchers can do when their values (inevitably) influence their research is to disclose them. Researchers do this so that those who use research can take the researchers' values into account in assessing the research. Is this reasonable? Would it have helped here?

7. Researchers often criticize the methods employed by other researchers. Does the **Preamble** suggest that this is inappropriate? How can we distinguish between those cases in which such criticism is appropriate and those cases in which it is not?

ISSUE

Standard 6 requires that researchers report their research results to the research community to *allow knowledgeable, trained researchers to understand and interpret them.* In our initial discussion of **Standards 5, 6,** and **7,** we suggested that these standards serve the marketplace of ideas. Furthermore, the marketplace of ideas requires that research results be reported adequately to allow other scholars to appraise them. However, these standards make no reference to appraisal, and this raises several questions.

One question is whether it is permissible to read this intent into the standards when a literal reading of its provisions requires reporting that is sufficient only for the purposes of understanding and interpretation. These purposes may require a lower reporting level than required for an independent results assessment.

Second, it is not always clear what needs to be reported in order to permit a reassessment. Sometimes scholars differ about what is relevant in evaluating an argument.

Finally, it may be that a reassessment might require extensive publication of raw data or interview transcripts. How much is it reasonable to expect people to report, and to what extent should we trust scholars to code and interpret their data accurately?

Case 2

Professor Julian Reed, a noted researcher in mathematics education, was also the owner of a prosperous restaurant. His most recent study was based on interviews of several waiters and waitresses at his restaurant and focused on how they did arithmetic on the job. Several of the subjects developed interesting heuristics for computing sales tax and adding figures, most of which ended with $.95. In writing up his results, Professor Reed didn't report that these subjects worked in his restaurant. Should he have reported this fact?

Discussion: This question requires a judgment as to whether the employer–employee relationship involved was important for readers to know in order to judge the research. An argument that it should have been reported is that the desire to please their employer, or the fear of displeasing him, is a factor in how the subjects responded in the interviews. Given this possibility, the relationship between the investigator and the subjects should have been reported. It is a relevant factor in assessing the work.

The case against this is that although there was some possibility that the relationship might have affected the responses, there are few reasons to suppose that this was likely. Moreover, there are any number of things that *might* have affected the response, not all of which could have been reported. In our judgment, it would have been desirable for Professor Reed to note his relationship to the subjects. However, since this is a matter of judgment about which reasonable people might disagree, we do not regard Professor Reed as behaving unethically for not having done so. He might, however, have asked the editor of the journal who published his work about the matter.

QUESTIONS

1. We have suggested that because the research subjects worked for Dr. Reed, the results might have been influenced, but it is not obviously the case that he should have reported this fact. Do you agree?

2. Are there other ethical issues involved here? Might Dr. Reed's subjects have felt coerced to participate in his study? Do AERA's standards provide adequate protection against such coercion? (See **Part II, Standards 1, 4,** and **5.**)

3. Reporting the employer–employee relationship would have required little space in Dr. Reed's paper. Is this a relevant consideration?

4. We have claimed that researchers should report their work adequately so as to permit an independent assessment of its merits by other scholars. This is implicit in **Standards 5, 6**, and **7**. This is because they serve not only the value of honesty in reporting results but also those values associated with the marketplace of ideas. Recall that in our introductory comments on the standards, we argued that the purposes and larger principles that they served were appropriately appealed to in interpreting them. This is how we found independent assessment in the standards despite the fact that it does not appear in the text. Do you think this reading is appropriate? Is it important that the standards have no legal force?

5. In some cases, when an independent assessment would require reporting vast amounts of raw data, it is impracticable. To what extent does the appraisal of research assume trust of the researcher's integrity? Should researchers be expected to provide the rawest data to other scholars on request? What problems might this raise in confidentiality?

I S S U E

Education researchers are more naturally inclined toward finding ways to improve education than toward making it worse or preserving the status quo. Consequently, they are more interested in reporting positive effects of experimental interventions than in reporting evidence about what didn't have an impact. Yet good evidence that something didn't have an educational effect may be important. Are researchers responsible for reporting non-significant effects as well as significant ones?

Case 3

Dr. Flanders sealed the envelope containing the article submission and handed it to her research assistant to take to campus mail. She had just finished writing up the results of her research evaluation of the Creating Character Program, and she was confident that the findings were strong enough to ensure publication in a leading journal. The evaluation had identified statistically significant relations between program features of the Creating Character Program and five predicted student behavioral outcomes. These outcomes were significantly more frequent in the student population where the program was implemented than in the control school student population. "You may see your name in print before graduation!" She said optimistically to her students.

Skip Tinker looked puzzled. "I didn't even realize we'd finished writing up our findings," he said. "We've done analyses of the twenty selected program elements and the ten predicted outcomes, but I've only completed the tables where we found statistically significant correlations. That's only a small part of the data, and we hadn't even talked about how you wanted to present all the other information. How can the article be done yet?"

Flanders smiled. "We don't need to do that. The other factors and outcomes are listed in a footnote, and what's not significant is not going to get this article accepted for publication. People care about what does work, not what doesn't, and the journals only publish findings when researchers find significant effects. You can file the other stuff away. We've got another project to do."

> **Discussion:** Researchers normally focus on reporting statistically significant correlations between variables because they may possibly reflect causal relationships. Causal relationships are important because they help explain how education takes place, and they may offer the possibility of making changes that produce beneficial results in the educational system. Research analyses frequently involve many variables and the relationships between them,

and it is often impractical for a research report to present information regarding all of the possible relationships among the variables studied.

According to this line of thinking, selective reporting of the significant relationships among variables seems appropriate because it tells the reader what may have caused something to happen and how educators might use what works. Nonsignificant relationships, on the other hand, are so many dead ends; such relationships represent myriad features of the situation that have no relationship to the desired outcomes, and consequently they are of little interest to people who want to understand or change education.

However, research findings reporting no significant relationships or no effects among variables are not entirely worthless. If they reflect variables that are often thought to be powerful influences on the quality of education, then reporting that they had no effect in a given research study might be interesting to other researchers and educators. Furthermore, if particular elements of an education program are touted as being essential, yet they do not demonstrate a relationship to the program's intended results, then the knowledge of that lack of a relationship may be of interest to potential program clients. In such instances, omitting research findings may well constitute a misrepresentation of the program and the research results. A problem here is that a "no effects" finding is usually not as attractive to journal educators as an "effects" finding. Moreover, distinguishing the useful or important no effects findings from the potentially infinite no-effects findings that are not interesting is a task requiring judgment. This task cannot be resolved by the application of a mechanical procedure or rule.

QUESTIONS

Standard 2 prohibits researchers from misrepresenting research findings, and **Standard 5** declares that researchers should refrain from selectively communicating their findings. **Standards 6** and **7** direct researchers to provide complete and not misleading reports of their research findings.

1. If a researcher reports "positive effects" findings and omits "no effects" findings from a research study, is this a misleading characterization of the experimental intervention power?
2. Do research journals and others making publication decisions have an obligation to be impartial to research reports with "no effects" as compared to "effects" findings?

ISSUE

Researchers are often asked to advise government. Often the advice they give will be reported and discussed in the media. Because researchers are often committed not only to their results, but also to their recommendations, they may report recommendations to government and the public that are more intended to ensure their adoption rather than an informed debate. Are there circumstances that justify such reporting?

Case 4

The members of the Finance and Equity Panel (FEP) had been appointed by the Commissioner of Education from a list of nominees recommended by the Governor, by the leading majority member and minority member of each house of the state legislature, and by representatives of diverse stakeholders. Everyone agreed that it was a balanced committee, and it needed to be.

The fiscal issues facing the state's school system were both complex and contentious. Hundreds of millions of dollars were at stake. The legislature was unable to come up with the changes that its courts had demanded of it, despite six months of arguing and political infighting. It was hoped that because FEP was balanced and bipartisan and its members were all widely respected people, it would be able to make recommendations that would break the deadlock. Its members had argued long and hard about the issues. While FEP was unusual in its openness to evidence and was not split by partisan concerns, it was nevertheless deeply divided on what to recommend. In many cases, FEP had commissioned papers to resolve technical issues, but often the paid experts disagreed. Moreover, FEP often discovered that, even when the data had been analyzed and its results agreed on, the policy issues remained open. Policy decisions often depended on a controversial view of equity, or on how to strike a balance between conflicting values. These were issues that no amount of number crunching was going to resolve.

FEP proceeded by taking votes on a series of policy recommendations. No outcome was unanimous. But in the end, FEP produced 11 recommendations. The result of these recommendations was that significant fiscal resources would be shifted from the state's wealthier districts to its poorer districts, and from suburban areas to urban areas. The recommendations would be highly controversial and politically difficult. Since their implementation depended on the prestige of the committee, the Chair asked for a final vote on the recommendations and requested that the vote be unanimous. Despite the fact that most of the members of FEP disagreed with some of the recommendations, and a few members had severe reservations about the set, everyone went along.

FEP reported its results in three ways. First, it produced a 500-page report of detailed analysis and argument, a report that it was assumed few would read. Second, it produced a five-page executive summary that reported FEP's recommendations along with a claim that they were unanimously accepted. Finally, it produced a 500-word press release. The headline, which FEP also produced, hoping that newspapers would adopt it, read "FEP Unanimous: City Schools Need More Money." The article focused on how the quality of urban education was a first priority for the viability of the state's economy and how FEP's recommendations would move urban education forward into the next millennium. There was no mention that FEP's recommendations would mean higher taxes and lower school budgets for most of the state's suburban schools, nor that many of the members of FEP had serious reservations about whether urban schools could or would spend the extra money to benefit poor children. It was clear to all members of FEP that any misgivings or disunity by FEP members would be exploited in the debate on its upcoming recommendations and would very likely result in another deadlock in the legislature. It was crucial to the success of FEP's recommendations that they be presented as objective scientific research.

Professor Paula Calloway, a school finance professor at State University, was a member of FEP. She was dubious about many of its recommendations. Shortly after the report was released, a reporter from the state's largest daily called her. "What do you personally think of these recommendations?" was the first question. Her only answer to the question was, "I fully support the FEP recommendations." She referred all other questions to the committee's chair.

> *Discussion:* What Dr. Calloway actually thought was that providing poor children in urban areas with the same resources that were available to rich children was a matter of "simple justice." She meant by this that providing equal funding for all children of the state was fair, regardless of whether extra funds had a beneficial effect on the achievement of children in poor districts.
>
> She believed it to be unjust that some children got a better-funded education than others because of where their parents could afford to live, regardless of how much educational dif-

ference money made. She also thought that money made little difference in educational outcomes. Her reading of the evidence suggested that the major determinants of educational success were beyond the control of schools. She was, however, unwilling to say this.

Dr. Calloway has four reasons. First, if she does say this, her comments may destroy the FEP's work. Second, all of the documents needed for scholars, reporters, and the public to judge the FEP's conclusions and to understand their arguments and disagreements are available. She was just being asked to do the reporter's work for him. Third, she believes that there is an implied agreement on the part of the committee's membership to publicly support FEP's conclusions, and she feels that it is most appropriate for any report commentary to come from the FEP's chair. Finally, she feels that the reporter is more interested in reporting a controversy than in reporting what will assist people in understanding the issues.

We respect these reasons. However, we also think that Dr. Calloway might have responded in a way that better served the aim of informing the public. She might have said, "I support FEP's recommendations because they are the product of competent and conscientious deliberations. But I must also acknowledge that I am not fully convinced that extra money for urban areas will quickly result in higher achievement for urban children. This is, of course, a difficult issue on which reasonable people might disagree."

Such a response might lessen the chances of FEP's recommendations being enacted, but it serves the values of the marketplace of ideas and enhances the quality of public deliberation about education. FEP is not the state legislature. One view of its proper role is that it should educate the legislature, but not seek to influence its deliberations by giving its recommendations more force than the evidence warrants.

QUESTIONS

1. What is the scope of educational researchers' responsibility to inform public debate about controversial issues? Has FEP met its responsibility? Are there occasions when researchers might simplify their conclusions, or appear more certain than they really are, to facilitate a decision?

2. Has FEP violated **Standards 5, 6,** or **7** in the way it has informed the public?

3. What do you think of the following argument? Researchers have the responsibility to do their best work. They also have the responsibility to see that their research is acted on in a responsible way. Education, however, is a highly politicized activity in which many actors have little regard for research but are willing to use it to pursue their interests. It is not an arena in which researchers can report their results and expect that they will be used fairly and judged reasonably. The public, moreover, is not able to assess research with any care, but is easily mislead by it. Thus, in the political environment in which FEP must report its results, it is reasonable for FEP to report its recommendations in a way that maximizes the prospects that they will be implemented. While FEP's results and recommendations are controversial and far from certain, they are supported by professional consensus. Moreover, every member of FEP believes that its recommendations are an improvement over the current state of affairs. If FEP reported its findings with any hint of doubt or suggestion of conflict, it would ensure that self-interested parties would defeat its well-intentioned recommendations. Thus, FEP's way of representing its results is more than justified.

4. It may be that some suburban legislators who are convinced that urban schools need more money would welcome FEP's recommendations because they provide "political cover" for decisions that might be resisted by their constituents. Should FEP be willing to provide such cover?

5. Should FEP be viewed as a self-interested party?

6. What should Dr. Calloway tell the reporter?

ISSUE

Can **Standard 8** be understood to forbid affirmative action?

Case 5

For reasons unrelated to the topic of the research project, the principle investigator, Cassandra Phillips, deliberately chooses to hire or promote a competent Hispanic female instead of a slightly more qualified Anglo male. Phillips does this to bring about greater ethnic and gender balance on the research team and to address what she perceives as a history of social injustice against Hispanics.

Discussion: Has Dr. Phillips violated **Standard 8**? It seems that the answer is yes. The emphasis in the standards is on using attributes that are relevant to evaluating academic or research competence. Yet **Standard 8** might only create a presumptive duty that may be set aside for good reasons. If **Standard 8** creates only a presumptive duty that may be set aside for sufficient reason, we need a theory regarding those reasons that provides sufficient warrant for not following the standard.

Such a theory of "excuses" or "justifications" is not provided by the standards. Two such justifications for affirmative action are that, by increasing the diversity of voices involved in academic life, the marketplace of ideas is enhanced, and, by hiring members of those groups that have been the victims of a history of discrimination, compensatory justice is served. Because the standards do endorse intellectual diversity and value the marketplace of ideas, there is a warrant in the standards for the first of these arguments. It should be noted that AERA policy explicitly endorses affirmative action; however, it does not define it.[2]

Case 6

Dr. Justin Clark has normally relied on the formal record of academic training to determine the competence of a prospective employee to perform statistical analysis. He has narrowed a current job search to two qualified candidates, one of whom is a member of a minority group.

If Dr. Clark follows his normal procedure, he will not hire the minority candidate because the minority candidate has the lower grade point average of the two. However, Dr. Clark has a file of work for each candidate, and it would be possible to have each candidate in for an interview. Thus, Dr. Clark could take a deeper look at the qualifications of each candidate. Moreover, Dr. Clark believes that because minority students often come from disadvantaged backgrounds, they may get off to a slower start in their academic work. It is thus quite possible that if he looks at each candidate's qualifications in more detail, he will find the minority candidate to be more qualified.

Discussion: Is the formal record of taking courses and earning grades sufficiently relevant to the evaluation of academic or research competence, or does **Standard 8** require something more, such as use of a valid and reliable test of the candidate's statistical skills or a direct examination of a candidate's work? The question may be important because reliance on formal academic credentials may have the consequence of discriminating on the basis of race or social class. Even if discrimination is not intended, there may be a disparate effect. Here it should be noted that Dr. Clark is not proposing to prefer a less-qualified candidate because that candidate is a member of a minority group. He is proposing to alter his procedures to look more deeply into the qualifications of each candidate than he normally would.

QUESTIONS

1. In the first of these two affirmative action and disparate effect cases, we suggest two theories that might serve to justify affirmative action. Are there others?

2. In your view, do any of these theories succeed?

3. Does the fact that AERA members, as professional researchers, have a duty to support and sustain the marketplace of ideas suggest that the "diversity of voices" theory is more appropriate for AERA than the "compensatory justice" theory?

4. Suppose that Dr. Clark does examine each candidate's qualifications in more detail, and, because he finds that the minority candidate is more qualified, hires her. Might the candidate who was not hired argue that she was discriminated against because of her race because Dr. Clark adopted a different procedure when a minority candidate was a finalist than he would have otherwise, and if he had followed his usual procedure, she would have been hired?

5. Suppose that it is the minority candidate who has the higher grade point average, but since Dr. Clark happens to have a sample of each candidate's work, he examines this work carefully and concludes that the white candidate is more qualified and hires her. Would you still draw the same conclusion?

6. Are personnel policies that require employers to look more deeply at the qualifications of minority candidates justified?

ISSUE

Standard 8 requires that people be hired on the basis of possessing relevant attributes. Although it seems clear that the ability to do statistics usually is a relevant attribute and race is not, there are many ambiguous cases.

Case 7

Professor Cleaver heads a large soft-money operation, the Agency for School Productivity. This agency hires a large number of people to do various research tasks. Here are some of the attributes that raise questions about what characteristics of people are job related: people addicted to drugs or alcohol, an interviewer who is HIV-positive, a person with an emotional disability or severe body odor, and a Turk whose employment is strongly opposed by an Armenian who is currently a member of the research team on which the Turk would work.

Discussion: Taking addictions into account may not violate **Standard 8** if these addictions affect the research competence of the person, as would be the case if the addictions led to unacceptable behavior involving mistakes in handling the job. But what if these addictions only reduced productivity because of frequent absences from work? The standard speaks of "competence" without specifying whether competence includes productivity. Because productivity is a standard element of competence and there seems to be no ethical consideration leading to the conclusion that productivity should be excluded from competence, we conclude that **Standard 8** permits an adverse employment decision based on addiction when that addiction affects productivity. However, it does not follow that moral disapproval of addiction, apart from an effect on performance, justifies such a decision.

Being HIV-positive is not relevant to evaluating a person's competence to properly conduct an interview. Yet the researcher might be concerned that if it were known that the interviewer was HIV-positive that adult subjects would refuse to participate, or that parents of minor children would refuse to permit their children to be subjects of the research.

A person may have a personality disorder or body odor and be quite competent in running a computer-based analysis of a database. Yet working with such people may be difficult. Is a refusal to hire people with whom it is difficult to work a violation of **Standard 8**? Is a refusal to hire these people without attempting to make a reasonable accommodation a violation of the standard?

These questions are not answered by the plain words of the standard, and they raise a more general problem. How is **Standard 8** interpreted in connection with other considerations relevant to hiring, retention, and advancement decisions? Does **Standard 8** have priority over considerations regarding a smoothly working research team? One way out of the dilemma is to interpret the term "competence" to include the ability to work comfortably with other people. But this opens the door to the discrimination that **Standard 8** prohibits.

Standard 8 seems to preclude Professor Cleaver from granting the wishes of his or her Armenian employee that he not employ Turks. However, hiring a person who is highly distasteful to another member of a research team can be disruptive. We are left with the unresolved question of the way in which **Standard 8** works with other relevant hiring considerations, such as the desire to build a compatible research team. If **Standard 8** provides only a presumptive duty that may be set aside for sufficiently good reasons, we then need a theory regarding such reasons that provide a warrant for not following the requirements of the standard.

We might think about these attributes in the following way. We might argue that we should not permit attributes to be considered job related even if they undermine effective team building, or otherwise have a negative effect on the workplace, if they do so only in virtue of inappropriate reactions to these attributes. This, in turn, requires us to have a view of what makes a negative reaction to certain attributes unreasonable—a matter that itself raises considerable complexities.

For example, we might claim that it is unethical and unreasonable for Armenians to harbor hostility toward all Turks. Thus, it would be unethical for Dr. Cleaver to permit the fact that such prejudice exists on his research team to count as a reason for not hiring a Turk, even if it might affect the smooth working of his team. We might also claim that when a given attribute is beyond the capacity of the individual to control, we have a prima facie duty to try to accommodate it. Thus, we might accept a duty to accommodate someone with a personality disorder if we can judge that this attribute is beyond the individual's control.

In contrast, we might claim that a negative reaction to someone with extreme body odor is not unreasonable both because body odor, assuming that it is not the result of some medical condition, can be easily controlled, and our reaction to it is difficult to control. These examples, however, suggest that any standard employed in such cases will raise complexities of interpretation. Moreover, this theory goes beyond what is plainly found in the language of the standards.

QUESTIONS

1. It seems that there are attributes that do affect productivity and might be viewed as job related but that are also attributes that we might wish to include on a list of protected attributes. It also seems to follow that some attributes should be protected, regardless of whether they are job related. What attributes are these? Why might we wish to protect them?

2. Are there attributes that deserve special protection? If so, why? For example, are there special reasons to protect religion or race? Might we want to protect possessors of such attributes

from discrimination even when there are contexts in which these attributes might affect job performance?

3. Some attributes affect performance because of how others react to them. When is it permissible to consider such factors? When is it not?

ISSUE

Standard 9 requires candid personnel recommendations. Is that always possible?

Case 8

Sara Menlow was asked to write a recommendation for Tom Ozgood. Ozgood has been an able student. He has applied for a position at the Northern Lights Lab, a prestigious research center, and Dr. Menlow believes he is fully qualified. He is a good student, but he is not the best student she has had in recent years. However, last year, Dr. Menlow recommended a student of similar ability to the lab and provided a candid recommendation for her. This student was not hired by Northern Lights. In fact, much to Dr. Menlow's surprise, the student got no position at all. Dr. Menlow hadn't thought much about this until she met the person who had been hired. This person was not nearly as capable as her student who had been rejected for the position.

She had called a friend at Northern Lights to ask about this. His response was this: "When we post a position, we get fifty applicants. The recommendations for at least twenty of these claim that this is the best person the writer has ever trained. Ten applicants are known to have walked on water at least twice while they were students, and five more will soon be candidates for the Nobel. When a recommendation says that the person is merely good, that is the kiss of death. Sara, your honesty is killing your students." Dr. Menlow is now entertaining the following thought: "If I provide a candid recommendation about Tom, I will, in effect, misrepresent his qualifications in comparison to other applicants because I now know that other writers will not be candid about their students. What counts as telling the truth about Tom is writing a recommendation that locates him accurately in relation to other applicants. To do that I must tell the truth by lying."

> *Discussion:* We believe this is a real dilemma, one that has no good solution for Dr. Menlow. Many scholars do seem to provide recommendations for their students that are inflated. Some may be motivated by a desire to help their students. Some may even have accepted Dr. Menlow's view. It may be that there are enough people who write gilded recommendations that the system has become unfair to those whose advisors are candid. Moreover, in one sense, Dr. Menlow's argument is correct. Employers who receive a large number of applications must rank them partly on the basis of recommendations. If there are quite different standards of candor, those candidates with candid recommendations will be systematically underrated. If recommendations are "norm referenced," and there is much dishonesty in the system, it becomes nearly impossible for the candid writer to tell the truth. One response—we believe the best one—is to note that the only cure for this problem is for everyone to be candid.

QUESTIONS

1. Those who write recommendations are commonly selected by the candidate. Is this a good idea? If not, how might it be changed?

2. A few academic departments generate collective recommendations for their students that are a consensus of the department. Is this a good idea?

ISSUE

Previously, we discussed cases of harassment in which one person directed his or her behavior at another specific person. Some people do not limit the applicability of the term "harassment" to such personal encounters. Some institutions have tried to inhibit harassment by enacting sweeping prohibitions against hate speech.

Case 9

Professor Violas, who in **Case 16** had posted a notice attacking a particular gay person, posts another anti-gay, anti-lesbian note on the bulletin board directed to no specific person.

> *Discussion:* These cases open the complicated topic of hate-speech codes. Are educational researchers obligated by **Standard 11** to take steps to implement hate-speech codes? Some might argue that such a code is one way to "avoid" harassment. To read **Standard 11** in this way opens up complicated issues, such as what formulation of such a code does **Standard 11** require? Some codes are vague and broad, whereas others are limited to specifically defined speech acts, such as the utterance of words that are intended to insult or stigmatize an individual or group on the basis of their sex, etc., and uses words that incite an immediate breach of the peace.
>
> It is important to note that the courts have struck down even the most narrowly drawn hate-speech codes as a violation of the free-speech clause of the First Amendment of the U.S. Constitution. The more broadly drawn a speech code is, the more it can have a chilling effect on the free exercise of academic discourse.
>
> These judicial rulings, which generally rely on the U.S. Constitution, are applicable only to public universities. Thus, the constitutional concerns that a hate-speech code would raise only operate to limit a broad reading of **Standard 11** in public universities. Educational researchers in private universities would not, as a technical legal matter, be limited by the U.S. Constitution. However, even in a private university, researchers who feel obligated by this reading of **Standard 11** to establish a hate-speech code should pay attention to the effect the code has on freedom of speech in general and academic freedom in particular.

QUESTIONS

1. The breadth of **Standard 11** may require researchers to avoid hate speech even if it is not targeted at a specific person. Does the fact that the code is not enforceable eliminate the tension between an injunction against hate speech and potential First Amendment rights? Might there still be a "chilling effect" on speech, independent of enforcement?

2. The assumption of this case is that the standards might require researchers not only to avoid the conduct proscribed, but also to support policies that prohibit such proscribed conduct. Does **Standard 11** have this force?

3. Why would hate speech be constitutionally protected speech? Does hate speech contribute to the marketplace of ideas? If so, how? If not, why not?

ISSUE

Standard 12 protects good faith whistle-blowing. When is whistle-blowing not in good faith?

Case 10

Professor Walsh has an enthusiasm for whistle-blowing. Some instances follow. Which are instances of "good faith" whistle-blowing?

- Professor Walsh knowingly files a false report to the dean of the school regarding a violation of the standards.
- Professor Walsh, without any personal investigation of a rumor regarding a possible violation of the standards, files a report of a violation.
- Professor Walsh, hearing a rumor of the violation, makes a few cursory inquiries and then files his report with the dean.
- After a thorough investigation that produces reasonable evidence, Professor Walsh files a report of a violation knowing that the report will cause difficulties for Professor Bell, with whom Professor Walsh has had a long-standing personal and professional feud.
- Professor Walsh, hearing a rumor of the violation, makes a few cursory inquiries and then files his report with the dean, knowing that the report will cause difficulties for Professor Bell, with whom he has had a long standing personal and professional feud.

Discussion: The first of these examples is not good-faith whistle-blowing. It can be argued that in the second, Professor Walsh acted in reckless disregard of the truth and that he did not act in good faith. In the third example, we can say Professor Walsh acted negligently, but whether a negligent report is not made in good faith is a harder question. In the fourth example, Professor Walsh reported accurately and on good evidence, but he acted out of hatred. Again, it is not obvious from the standard whether imposing a penalty on Professor Walsh would be justified. But to allow a penalty in this case would serve to frustrate the enforcement of the standards in a situation in which the standards were violated.

Finally, in the fifth case, we see Professor Walsh acting negligently because of his animosity toward Professor Bell. This is also a hard case. The question is whether the reason for the negligent investigation should make a difference with regard to whether a penalty for Professor Walsh is in order.

QUESTIONS

1. Does **Standard 12** create an obligation to engage in whistle-blowing when people have knowledge of a standard's violation? If not, should there be such an obligation?
2. The standards of **Part I** are rooted partially in the belief that the credibility of educational researchers depends on their being both competent and ethical. Does this imply any obligation for researchers to police their field? If not, then who should police the researcher's field?

PART II

RESEARCH POPULATIONS, EDUCATIONAL INSTITUTIONS, AND THE PUBLIC

The Preamble, the Standards, and Their Rationale

Preamble

Educational researchers conduct research within a broad array of settings and institutions, including schools, colleges, universities, hospitals, and prisons. It is of paramount importance that educational researchers respect the rights, privacy, dignity, and sensitivities of their research populations and also the integrity of the institutions within which the research occurs. Educational researchers should be especially careful in working with children and other vulnerable populations. These standards are intended to reinforce and strengthen already existing standards enforced by institutional review boards and other professional associations. *

---

* These standards should not be construed so as to prohibit teachers or other educational practitioners from studying their own practice. Whenever practitioners engage in research about their own practice in any form, they should do so in a manner consistent with the ethical guidance of the **Standards**.

STANDARDS

1 *Participants, or their guardians, in a research study have the right to be informed about the likely risks involved in the research and of potential consequences for participants, and to give their informed consent before participating in research. Educational researchers should communicate the aims of the investigation as well as possible to informants and participants (and their guardians), and appropriate representatives of institutions, and keep them updated about any significant changes in the research program.*

2 *Honesty should characterize the relationship between researchers and participants and appropriate institutional representatives. Deception is discouraged; it should be used only when clearly necessary for scientific studies, and should then be minimized. After the study the researcher should explain to the participants and institutional representatives the reasons for the deception.*

3 *Educational researchers should be sensitive to any locally established institutional policies or guidelines for conducting research.*

4 *Participants have the right to withdraw from the study at any time, unless otherwise constrained by their official capacities or roles.*

5 *Educational researchers should exercise caution to ensure that there is no exploitation for personal gain of research populations or of institutional settings of research. Educational researchers should not use their influence over subordinates, students, or others to compel them to participate in research.*

6 *Researchers have a responsibility to be mindful of cultural, religious, gender, and other significant differences within the research population in the planning, conduct, and reporting of their research.*

7 *Researchers should carefully consider and minimize the use of research techniques that might have negative social consequences, for example, experimental interventions that might deprive students of important parts of the standard curriculum.*

8 *Educational researchers should be sensitive to the integrity of ongoing institutional activities and alert appropriate institutional representatives of possible disturbances in such activities which may result from the conduct of the research.*

9 *Educational researchers should communicate their findings and the practical significance of their research in clear, straightforward, and appropriate language to relevant research populations, institutional representatives, and other stakeholders.*

10 *Informants and participants normally have a right to confidentiality, which ensures that the source of information will not be disclosed without the express permission of the informant. This right should be respected when no clear understanding to the contrary has been reached. Researchers are responsible for taking appropriate precautions to protect the confidentiality of both participants and data to the full extent provided by law. Participants in research should be made aware of the limits on the protections that can be provided, and of the efforts toward protection that will be made even in situations where absolute confidentiality cannot be assured. It should be made clear to informants and participants that despite every effort made to preserve it, confidentiality may be compromised. Secondary researchers should respect and maintain the confidentiality established by primary researchers. In some cases, e.g., survey research, it may be appropriate for researchers to assure participants of anonymity, i.e., that their identity is not known even to the researcher. Anonymity should not be promised to participants when only confidentiality is intended.*

RATIONALE

Research may include people involved either as research participants or as members of institutions where the research takes place. Researchers who involve others in their research take on certain obligations to these people who have independent activities and goals, and whose welfare may be jeopardized by their research participation. Institutional policies and laws have been designed to ensure the protection of research participants, and researchers should conform to these applicable laws and policies as well as be sensitive and humane in their relations with research participants. Researchers are also obliged to know the purposes and activities of the institutions involved in their research.

Three principles are usually associated with the ethical treatment of human research participants. These principles are embodied in institutional review board policies and procedures for the protection of human research participants, which the **Preamble** refers to directly as something the standards of **Part II** should uphold. These three principles are:

1. Respect for autonomy,
2. Beneficence, and
3. Justice.[1]

Respect for autonomy is the principle that whenever possible, people should be allowed to decide freely whether or not to participate in activities. If people's autonomy is limited or diminished, as is the case with children or mentally disabled people, then extra measures should be taken to protect their interests. Autonomy, in the context of research, implies the requirement of informed consent. This means that the intended research participant is informed about the project, understands it and the possible consequences, and voluntarily agrees to participate. Knowledge, decision-making capacity, and the freedom to choose whether to participate or not are the three necessary elements of informed consent.

The principle of *beneficence* is the idea of doing good and avoiding harm. In the research context, beneficence calls for a favorable balance of potential benefits as measured against the potential risks of the planned research. Benefits may include creating knowledge for its own sake or desirable results produced from the practical application of knowledge anticipated as research findings. Participation in research may also harm the participants, however, and research activities should be designed to avoid or minimize harm to the research participants. Potential benefits of the research should be maximized, and possible harms minimized using a risk/benefit analysis that is as objective as possible, and construes risk as the combination of the probability and magnitude of possible harm.

Justice is concerned with the fair allocation of rights, responsibilities, and goods as determined by the nature of the activity involved. In the research context, justice pertains to the distribution of burdens and benefits produced by the research activity and its results. Justice also concerns whatever rights and obligations are conferred upon people as a function of their involvement in research. Individuals or groups should not be included as research participants in ways that make them vulnerable to a disproportionately large share of the risks and burdens of research. Individuals or groups also should not be unfairly excluded from participating in promising research, where being excluded would mean that they or people like them could not obtain benefits resulting from the research findings. Vulnerable populations (e.g., the racial minorities, the economically disadvantaged, the sick, and the institutionalized) are groups whose particular availability as research participants make them especially prone to having to bear an inordinate share of research risks. At the same time, these vulnerable populations should not be left out of research either, if this means that

45

they or their group will be less likely to enjoy the benefits of positive research findings. The difficulties of balancing these two considerations heightens the importance of the autonomy by members of the relevant vulnerable population in determining what participation is most just.

The **Preamble** does not make direct reference to these underlying principles, but their influence is evident in its allusion to the necessity of respecting the rights, privacy, dignity, and sensitivities of research populations. The violation of a right is an act of injustice, and may also involve potential harm, the loss of benefits, or an infringement upon the participant's autonomy. Protecting people's privacy frequently protects them from harms or the loss of benefits that would result if sensitive personal information were made public, and the same is true for many people's other sensitivities. The idea of human dignity is related to respect for autonomy—allowing people to exercise their judgment in making important decisions about their lives. Autonomy is also relevant to the **Preamble's** mentioning the need to devote care in research involving children and other vulnerable populations. Since educational research commonly involves children who may not be able to provide free and informed consent, researchers must take on a special obligation to look out for the research participants' welfare, and to cooperate with others, such as the children's parents, to protect them. Since there are significant differences in people's outlooks, researchers ought to be aware that other people's choices, particularly with respect to the value of research, may be different from their choices. Respect for autonomy, beneficence, and justice are also relevant to the **Preamble's** statements concerning respect for ongoing activities in various institutions. Those activities are efforts to create various benefits. Furthermore, the people involved in those institutions should not be impeded from voluntary participation in those efforts, and have rights associated with them that would be unjust to abridge.

The standards further elaborate ways in which the three principles of respect for autonomy, beneficence, and justice are applied in research involving human participants. The right of informed consent in **Standard 1,** the right to withdraw from experiments in **Standard 4,** and the rights to confidentiality and anonymity in **Standard 10** all appeal to the principle of justice through their declaration that these are *rights*, and the first two of these rights reflect the importance of respecting participants' autonomy. All three rights also pertain to participants' vulnerability to potential harm, and thus introduce the principle of beneficence. The prohibition in **Standard 5** against exploitation also rests upon considerations of justice, and of reaping benefits at the expense of others.

Standard 1's assertion of the importance of informed consent is the leading representation of the respect for autonomy principle, but other standards also reflect this principle. As previously mentioned, the right to withdraw from research in **Standard 4** and the rights to confidentiality and anonymity in **Standard 10** concern preserving the individuals' ability to control their participation in research and to control others' access to personal information about themselves. The appeal for honesty between researchers and participants in **Standard 2** also relates to respect for autonomy, because a person who is deceived is unable to make decisions that are based on a knowledgeable understanding of the circumstances. The prohibition in **Standard 5** against coercing subordinates or students also follows from the principle of autonomy, since coercion to participate in research is a denial of the individual's freedom to choose whether to participate.

The principle of beneficence is most directly represented in **Standard 7** which calls for researchers to avoid research interventions that could harm the research participants. The importance of avoiding harm and promoting benefits is reflected throughout the standards and is often intertwined with the principles of justice and autonomy. **Standard 3** (concerning locally established policies) **Standard 6** (concerning being mindful of cultural differences) and **Standard 8** (concerning ongoing institutional activities) all refer to possible problems which may arise due to researchers' intrusions into existing activities in local institutions or cultures. Where a local institution or culture is involved, researchers also assume an obligation to respect the recognized goals and purposes of the institution or cultural activities that can produce benefits to the participants. The members of the institution and the public directly or indirectly support that institution's objectives, and researchers studying what goes on in such institutions and cultures have no special authority to thwart or redirect the institution's activities. Impeding these established institutional or cultural activities not only jeopardizes people's ability to achieve the intended benefits of those activities, but also may represent an unjust intrusion upon a community's collective autonomy to regulate its own affairs.

Educational research is also an institutionalized activity with its own goals, and the obligation to share the potential benefits of this activity with the public is represented in **Standard 9**. Educational research's basic and applied goals are to contribute to human knowledge and to improve education. In order to advance either of these goals, educational research must not only be carried out, it must be disseminated to the appropriate audiences for their use. These audiences include practitioners, who are able to make practical use of the findings, and the research community and its stakeholders, so the findings can be integrated into the understanding of the field.

Interpretation of the Standards: Issues, Cases, and Discussions

ISSUE

Potential research participants are generally entitled to know about the risks, benefits, consequences, and aims of a research investigation before they participate in research. Informed consent, the term used to identify the individual's decision to participate, is often obtained through a process in which participants or their guardians sign a form containing this information. This form documents that the participants or guardians were offered the information. Obviously, the information should be offered in a way that makes it accessible to the potential research participant, for example, in language they understand. But having access to this information does not necessary mean that the individual absorbs and considers it with the care it deserves. Is this the responsibility of the researcher, or of the potential participant?

Case 1

Dr. Vargas walked out of the principal's office whistling a tune. His research project was about to begin. He had left all the informed consent forms with Principal Rand, who had promised to include them in the school's regular mailing of forms to parents at the beginning of the year. Vargas had worked hard on the forms, and had to go back to his University's Institutional Review Board three times to get their approval. The forms gave complete and accurate information about the research, including the possible benefits and other relevant information. They were written at a literacy level below that of the parents whose children attend Principal Rand's school. Principal Rand had assured Vargas that the parents were always diligent about signing and returning forms they got in the mailing, because the included health forms had to be submitted before the children could start school. "They just sign them all, one after the next, and send them back," Rand had told him, "so you're sure to get nearly everyone's signatures. They don't even read half of the forms."

Vargas was confident no one would be harmed, and he had given the parents all the information they needed. Now all he had to do was to wait for the forms to come in, and his Science in Second Grade Research Project could begin.

Discussion: Providing all the necessary information in a form the prospective participant or guardian can understand is necessary and important. Institutional Review Boards often devote considerable attention to the quality of the consent form. However, obtaining a signature on a document containing the necessary information does not mean that the reader actually read and understood what the document says, and that understanding is necessary in giving truly informed consent. **Standard 1** regarding informed consent, implies that effective communication of the information to the participant or guardian must take place, which means that it's not sufficient to make the information available if there's a good chance that those consenting will ignore it. In order to exercise their autonomy through the mechanism of informed consent, the participants or guardians must know what they're deciding.

Vargas knows that the strategy he's using is likely to lead to uninformed consent in a considerable number of cases. Sometimes it's impractical to do something like meeting with each parent individually to be sure they've read and understood the form. In this case, the research apparently poses no risk of harm. Vargas cannot make every parent stop to consider what they are signing. However, Vargas should at least make a reasonable effort to draw parents' attention to this form, and perhaps send a separate mailing of the form.

ISSUE

Reasonable people may have different opinions about an issue. In some cases, people believe that they are better qualified to make judgments about that issue than the people with whom they differ. In such circumstances, one may ask whether those who consider themselves more highly qualified have a responsibility to educate the others, particularly if they stand to benefit from the others' apparent ignorance. If someone has a mistaken belief, must that belief be corrected before they can make an informed decision? Honesty is sometimes a question of what is said, and sometimes a question of what is not said. When should researchers permit prospective participants to be deceived or misled, if the researchers have not tried to be deceptive? Is allowing others to be misled ethical in the interest of pursuing a research project?

Case 2

"We have everyone's consent, Dr. Bunker, so you can start the evaluation of the Feeling Good Values Program next Monday. Good-bye, and thank you!" Dr. Bunker said good-bye to Superintendent Slate, and shook her head as she hung up the phone. Superintendent Slate and the people in the West Alta School system meant well, but seemed awfully naive. Bunker had evaluated scores of programs similar to the Feeling Good Values Program, and had never found significant positive results other than those coming from the participants' enthusiasm. She thought it was important to do an evaluation of the Feeling Good Values Program, because the program was actively marketed by a large entrepreneurial organization, and she was convinced the program was worthless. She had not said this to Superintendent Slate when she offered her services as an evaluator, because she hadn't been asked, and was afraid Slate might have second thoughts about obtaining the evaluation. The people at West Alta would be disappointed, but it was their own fault. Besides, they had already paid for the program.

Discussion: Dr. Bunker is not obliged to convince everyone participating in the project of her judgment of the chances of the program's success before she begins the evaluation. **Standard 1** calls for effectively communicating relevant information about the research project, but not for convincing everyone to hold the same view about it. The idea of informed consent implicitly recognizes that there is room for some individuals to decide that a research program is worthwhile, and for some individuals to decide otherwise. **Standard 2** requires honesty between researchers and participants, so Dr. Bunker is obliged to be truthful about what she knows about evaluations of similar programs.

The requirement of honesty, taken with the requirement for informed consent, means that she is obliged to communicate to Slate and others involved what the existing research suggests about the likely outcome of the research evaluation and the possible repercussions. There is no need to deliberately mislead the participants, because the research project can be carried out even if the participants are aware of what evaluations of similar programs have shown. Honesty also requires Bunker to design an evaluation that permits the Feeling Good Values Program to demonstrate significant results if the program is indeed effective, because this is clearly why the school officials have agreed to participate. She is not, however, obliged to tell them her own opinion about what the outcome of the research will be, nor is she obliged to try to convince the participants that their program is probably worthless before the evaluation begins. The research is supposed to shape that conclusion.

ISSUE

Some research cannot be carried out without deception. In some cases, knowing what the research is all about will make it impossible to investigate what the researchers are trying to study. If the participants know that the research project is testing their honesty, for example, they are not likely to cheat. In other cases a full disclosure of the design and purposes of a research investigation may influence the research participants' behavior to make it not representative of people's normal reactions to the conditions being studied—making the research less valuable. In some cases, a research project may be designed so that the research participants are told that the research will involve some deception. What information may researchers withhold from participants, knowing that they will be misled to some degree on the nature of the research in which they've agreed to participate?

Case 3

Dr. Lynn was an enthusiastic supporter of the First Amendment of the U. S. Constitution and a life-long member of the American Civil Liberties Union (ACLU). He was delighted in the late 1960s when the Supreme Court handed down rulings that extended such rights as free speech and free press to students in schools. However, as the years went by and he did various fieldwork projects in schools, he became increasingly dismayed by students not seeming to know or care about the rights they had. He decided to conduct a research survey designed to discover what students knew about their rights and what opinions they had about what rights students should have, and use the research evidence to support better civic education. Dr. Lynn asked a former student of his, Grace Forest, who was now principal of Middle America High School, if she would arrange for him to give the questionnaire to a sample of students. She was happy to help.

The informed consent form Dr. Lynn provided said only that students would be asked to take a test designed to measure their knowledge of First Amendment rights. It made no mention either of the fact that it would also ask them what rights they thought they had or believed they should have, or of the advocacy use Dr. Lynn planned for the results.

When the questionnaires were being given out, however, the principal chose to make a little speech. She told the students that Dr. Lynn, her former teacher, was a well-known crusader for free speech and that she had agreed to allow him to give out his questionnaire because she thought it was important for students to know and value their rights.

After the questionnaires were collected and the students dismissed, Dr. Lynn told his former pupil that he wished she hadn't made her speech. "I'm very much afraid it will bias the students' responses." "Nonsense," she said, "Isn't the point of the First Amendment to allow citizens to be fully informed?" Dr. Lynn acknowledged that this was the point of the Amendment. As he walked though the school parking lot, however, he tossed the questionnaires into the trash.

Discussion: **Standard 1** calls for the informed consent of research participants and insists that this consent extend to the investigation aims. **Standard 2** calls for honesty in the relations between researchers and participants, but here full disclosure of the research objectives probably is inconsistent with the validity of the research.

Dr. Lynn and Grace Forest are both authority figures to these students. Therefore, telling the students that they have a positive view of students' rights is quite likely to bias the students' responses to survey questions about those rights. In this case, it is unlikely that any harm will result from failing to fully inform participants of the research purposes, so it's not really an issue of not warning participants of anticipated risks. Probably the strongest argument made for fuller disclosure of the researchers' aims would be that if some of the students' parents knew that the research might be used to support Dr. Lynn's positions on student rights, they might not want the students to participate. Dr. Lynn could mitigate this problem by keeping the students' responses anonymous. Since there seems little chance of harm to the students and fuller disclosure would bias the research results, the degree of disclosure provided in the informed consent form seems reasonable. It is likely that this is a case where the "deception" qualification of **Standard 2** is permitted.

ISSUE

Researchers do not always agree with the policies, procedures, and values of the people whom they study. This is not surprising in a world where people from different cultures with different values create and participate in educational institutions with various missions. However, this may lead to problems because researchers or research participants may engage in practices during research activity that either researchers or participants find objectionable. When should researchers defer to the preferences of research participants about appropriate behavior, and when are they free to follow their consciences?

Case 4

Frank Chance looked uneasily at the condom in Sister Maria's hand. It was the brand of contraceptive he'd been giving to the research participants at his clinic who came in for abortion counseling. It now looked like he was going to have some explaining to do. Chance was doing a study comparing an "abstinence only" with an "abstinence or responsible sex" program, and the participants in the latter program group were receiving free contraceptives on request. He had the consent of all the research participants and their parents. Part of the study included comparing the academic achievement of the research participants, and some of the participants were students at the Roman Catholic high school where Sister Maria was teaching.

Chance had told school officials from the schools where the research participants were students that all study participants were encouraged to be abstinent, but had not told them about the contraceptive distribution. The sex education programs were being delivered at Chance's clinic, and not at the schools. Furthermore, the school officials were not research participants. This was going to be embarrassing, Chance decided, but he believed he wasn't doing anything wrong.

Discussion: This case raises questions about honesty and honoring the moral preferences of others who have been asked to participate in a research study. **Standard 2** calls for honesty between researchers and other institutional representatives unless deception is both necessary to the study and it is still justifiable. However, it is doubtful that this study is only possible under deceptive conditions. **Standard 3** (concerning local policies) **Standard 6** (cultural differences) and **Standard 8** (institutional activities) all speak to the importance of respecting established interests of institutions or groups of people who are affected by the conduct of research.

Chance certainly knows that the Catholic Church has a contrary position on the use of contraceptives, and that the school probably has a formal policy regarding cooperation with institutions that sanction the use of contraceptives. While they were not research participants per se, school officials were contributing to the implementation of the research study, and were entitled to know all elements of the study. Chance should have told the school officials and let them decide whether they were willing to cooperate in the study.

ISSUE

Researchers sometimes devote considerable effort to research studies. If research participants decide to withdraw from a study part way through, the researchers involved have probably wasted their time. In research involving a quantitative analysis of the research data, too many participants dropping out of a study weaken the researcher's ability to draw statistical inferences about the research population. In qualitative research, even a single research participant's dropping out may mean the researcher loses a large part of the findings that he or she was hoping to report. And at the outset of the study, if the research participants knew what they were getting into when they gave their consent, it seems that they have some commitment to see it through. Is there a limit to the point at which research participants have the right to withdraw from research?

Case 5

"And another thing," said Abby Jones, as she stood up to leave Dee Stevens's office, "I'm not going to be coming by here any more to talk with you. What with the baby, and school, and my job, and everything, it's just too much. I appreciate the money you give me, but I earn more at my job, and I don't have any time to play with my daughter or go shopping or anything. Besides, we've been doing these meetings for a few years now, and I'm not telling you anything I haven't told you before. I'm sorry, but I really can't do it."

Dee fought down her internal panic. She had been doing a qualitative longitudinal study of inner city teenage mothers and their education for three years on how they experienced school and their social situations before and after their children were born. She had another year to go, and Abby would be the third of the five original participants to drop out of the study.

Abby Jones had provided a wealth of insights into her own situation, and how having a child had changed her perspective on the significance of finishing high school. But the study called for Dee to follow the mothers until they graduated or turned eighteen, and Abby hadn't done either yet. Dee's study would be seriously weakened if Abby did not continue. Dee wanted desperately to argue with Abby to continue, but she hesitated about whether she could do that. Wouldn't she be coercing Abby if she tried to persuade her not to withdraw?

Discussion: **Standard 4's** statement about the right to withdraw clearly indicates that Abby is entitled to drop out of the study if she chooses to, regardless of the importance of her participation. Dee may try to persuade her to continue, based in part on whatever she had previously said to Abby about participating in the project. If Dee had discussed the project's length and the need to collect information for the full period of the project, she could remind Abby of that discussion, and of Abby's decision to go forward. She could also try to revise their relationship, and offer to make the meetings more convenient to Abby to make it easier for her to continue. She could offer a modest increase in the compensation she provides to match whatever Abby earns at her job. She could also ask Abby not to make her decision final, and hope that Abby's desire to withdraw is only temporary. In anything she does or says to try to persuade Abby to continue in the study, she must not do anything that would resemble coercing Abby's participation. This is prohibited by **Standard 5**. Dee cannot try to overrule Abby's voluntary informed consent, which is reflected in **Standard 1**. If Abby still wants to withdraw then she may do so, no matter what effect her withdrawal has on the quality of the research project.

ISSUE

Undergraduate students represent an attractive research population for university-based researchers. They are readily available in large numbers, usually healthy, and the similarities of their age, educational level, and other characteristics make them a potentially useful group of research participants. University researchers are also used to working with this population. Such researchers, however, are in positions of authority with the students, and this raises the question of whether faculty researchers coerce their students into participation in research by virtue of their relationship with the students. At some institutions, the faculty set up pools of research participants which are shared by several faculty researchers to avoid the situation of students having to decide whether to participate in their own professors' research projects. Should participation in faculty research projects be a part of undergraduates' coursework?

Case 6

"If you don't want to be part of the research participants pool that's fine," said Professor Presser as he looked down at the young freshman in front of him, "It is not a course requirement. I do hope you heard me say that being in the research participants pool doesn't mean that you will participate in any of my research projects, but only that you will be in one of the research projects directed by the Department faculty. We can't say at this point who will be selected to participate in each study. Of course, the Department considers participation in a study to be an important educational experience that is integral to your studies. Because participation does take up participants' time, if you decide to stay out of the research participant pool, your alternative course assignment will be to write a five-page research paper for this course on the *Zimbardo* experiments." He smiled kindly at her. "I'm not sure you'll learn as much writing the paper, but that's your decision to make."

Louisa smiled back uncertainly. She thought Professor Presser seemed nice, and she knew that most of the other students were choosing to participate in the pool rather than write the paper. But she wasn't enthusiastic about giving up the option of writing the paper even before she knew what kind of study she might be in. What if they asked her personal questions? She didn't want to write an extra paper, though. "Gee, Professor Presser," said Louisa Audonomi, "What would you do in my situation?"

> **Discussion:** Including students' participation in a research project as part, even an optional part, of an academic course violates the stance in **Standard 5** against coercion. Even if students are not participating in their professors' research and there are alternative ways to meet course requirements, presenting students with such alternatives in the context of their course-taking still needlessly diminishes the students' decision-making autonomy due to the influence the faculty possess over the students. The alternative assignment represents an incentive that students want to avoid. Furthermore, students may find themselves in this dilemma because the course is required for a major or fulfills a distribution requirement. A preferable policy would be for the Department to advertise for volunteers. The faculty could point out to their students any educational value they associated with participation in such research in their advertisements or in the informed consent process. They could then let the students decide if they want to participate in the activity, based on those and the other relevant considerations.

ISSUE

Coercion need not be intentional to be effective. Even if the researcher takes steps to avoid pressuring a potential research participant into participating, the potential participant may still feel pressured. If the researchers have tried to minimize their coercive influence, does this make it acceptable? Is it permissible for researchers who do not intend to coerce the participation of human research participants to carry out a research activity in which the research participants are still coerced into participating?

Case 7

"OK, class, I'm now giving you one more chance to get out of this research activity before we start. Does anyone want to go to study hall for the next 45 minutes instead?" Mrs. Proxy paused, and looked across the room at the students in her senior Civics class. She had agreed to give up one class period to let the students participate in a research survey, but she wanted to make sure nobody filled out the survey who didn't want to. She had asked the researcher to stay out of the room while she gave the students a chance to decline, so that they weren't put in the position of saying no in the researcher's presence. She had read the students the consent form they were to sign, and had collected the signed parent consent forms already.

Chris did not move from her seat. She didn't want to refuse to fill out the form, but she didn't want to do it either. Her grades were right on the borderline for whether she could participate in varsity sports, and she didn't want to do anything that might cause Mrs. Proxy to lower her credit for class participation. She didn't think Mrs. Proxy would do it on purpose, but it might influence her even so. But what if the survey asked questions about things at home? That was something Chris didn't really want to answer questions about. Chris began to sweat.

> *Discussion:* While intended coercion may be more blameworthy than unintended coercion, any coercion precludes informed consent by the potential research participant. **Standard 5** prohibits researchers from using their influence to compel others to participate regardless of whether the exercise of that influence is deliberate or not. There may be settings or people who, simply by virtue of their role in the participant's life, exert a coercive influence. Because Proxy is in a position of authority over Chris, she has a coercive effect even if she doesn't mean to. In this case, the problem could have been avoided by having someone else request the students' assent and administer the survey, so that they could feel free either to participate or not.

ISSUE

The interests of a research population in participating in research depend on whether the focus is on the risks or the benefits. If the research promises substantial benefits, then it is sometimes important for a specific population to be included in the research to ensure that the research findings apply to that population. However, the basic purpose of research is to discover knowledge that may then be applied to benefit others. Therefore, the role of the research participant is essentially one of being used for a larger purpose. And if the research can be done in such a way as to not require the participation of a vulnerable population, and yet have the findings apply to that population, then using a vulnerable population when it could be avoided becomes suspect. Is singling out disadvantaged students for study as research participants exploitation?

Case 8

"You're a racist, that's what you are! You have no right to use these children as guinea pigs for this under-funded program. You wouldn't for a moment consider using this program with middle-class white students. I'll have no part of this exploitation!" Bobby Engles walked out of Dr. Whits's office. Dr. Whits was troubled by Engles's accusations. Whits's proposed research project was to study the effects of the Bare Bones Science Curriculum on students at three schools where nearly all the students were disadvantaged black youngsters. Whits thought this was a good idea, because the Bare Bones program provided students with laboratory learning experiences with a minimum of resources. Its designers had worked hard to construct interesting experiments that could be done with inexpensive and readily available materials. If it proved successful, schools with disadvantaged students and limited resources should be especially interested in the program.

Engles's accusations came as a shock. Bobby argued that the research should be done with middle-class children first to see if the program had any harmful or beneficial effects, because these middle-class schools and the parents of these children would be more able to compensate for any detrimental consequences. Such schools might want the program also. Why make the disadvantaged children take the risks first if the program showed no benefits to the advantaged students?

> *Discussion:* Whits's dilemma represents an important tension in the selection of research participants from vulnerable populations. This concern is reflected in the ambiguous character of **Standard 6** which calls for researchers to be "mindful" of differences of various research populations. What does it mean to be "mindful" here? On the one hand, the history of research reveals that vulnerable populations carry too much of the burden of risks in some dangerous research projects. On the other hand, that same history of research also suggests that research has focused too much attention on research designed to address the needs of already advantaged populations, compared to the findings oriented toward the needs of disadvantaged populations. Research that promises the most beneficial findings gains validity if the research participant population includes people with the same characteristics as those who benefit.

> On Whits's side, it could be argued that if the research is done with participants from an advantaged population, research to see if the same effects extended to disadvantaged populations might never be done. If the research shows benefits for the advantaged students, people may assume that it works for disadvantaged children. If no benefits are discerned for the advantaged students, there may be too little interest by researchers or sponsors to see if the intervention does have a positive effect only on a particular disadvantaged population. Of course, the research participants are not the primary intended beneficiaries of the research activity. Research participants are always being "used" for some purpose beyond their welfare by definition, even if it happens that they are lucky enough to benefit.

> Whits could contemplate a number of options to remedy the situation. First the research participant population could be expanded to include students from both advantaged and disadvantaged populations. Second, Whits could go back to the institutional review board, and ask if this issue had received full consideration when it was approved initially. Third, Whits could set up a meeting of representatives of the community in which the research would be carried out and ask for their response and endorsement. Fourth, Whits could pay attention to the question of whether harm could come to the participants, and if so, whether some remediation or compensation for the research participants should be built into the project from the beginning.

ISSUE

Standard 7 restrains research that might have negative social consequences. It illustrates these consequences by interventions that deny students important instruction. It is noteworthy that it does not absolutely prohibit such research. When can we take risks with the educational welfare of students to gain important new knowledge?

Case 9

Dr. Spencer is a noted researcher of reading. He has developed several well-known and widely used reading programs. He has recently developed a new approach to teaching reading for the late primary grades that he wants to evaluate. In the past, Dr. Spencer has found that one problem in interpreting his data is that students learn to read throughout the curriculum, not just during the period specifically devoted to language arts. Teachers frequently and generally interject reading instruction into other subjects of the curriculum. For example, teachers teaching science often spent time helping students work out the pronunciation of new scientific vocabulary. Other research has indicated this instruction may strengthen students' reading skills. From Dr. Spencer's standpoint, however, this "random instruction" makes it harder to determine whether student gains on reading tests were attributable to his programs. So Dr. Spencer has developed a research design to deal with this difficulty. In essence, he is going to do a study comparing four groups of students. Group A will be taught the old reading curriculum. In addition, teachers will be free to teach reading in conjunction with other subjects as they have always done. Group B students will be taught the old curriculum, but their teachers will not teach reading elsewhere. Group C students will be taught according to the new Spencer curriculum, and group C teachers will be allowed to provide reading instruction as they choose in other subjects. Group D students will be taught using the Spencer curriculum, but teachers will not teach reading elsewhere. Using this design, Spencer believes that he can show the effectiveness of his new approach.

Discussion: Here it seems that Groups B and D are to be denied instruction in reading that they currently receive. This seems a case of what **Standard 7** is intended to restrain. Dr. Spencer is proposing to withhold valuable instruction from two groups of students, intending to study the effects of his new program better.

It is not, however, entirely clear whether Dr. Spencer is violating **Standard 7**. First, **Standard 7** does not contain an absolute prohibition of all research that might have harmful consequences. It requires that they consider and minimize risks. Presumably, researchers are invited to consider whether the research is important enough to justify some risk.

Some comments on the relationship between **Standard 1** and **Standard 7** may be in order. That **Standard 7** (as well as the other standards that seek protection for research participants, e.g., **Standard 5**) is included suggests that the informed consent provided **Standard 1** is not sufficient protection for research participants. Researchers may not engage in studies that have significant risks simply because participants are willing to accept them. In this case, because Dr. Spencer's research does deny some students valuable instruction, **Standard 7** seems to require that Dr. Spencer accept a weaker design that does not withhold instruction unless he can show that his research is important enough to warrant the risk involved. Otherwise, some dilution of his design tightness serves the minimization of risk requirement of **Standard 7**. He may not, under **Standard 7** justify significant risk by claiming that participants have agreed to accept them. (See also the discussion of **Hard Case 6**.)

ISSUE

In medicine, the traditional admonition to be cautious is expressed as "Do no harm." When in doubt, medical practitioners are advised not to intervene unless they are confident that their interventions will be at least benign, if not therapeutic. But research, in medicine or in education, often takes place in circumstances where no one knows if the contemplated intervention will produce any harm, or whether the intervention would be any better or worse than current standard conventional practice. Unfortunately, sometimes the only way to find out is through experiment. How should researchers address the question of whether a proposed intervention will cause harm?

Case 10

"You're asking me for money for bats and boxing equipment for a nonviolence program?" Principal Dunn was shaking with rage as she looked at Cathy Ardix's purchase requisition. "You're supposed to be stopping student violence at Verdun Middle School, and it looks like you're arming them! How am I going to defend this to the people in the Superintendent's office?"

"By explaining how the Beating the Odds program works, of course," said Cathy Ardix, "because this program is built upon a sound theory of controlling aggression, and the research evaluation we're going to do on this program will provide empirical evidence, too. You can't teach students to stop feeling angry and aggressive, but you can teach them to channel their violent impulses in harmless directions. The Beating the Odds program will identify students whose background indicates they are at risk of being violent, and offer them opportunities to vent their anger by using the bats on heavy punching bags. Then they'll share their feelings with the other students in the program. That way they'll learn that we understand their anger, that other students feel similar angry feelings, and that there are acceptable ways to express violent urges to not hurt anyone or get them in trouble. Students will learn empathy and self-control."

"So what you're telling me is that there's a theory behind the program, but it's not been tested?" said Dunn. "What if this program encourages the students to violent action when they have violent impulses? Is that a sound theory? And have you thought that we're going to be using student records to single out the most potentially violent students, even if they haven't actually done anything wrong? Did you think about how maybe the group discussions will encourage them to reinforce each other's violent attitudes? Don't you think this might have a negative impact on teachers' or other students' expectations of behavior they'll see from these students? *Beating the Odds* seems like a bad idea to me!"

> *Discussion:* Dunn has a commonsense rationale for the possibility that this program will produce negative results, and **Standard 7's** injunction against harmful research techniques clearly applies here. When people have reason to consider something as negative as violent behavior as a possible outcome, extra precautions become reasonable. Other approaches that do not seem as risky should be tried first. Unless there is supporting evidence of positive outcomes from similar programs with adults as research participants, it is hard to see how such a program could be justified.

ISSUE

The positive outcomes of applied research activities do not necessarily coincide with the legitimate goals of the institutions where that research is carried out. Schools, for example, may have activities that are designed to produce one kind of educational outcome, while researchers may be interested in an outcome that is in conflict with the schools' goals. Should researchers overlook the relationship between other school objectives and the consequences of implementing their research projects in those schools if the research is otherwise ethical?

Case 11

Dr. Dere was ready to launch the second stage of the Reading 4 All program. The first stage had been very promising, with students in the pilot treatment group reading significantly better at the end of fourth grade than students in the same school when the students had been in the program for two or more years. The second stage of the research project was supposed to have 10 primary school classes participating, and would enable Dr. Dere to test the program to find if it would improve reading for both boys and girls and for both disadvantaged and advantaged students.

Dr. Dere felt lucky that so many teachers in the targeted schools were willing to participate, especially because the school system's Driving Curricular Success Initiative (DCSI) was designed to have language arts learning objectives reflected in school assessments that the teachers were supposed to use to orient their curricula. The teachers and parents working with Dr. Dere were cynical about the Initiative and were excited by the success of the Reading 4 All's pilot stage. So what if the learning objectives don't match up, they said; this is a program with evidence of effectiveness that the DCSI simply doesn't have. Let's go with what works!

Discussion: **Standard 8's** statement about the integrity of ongoing institutional activities implies that it would be unethical for Dr. Dere to knowingly thwart the legitimate activities and policies of the school system without discussing his planned project with appropriate school officials. If Dr. Dere were to carry out the project, it might lead school officials to misinterpret the evaluation results of their own initiative and make a poor decision as a result. Dr. Dere does not have the authority to decide what initiatives the school system should support, and it is not even clear that Reading 4 All is a better program than DCSI. He is obliged to discuss this project with appropriate school officials and obtain their approval before going forward.

ISSUE

The benefits of research findings depend on people having access to them. Research findings that contribute to knowledge in a given area have to be reported to the relevant research community to advance the field. Research findings with practical implications must be communicated to people who are in a position to implement change based on research knowledge. However, depending on the circumstances of the research activity, sometimes no one who has the findings has a strong interest in publishing them. Sometimes the findings are contradictory, or show no link in a hypothesized relation, or show no improvement from an implemented reform. What are researchers obliged to do to report disappointing research results?

Case 12

"No news is no news," thought Dr. Mum wryly to himself, as he shut the door to his office for the last time. For three years he and his team of researchers had dedicated their professional lives to evaluating a promising educational reform strategy in a suburban school district, but the research findings did not show the hoped-for positive impact on student achievement. He had filed a report with the school district officials who had paid for both the program and the evaluation, but he did not expect them to broadcast widely a story about their expensive failure. Dr. Mum and his research team had also submitted the results of their study to several professional journals, but while the reviewers commented that their technical work was flawless, no one recommended publishing a study with a finding of "no effect." Dr. Mum had accepted a position at another university in another state, and did not expect to be working with the same school district again.

Discussion: **Standard 9** calls for researchers to communicate their research findings via appropriate means to interested audiences. Dr. Mum should make a good faith effort to provide his team's research findings to someone interested in the quality of education in the school system who does not have a vested interest in the program's success. The clear purpose of the project was to improve education in the school system, and if Dr. Mum only gives his report to people who have an interest in ignoring it, the practical value of the research will be wasted. Depending on who supported the program originally, Dr. Mum could send it to other school officials, such as school board members who were not originally involved in the development of the program, or to the concerned public through the local parent association or media.

A finding of no effect is often less interesting from a scientific standpoint because there are more potential factors that do not produce a given effect than those that do. However, if the program represents a strategy other researchers and reform developers are likely to replicate, the scientific merits of providing research findings that will make people think twice about developing and implementing a similar reform may make publication worthwhile.

In addition, if the program represents a fairly common approach, and lending its professional scientific prestige adds to the weight given to the findings, a journal may publish the findings as a public service. Effectiveness and efficiency might be best combined by Dr. Mum's sending the reviews rejecting the study to the appropriate people in the school system so that they are aware of both the findings and the research community's views of the study's technical rigor. (**Standard 9** is similar in content to **Standard 5** in **Part I**. See also **Part I, Case 6** and **Hard Case 2**, for related discussion.)

ISSUE

Preserving anonymity or confidentiality can be difficult, depending on the circumstances of the research. In anonymous research, the researcher has to take steps to ensure that the information provided by research participants doesn't disclose their identity to the researcher. When information is obtained under a promise to provide confidentiality, the researcher agrees not to reveal the identity of participants or what the researcher has learned about individual participants to others. Taken together with the desirability of reporting the research findings, particularly in circumstances where the audience for those findings knows one or more of the research participants, the researcher has to balance carefully the goals of reporting useful information and not inadvertently disclosing a research participant's identity. It's not simply a matter of substituting something else for the research participants' real names.

Case 13

"This vignette is classic!" chortled Dr. Trent, as he showed the survey form to his colleague. "It's a perfect case of teacher expectations shaping the assessment of student abilities. The anecdotal detail in this account of the principal's telling the teachers that those disadvantaged students were gifted as well as having reading disabilities, and the report of how the teachers then reacted, is just fantastic. I'm going to use this response verbatim as the opening of the book in which I'm reporting the survey results."

"Oh no you're not," said Eva Vincento, as she looked at the survey form. "These details are too good. If the teachers who are in this story read the book, they'll recognize it right away. You promised the survey participants complete confidentiality, including that principal and those teachers, and this will give away their participation in the research. Those teachers will be mad, and the principal could get in trouble. You've got to alter the details of the account enough to prevent easy identification of participants."

Discussion: Anonymity is the idea that the research participant's identity will not be known to anybody, including the researcher. Confidentiality, however, requires the researcher who knows the participant's identity not to reveal it to anyone else. If the researcher knows that the information the research participant provides will identify the participant, then the research participant's confidentiality is not being preserved.

Standard 10 asserts that research participants receive confidentiality unless that confidentiality is expressly waived. Of course, researchers cannot always anticipate what information, if published, will identify the research participant to some reader, and this should be pointed out to potential research participants during the consent process. However, researchers should make reasonable efforts to preserve confidentiality, to the extent that this is practical.

ISSUE

Anonymity and confidentiality are significant because research participants sometimes have information that they do not wish to make public. Sometimes this information is private, sensitive, or personal, and sometimes it is information that might cause harm to the research participant if it becomes public. Research participants provide researchers with such information on the condition that researchers not divulge the information to the public. In some instances, this information may be of concern to others, and pose a threat to the welfare of other people. However, if people know that researchers will abandon their promises of confidentiality whenever they believe the confidential information identifies a threat to someone else's welfare, then the likely result is that potential research participants will refuse to participate in research where such information may not be protected. Should researchers protect the confidentiality of information concerning research participants no matter what they find out about them?

Case 14

"So now you know," said Mr. Ibanez, "what are you going to do about it?" John Sundell looked at him uncomfortably. Sundell was studying the career patterns of school administrators, and in researching Mr. Ibanez's former jobs had found a record of allegations of sexual harassment against Ibanez at a former job. The allegations were based largely on rumors that had not been thoroughly investigated. Yet, there was a pattern. Nothing had been proven, and Sundell doubted that anyone in the school district where Ibanez was now a school principal knew anything about it. The informed consent form for Sundell's research study included a promise of confidentiality to the research participants, including Ibanez. Sundell was also confident that the school board that had hired him would want to know about the allegations. Sundell's research indicated that Ibanez had not disclosed this information to the school board when he had been asked the appropriate questions. From Sundell's perspective, the issues looked pretty cloudy.

Discussion: Sundell has promised Ibanez confidentiality, and **Standard 10's** provisions concerning confidentiality oblige him to keep his promise. Sundell would never have looked into Ibanez's records and known about the misconduct allegations without Ibanez's agreement to the consent form. Without Sundell's promise of confidentiality, Ibanez and other research participants would not have agreed to participate in the study and the research would not have been carried out. Besides, Sundell has only unproven allegations and hearsay evidence to go on. Sundell should remain silent.

If Sundell had convincing reasons to believe that Ibanez was dangerous to others, he might have a moral justification, perhaps even an obligation, to violate the relationship of confidentiality. However, it may be that such justification should be compelling, indicating that harm is likely to result to a particular person rather than in speculation about how a person of allegedly bad character might act. Here grounds for overriding the obligation to confidentiality are likely to be contentious. The standards are silent on this issue, however, and simply declare a blanket obligation to preserve confidentiality to the extent that it is practically possible. Of course, if a researcher were concerned about such a possibility arising, the researcher could make explicit in the procedure for obtaining research participants' consent that the promise of confidentiality only extends to private information disclosed by the research participants and not to information that indicates potential harms to others. By anticipating this circumstance, researchers may avoid being caught between the standards' obligation to respect confidentiality and an obligation to warn someone who is unknowingly in danger of being harmed.

ISSUE

The **Preamble** requires that researchers respect the privacy of research participants. **Standard 10** requires that researchers take steps to preserve the confidentiality of both participants and data. How does this apply to student records?

Case 15

"Look," said Dr. Klees, a professor from Taylor College, doing research for an article he planned to submit to a scholarly journal, "I need access to your student records so that I can know whom to interview. My research requires that I interview at-risk students. I need to know who is failing and has been a disciplinary problem. I'm perfectly happy to get the informed consent of the parents of the students I interview, but I can't know who that is until I have identified the students who fit my parameters. My notes will be strictly confidential. I have taken steps to ensure that they are protected at all times. Not even my research assistant has access to them. All I need is an afternoon with your files."

> **Discussion:** **Standard 10** requires that researchers take steps to protect the confidentiality of data. Dr. Klees has agreed to do this. However, current law (the Family Educational Rights and Privacy Act) requires that schools limit disclosure of personally identifiable information from student records. If Dr. Klees wishes to inspect student records, unless he meets some specific conditions, like doing research at the request of the school to improve their instructional program, he must get parental consent to do so. **Standard 10** places a burden on researchers to protect not only the confidentiality of their data but also the anonymity of data about participants where appropriate. Moreover, the **Preamble** includes the broader requirement that they respect the privacy of research populations and the integrity of institutions in which research occurs. This means that researchers must respect the right of students to have their records remain private even from researchers who would fully protect the confidentiality of their data. In some cases, researchers may be able to have access to student records indirectly if those in the school who have legitimate access to those records are able to report useful data to researchers without revealing identifiable information about any students. Providing the G.P.A. of the senior class would be such an example. However, this is not such a case. Dr. Klees has no alternative but to seek parental permission to review the record of each student whose records he wants to look at.

Hard Cases

ISSUE

Can technical or practical considerations override the requirement for obtaining the informed consent of human research participants?

Case 1

Dr. N. G. Near stared angrily at Don Cramer, the administrator responsible for managing the review process for the Institutional Review Board (IRB) of Public Good University.

"Are you telling me that the IRB may decide to make me get parental permission and student assent for every student who is asked to fill out the *What's OK? Assessment Survey*?" I can't do that—it's crazy! First of all, this is for the students' own good—they're filling out a survey so we can accurately identify the frequencies of dangerous behavior to which these students are vulnerable. This is so that the school system can target their programs to eliminate the real pervasive problems. Second, we are sending a letter to the parents explaining this and offering them a chance to have their children not participate. Third, if any student says they don't want to fill out the survey, they don't have to. Fourth, we are keeping all the individually identifiable information confidential, and are only turning over aggregated data, so nobody's individual response will be presented to anyone."

"It's not practical for us to get parental permission from the parents and assent from all the students; it would seriously damage the quality of the research findings. The students in this study go to school in the inner city, many of their parents are disadvantaged, some are illiterate, and our going through the process of asking each parent individually is bound to increase those declining to participate. The disadvantaged parents' children are probably the ones we most want to include because those children are most likely to be at risk. With more people declining to participate, the validity of our conclusions will be diminished. And the cost of getting those permissions will be astronomical! I don't have room in my budget to pay for this!"

Don Cramer looked coolly at him. "I appreciate your concerns, Dr. Near, and I am sure that the IRB will, too. I just can't say that the IRB is sure to approve the proposed research plan. The IRB members take the idea of informed consent quite seriously, and your plan does not include it. Your research is designed to guide programs for the school system in the future, and it is not yet decided that anything specific will be done to benefit all the students taking the survey, so it's not clear that students are participating for their own benefit. Since some parents won't even see the letter being sent home, much less read and understand it, we can't be confident that every parent will make an informed decision about their children's participation. The students are likely to feel coerced into participating, even if they are told they can decline. And we cannot be absolutely sure that the data will remain confidential, or that there are no other risks involved in participating.

"It may be that the strength of the study depends on a high rate of participation, but even so, students have no obligation to participate in the generation of the best quality study possible. And as for the practicality issue, you know as well as I that it is possible to create the conditions in which everyone could make a voluntary and informed decision; it simply costs more money. That may just be the price you have to pay in order to treat your research participants ethically."

Discussion: **Standard 1** requires researchers to obtain the informed consent of research participants. And it does not specifically recognize any need for exceptions. However, **Standard 2** does suggest that a measure of deception might be permitted if it is a requirement of good research. Hence it seems reasonable that informed consent is not an absolute (moral) requirement and might be modified by sufficient reasons. However, if researchers plan to involve human participants in research without obtaining their informed consent, the burden is on them to show that the research is worth doing, and that there are good and sufficient reasons why the absence of informed consent may be acceptable.

The federal regulations governing such situations do provide some flexibility because they allow research to be conducted if the risks are minimal and obtaining consent is not "practicable." Research on emergency treatments, research involving deception, and research with people who both lack the capacity for informed decision-making and have no qualified guardian are examples of the type of research where informed consent is not practicable. At the same time, not being practicable is not the same as being inconvenient. The question in cases like this one involves judgment of when the practical difficulties reach a level at which it is reasonable to judge that obtaining informed consent is not practicable. This will depend on the nature of the research project and exactly what it would take to secure research participants' informed consent.

Researchers can also demonstrate a good faith effort to ensure that they are not just avoiding asking for consent because they are afraid they won't get it by exploring other means to determine willingness on the research population they plan to study. One way to do this is to set up a group of people representing the community who are members of the population(s) to be studied and ask them to review the propriety of what the researchers propose to do.

QUESTIONS

1. How would you decide this case? Is gaining informed consent not practicable, or merely inconvenient?

2. Should the importance of the research be a factor in deciding whether there might be sufficient reason to permit research where gaining informed consent is impracticable?

ISSUE

Sometimes researchers discover something in collected research data that shifts the researchers' attention from one question to another. If the new question was not described as part of the research project for which the participating research participants gave their consent, does this mean the researcher would have go back to the research participants for their consent to pursue the question? Are researchers bound to not change the focus of research involving human participants if the participants' consent is no longer obtainable?

Case 2

"It's not just significant, it's meaningful!" said Tink Akins to himself, looking at the data on his computer screen. He had been studying the results of a qualitative and quantitative study of cooperative learning at the high school level for over a year and had finally found something major. After going over the student interviews repeatedly, he had noticed that they included information about which students were friends with each other, and he had figured out how to re-analyze the data to look at the relationship of gender, membership in a specific peer group, and academic achievement. The results were far more profound than the effects of the cooperative learning activities. This was publishable stuff!

"Uh oh," thought Akins to himself, "I've got a problem." Akins had used a consent form that was quite specific about the purposes of the investigation, and the form made no mention of Akins's current topic. Akins thought the students might be sensitive about the information they'd shared in the interviews about their friends, and there were quotes from the interviews that he would want to include in an article reporting the findings. Unfortunately, at this point, he could no longer contact the research participants to ask their permission to include the new topics in his report findings. Did that mean he had to forget the whole thing?

> **Discussion:** Akins is caught between his responsibility to report significant research and his obligation to inform research participants of the nature of the research they are involved in. **Standard 1** includes in the research participants' right of informed consent the idea that research participants should be told the aims of an investigation. Akins's review of the data shifted his focus from the original aim. **Standard 9** and the **Foreword** both imply that when researchers discover something significant, especially if it holds the promise of benefiting the practice of education, then researchers are obliged to make their discovery public. Akins's situation seems to compel him to violate one standard in order to fulfill the other.

QUESTIONS

1. Could Akins have avoided this dilemma in the first place? Could he have kept a record of everyone he interviewed, so that he could go back and ask for consent to publish findings about the new topic? Could he have used a more open-ended consent form which listed possible topics that might be included in the research analysis based on the anticipated interview topics? What about having the consent form allude to whatever topics arose in the course of the research that were related to the understanding of education? Would such a consent form be sufficiently informative to make the participants' consent informed?

2. Can Akins make the following argument? "The description of the aims of my research provided in the informed consent form was full and accurate to the best of my ability. Consent from participants was obtained in good faith. Because I found something that I did not anticipate does not change the fact that these were the aims of my research and generated the procedures followed and the data collected. My involvement with the participants was exactly and only what we agreed. The fact that these data now support an unanticipated conclusion does not change this."

3. Suppose the unanticipated result is controversial and of a nature that it is reasonable to believe that many of the participants would have refused to participate if they knew that this matter were under investigation?

4. If Akins is trapped by the dilemma, how should he decide what to do? The problem of unanticipated findings is bound to arise occasionally, even in the most carefully designed study. Here a judgment has to be made about the sensitivity of the participants' participation and the significance of findings. Certainly Akins should be especially cautious about presenting any information that might be linked to any individual research participant. Akins probably should not make this decision on his own, but should consult with the Institutional Review Board (IRB) that approved the research, or with other qualified people not involved in the project.

ISSUE

Who represents the community's view of appropriate research questions?

Case 3

Mayor Publius looked at Dr. Terry Gates's list of review committee members to advise her about the community's likely response to her proposed Teenage Survey Project. Dr. Gates had convinced her university's IRB that the survey she proposed to do involved a large enough number of respondents to make it impractical for her to obtain parental permission and student assent from all of the participants. However, the IRB had insisted on a number of measures designed to protect the research participants, including that she consult with representatives of the community involved to ascertain that there would be no objections from the community on the nature of the survey questions she proposed to include.

The review committee included the Mayor, a minister of a local church, the head of the PTA, the high school principal, and a physician with a general medical practice in the community. The committee members were all respected, longtime members of the community who knew it well. Still something about this review process was troubling him.

"Tell me, Dr. Gates," he said, "just how do you want us to decide what we think of this survey?" Are we supposed to tell you whether we think this survey is OK ourselves, or whether we think people in town will think so? I for one think research is important, but there are other folks who might not. And some of these questions might seem insulting or nosy to some people, even though I think I understand why you need to have them."

"I don't think there should be any question, Mr. Mayor," said Reverend Layson. "We are here because we're considered to be leaders in this community, and we should lead. If Dr. Gates just wanted anybody's opinion she would have picked the committee at random. But she's chosen people whose occupations reflect a long-standing interest in the welfare of the people in this town, and I think we should view it as a trust of our judgment to recommend whether they go forward."

The mayor looked around the room. What he saw was white, middle-aged, well-educated, upper-class men with no public history of scandalous behavior. They knew the community, and worked hard on its behalf. But did they represent it? Would they recognize a sensitive question when they saw it? Were any of them black, female, non-citizens, gay, poor, adolescent, HIV positive, sexually active with multiple partners, or with a criminal record? What "community" was supposed to be consulted here?

Discussion: As the previous case suggests, community representatives may be an appropriate mechanism to rely on when informed consent as required by **Standard 1** is impractical. The purpose of such a committee of representatives is to provide participants the protection that would be normally provided by informed consent. Any effort to consult with community representatives about a proposed research project must grapple with at least two elusive questions, namely, how to identify the relevant community, and what qualifies someone to represent the community appropriately. Individuals are often members of several groups that might be called a "community," and particular research projects often draw their participants from several different communities.

Membership in a community is determined in a variety of ways, for example, by natural characteristics such as age, gender, or race, or by choice, such as marital status or residency, or in other ways, such as culture, ethnicity, or assignment to a school based on residential location. Membership in a community according to any of these characteristics may influence someone's assessment of relevant risks of a given activity, their attitude toward social welfare, and other factors affecting their perception of the merits of research and willingness to participate in it. It is often practically impossible to have the majority of a group of people consulted about the propriety of a research project come from the "community" in every relevant sense of the term. And it would be practically difficult to establish separate consulting groups for each community identified in the proposed research participant population. And yet, the idea here is to find a way to identify what the community's reaction to the proposed research will be.

Similarly, there is more than one criterion worth considering in deciding who would be a good community representative. The most immediate criterion is to identify someone who is a typical member of the proposed research population. Such a representative will provide a direct response from one member of the community, reflecting at least some of the characteristics of that community's perspective. However, community members are not necessarily well-informed about the general characteristics and variations within their community, and they may be hindered by the particular consultation process from providing a reaction that reflects the best interests of the community. Experience, knowledge, and dedication to the community are all significant factors, and it is difficult to be confident that any particular individual possesses them all. Whether it is best for people to speak for themselves, or whether it is best for someone who is a knowledgeable and experienced advocate of a particular group to speak on their behalf, will vary from situation to situation.

QUESTIONS

1. Some potential research participants may not wish to participate in a study for reasons that have little to do with their membership in a given community. Does this procedure adequately protect them?

2. We suggested in the discussion of the **Preamble** that there were three principles that governed treatment of participants. These were respect for autonomy, beneficence and justice. Does the procedure described above satisfy each of these principles? In particular, can a procedure that works by consulting "representatives" of a group satisfy the principle of autonomy?

ISSUE

More and more regular classroom teachers are becoming active members of research activities often under the name of "action research." Along with making themselves the participants of research, of course, they also involve their students in their research. This raises the question of whether students have any choice about becoming part of an action research project and whether this is ethical. May teachers carry out action research with their own students?

Case 4

"Let me get this straight, because I'm a little confused here," said Pat Tern to Libby Peterson. Pat felt a mixture of shock and mounting anger. "You're telling me that I shouldn't be doing my action research project with my own seventh grade students? Wait a minute. I'm a professional teacher, and my job requires that I do my best to help these kids learn. My action research project is designed to improve my students' educational experiences, and you can be sure I wouldn't be doing this if I didn't think it would, and that I'd stop the first moment I thought any student wasn't doing so well. And my plans for recording and reporting the data take into account the confidentiality issues I have discussed with the students and parents. What do you want me to do, carry out the project with somebody else's students? Don't you think I'm going to be more worried about the welfare of my students, whom I know and am emotionally attached to, than any others? And besides, when do you expect me to do this—during the 11 P.M. to 7 A.M. shift? The only practical way for me to do this is as part of my regular work. What is your problem?"

Libby Peterson stubbornly pursued her point. "There is no way that you can say that these students have any choice about participating in this project. I know you explained it to all of them, and to the parents, and that nobody objected. And I know that you don't mean to be doing anything that is not in their best interest. But face it, Pat, if somebody felt uncomfortable about it, particularly a student, the fact that they are emotionally attached to you means that they're being pressured to do it. And you know as well as I do that this project involves keeping a record of what happens, and regular meetings with the other teachers who are doing the project. That's time you could be spending thinking about other ways to help your students, and you don't have a lot of extra time. You're deciding for them that they're going to be part of something which may limit your teaching effectiveness and which they didn't come to school for. Maybe you just shouldn't do it at all."

Discussion: Voluntary consent is a fundamental principle for participants' joining in research. People are not obliged to serve as research participants, and may refuse to do so without regard for the basis of their unwillingness. If people are pressured to participate in research, either because they anticipate undesirable consequences if they refuse or because of undue inducements to participate, then they cannot have freely given their consent. This principle of avoiding coercion applies even in circumstances where no one has deliberately made an effort to attach any external consequences to the participants' decisions. **Standard 1** calls for informed consent, which includes not being coerced, and **Standard 5** specifically prohibits researchers from coercing their students to participate.

At the same time, it is not clear that younger students have the capacity for fully informed consent. It is difficult to argue that research to benefit people incapable of consent should be avoided entirely, because this would mean that research populations incapable of consent could never hope to benefit from any such research. The point that research work will distract Pat Tern from her professional duties may be true to some extent, but other ordinary commitments will distract teachers in similar ways. It seems unreasonable to single out research activity as the potential distraction that is unacceptable. And certainly the practical situation of professional teachers is that action research is more feasible if they do it with their own students. The logic of prohibiting precisely those people who are already involved in the action of their own classrooms from participating in action research makes the conclusion of applying the principle of not coercing consent here seem problematic.

QUESTIONS

1. Is the degree of risk relevant here? The possible harm to students is fairly minimal. Is it possible to permit action research so long as the risks to the students are small?

2. Is the possible benefit to the participating students relevant? Pat Tern may become a better teacher who benefits her students as a result of participation in action research. Should this count, or should it be dismissed as an unproven possibility?

3. Is it relevant or true that the students are incapable of informed consent? If they're too young to make a mature rational decision, then won't their parents or guardians make their decision? Can the request for permission from the parents be arranged to minimize any sense of coercion that they might feel?

ISSUE

Researchers often have definite opinions about students' education. When it comes to students' educational chances, researchers may think that students should do something other than what the students choose to do. Should researchers decide how to represent their participants' real interests?

Case 5

"You should speak up, Connie!" said Ellie Rist to the teenager sitting across from her. Ellie was exasperated with Connie Vencion's attitude about the upcoming student-run high school fair, and she wasn't going to hide it. She'd been doing a qualitative research study of male and female Hispanic student involvement in school culture for more than a year and the pattern was obvious. The Anglo students put together one set of activities, and the Hispanic students another. The Anglo student activities were designed by an even split of boys and girls, but the activities designed by the Hispanic students were always decided by the boys.

Ellie was confident of Connie's practical sense and creativity, and she was sure that Connie could come up with better ideas for the fair booths than the boys had decided on. She knew that Connie and her girlfriends were going to end up doing most of the work both before and during the fair, and that the boys would get the credit among the students for whatever success resulted. Ellie thought this represented a perfect example of cultural norms working against the interests of members of the cultural group who were willing participants in their own exploitation. She knew she would make this comment in the research findings of her report, but that wasn't going to change Connie's life one iota. She wanted to encourage Connie to take the initiative, but she was conscious of Connie's unease.

Connie shifted uncomfortably in her seat. She liked and admired Dr. Rist, and she did not want to disappoint her. At the same time, she didn't want to follow her advice. She knew that the boys probably wouldn't appreciate her suggesting any different ideas for the fair booths, and she especially didn't want to put her boyfriend on the spot. Besides, she was happy to do the work for the booths with her friends, and she didn't see why this was such a big deal. She knew that the school principal always made sure that the Hispanic students got to put together some of the booths, and she thought it was nice that he and the teachers always came by to participate. But all this talk about independence and leadership didn't make sense. She wished Dr. Rist would change the subject.

Discussion: A legitimate purpose of educational research is to improve the condition of the population studied. While research is designed to contribute to generalized knowledge that can subsequently be used for people's benefit, applied research that also benefits the research participants is a positive result, particularly in view of the time, energy, and risk expended by those participants. Researchers sometimes have access to information that is not readily accessible to the research participants and that may support practical judgments benefiting research participants that those participants may not appreciate. This is particularly significant in circumstances where the research participants are prone to cultural prejudices that they have accepted without reflection and which move them toward decisions that are detrimental to their interests.

At the same time, it is also possible for researchers to impose their prejudices about what is best on the research participants without adequate justification. **Standard 6** reminds researchers to be mindful of differences in research populations, and specifically mentions both culture and gender as examples of such differences. Members of an advantaged class in a society have frequently made decisions on behalf of those who are relatively disadvantaged, only to discover later on that they have overlooked important considerations that made a different decision reasonable. What is obviously true to the researcher may turn out not to be obviously true.

QUESTIONS

1. Is Ellie Rist's view of what Connie should do entirely based on knowledge about Connie's educational interests, or is it based on a wider understanding of what is in Connie's best interest? Is Ellie Rist imposing her own cultural view of the role of women in society on Connie?
2. What form of interference on Ellie's part might be permissible? Should she be trying to change Connie's mind at all? If Connie does not change her mind, is Ellie entitled to take direct action, by speaking to the principal about student involvement in the school fair?

ISSUE

What risks associated with participants' ordinary lives may researchers allow their research participants to endure?

Case 6

"I can't believe you're going to stand by and let all those children run headlong into wasted lives." Sophie Hart shook her head sadly as she looked over the description of the experimental project Dr. Sal Mann was proposing to carry out. "I think it's great that you're going into these high poverty schools to evaluate the effectiveness of a coordinated approach to professional development, curriculum, and student performance assessment, along with a parental involvement program. The expertise and resources you're bringing are comparable to the programs in the best schools in the state, way beyond those of the schools in this area. It will be good to obtain data on the value of this approach for students in poor schools, so people can see that this program helps these students as much as it helps students in the schools where your approach is more common. But why do you have to sacrifice the interests of the students in the schools who will be serving as a control group? You know this means that those students will continue to get a poor education. The school officials have only agreed because now they have a justification for not reforming their program because they're participating in an experiment. You also promised to introduce the experimental approach at the end of the experiment if it proves successful. But in the meantime, students will get five years worth of bad education. Furthermore, by that time, for many of them, their educational fate will be sealed. You're contributing to the perpetuation of a failing system."

Discussion: **Standard 7** requires that participants be protected from harmful consequences. In an imperfect world, where some people do not have access to the same resources as others do, researchers who seek better solutions for those who are disadvantaged are sometimes presented with situations where they may be forced to choose among undesirable alternatives. Dr. Mann needs to have some comparison group of students who do not participate in the approach to establish whether it leads to improved learning. Comparing student learning under the experimental approach to student learning in a school system with better resources typical of a more advantaged school system may be a bad comparison. This is because it may not reveal the power of the experimental approach to improve student learning in schools with few resources. However, preserving the disadvantaged conditions of some students' education to provide a direct measure of how well students would do with and without the experimental approach seems to perpetuate rather than eliminate a situation where it was already concluded that the students are not receiving the education they deserved.

However, until the experimental approach has actually been shown to provide a better educational experience, there is no rational warrant for asserting that the experimental approach is better than the education that the students are already getting. It may be useful to compare this case with **Case 9**. In that case, Dr. Spencer was proposing to withdraw instruction currently provided for the sake of a better research design despite the fact that he had reason to suppose that it was effective.

In this case, a current program is left in place despite the fact that it is viewed as poor. The argument that failing to provide all students with the new program violates **Standard 7** rests on the presumption that it is known to be better than the current program. But this is what the research is intended to discover.

QUESTIONS

1. It appears that Dr. Mann is not reducing the level of resources of any of the schools he is investigating. He is only increasing the level of some schools but not others. Does this make a difference?

2. Suppose that to make comparison between schools sharper, Dr. Mann proposed reducing the resources available to an already low-resource school. Would this be acceptable?

3. Is the complaint that students are harmed, or that some are treated inequitably? Is such inequitable treatment harmful?

4. How important is it to the above argument that Dr. Mann is genuinely ignorant about whether his program is better than what is currently being done? In the medical context (to simplify a little), it is often thought that, in comparing treatment A to treatment B, the physician is required to give the treatment that is best if there is a consensus in the medical community identifying that treatment. This view requires genuine uncertainty between two treatments to give some

individuals treatment A and others treatment B. What is known is determined by community consensus. Is this a workable view for education? Does education have mechanisms for ascertaining professional consensus?

ISSUE

Sometimes changes in the educational practice go beyond changing the techniques used to achieve an established objective. For example, sometimes when changes are made in the curriculum this is done because there is a different view of the goals that the curriculum should serve. **Standard 7** requires that researchers be cautious about research that has negative social consequences, and it illustrates this by pointing out that some experiments might result in denying students part of the standard curriculum. How might this apply to cases where changing the curriculum is the point of a new curriculum?

Case 7

"The fact is, this program leaves out learning math facts!" declared Stan Lenon to the Point Bluff School Board. "And that means these children won't be able to make change when they grow up and get jobs at the grocery store. These consultants can say all they want about problem solving, but it looks to me like they are just creating a problem where it didn't exist before. This *Math Operator* program has cute games and fancy ways of going around in circles, but it doesn't ever ask the students to learn the basic facts of addition, subtraction, multiplication, and division. I swear the kids won't be able to add two plus two half the time, because they won't be able to figure it out without a solar-powered calculator, and those calculators don't work when it's dark!"

"Mr. Lenon has an unusually square view of what mathematics is really about," said Cal Sanderson, when it was his turn to speak. "The purpose of mathematics education is to construct a set of patterns that help students use numbers in meaningful ways, not learn how to spit out numbers mindlessly when someone holds up a piece of packaged meat and asks what it costs. Making change is for machines in the 21st century, so that people can turn their attention to thinking about real problems involving quantitative analytical strategies that machines haven't been able to master without guidance. The *Math Operator* program will help the children learn how to think mathematically, not how to exercise their memories. Let them learn that skill memorizing poetry. Our program and our performance assessment strategies are designed to assess meaningful learning, not rote memory."

Discussion: **Standard 7** warns researchers to avoid possible negative social consequences of research interventions. Its illustrative example concerns depriving students of important parts of the standard curriculum. If the *Math Operator* program omits teaching the basic math facts, then it is clearly leaving out part of the standard curriculum. Cal Sanderson would probably retort that this is not an important part of the standard curriculum, but such a claim is clearly at issue here. No one knows what the consequences will be for student achievement in mathematics or their long-term welfare as a consequence of omitting this component of the standard curriculum. Moreover, the issues raised may concern more than the nature of an effective math program. They may also concern what parents want for their children.

Here is one way to think about the problem. First, the researchers have a responsibility to discover whether the new program has a deleterious effect on the knowledge of math facts. Because a decline in knowledge of math facts would be viewed by some as a harmful consequence, they must assess this even if they believe that this is not a harm or that such harm as results may be balanced by a deeper understanding of math. If student knowledge is lower in math, the researchers would have to seriously contemplate re-instating this part of the standard curriculum. Researchers also should give consideration to whether a lack of student knowledge in this area is undesirable, either in itself or because it may have a negative impact on student learning which depends on this basic knowledge.

Second, because the new *Math Operator* program shifts the focus of mathematics education toward different and controversial goals, Stan Lenon and Cal Sanderson should discuss these issues in a forum, such as a school board meeting, to allow decisions by those concerned on what kind of education the school should provide.

QUESTIONS

1. This case suggests that one difficulty in applying **Standard 7** is that we don't always agree on what constitutes doing harm. How do we decide what's harmful?

2. One proposal is that when educational changes concern the goals of education, it is more appropriate to have decisions made democratically than made by experts. Researchers should collect facts relevant to the dispute, but then argue the case before a democratic body where the decision about goals will be made. Is this a reasonable division of labor? Why?

3. One response to the previous question is that facts should be determined by research conducted by experts, whereas values should be chosen democratically. Is the reason why it's difficult to decide what's harmful here that people have different values about math? Consider that Cal Sanderson's argument basically appeals to factual claims about what kinds of math people in our society will need to do, not to different tastes about mathematical knowledge.

ISSUE

When does a research training exercise become research in which the protection of any human participants involved becomes imperative?

Case 8

"And remember, everyone, the deadline for your research project paper is next Friday at 5 o'clock, and the paper will represent one third of your final grade. Good Luck!" Professor Mentor watched as her students walked out of the room, and then turned to look at Laura Header, who had come into the lecture hall sometime during Mentor's lecture and was sitting waiting for her. "What can I do for you, Laura?"

"You can tell me why you're allowing your students to engage in research involving human participants without their going through the University's Humans Research Participants Committee. You yourself just called what they're doing research, and I understand that some of the student projects you've approved involve human participants. Our university requires committee review and approval for all such projects, and you haven't even notified my office that these projects are going to happen, much less submitted them for review. I want you to put an immediate halt to all these projects until that happens; I'm not going to jeopardize the well-being of human research participants, or our institution's eligibility for federal funding, for the sake of these students' training."

Mentor felt herself getting angry. "That's just the point, Laura; it's not really research, it's an educational experience. This is not dissertation work where the students have to demonstrate the ability to actually contribute to the field of research. These are student projects that don't have a chance of ever being published, and they're not intended to be. The final product is a course paper, with a grade, and the purpose of the activity is to learn, not to contribute to the field.

I review and approve the students' projects as part of my role as a teacher, and I accept full responsibility for that. Your committee has enough to do reviewing real research protocols without interfering with the educational work that I do at this institution."

Discussion: The transition from student to full-fledged researcher is not an overnight transformation. One of the ways to learn something is to practice it, and students may be involved in educational activities which resemble research as a part of their education. If these prototypical research activities involve human participants, those human participants should be treated ethically. The inexperienced student researcher may be even more likely to overlook potential risks to which other people are exposed by their interventions. The probability that their work will not produce significantly valuable research findings that promise to benefit human society makes it all the more difficult to justify any inconvenience, much less any risk, to human participants.

At the same time, the distinction between education and research is a meaningful one. At some level it must be acknowledged that the supervision of research activity carried out under the auspices of education means that the responsibility for the student's activities is the teacher's. If a teacher assigns students something that involves other people, the teacher is responsible for taking adequate precautions to preserve the welfare of the people that the students are using. Furthermore, teaching the students how to protect the welfare of the people they interact with as research participants should be an integral part of the future professional researcher's educational experience.

QUESTIONS

1. Which of the standards of **Part II** are most at risk of violation by students who are doing projects that involve human participants? What precautions should be taken to protect participants?

2. When does a person become a participant? Suppose that a student doing a paper talks with an experienced teacher; is that teacher a participant? Suppose that the student "interviews" the teacher; is the teacher now a participant? Is there a difference between interviewing and talking with someone? Suppose that the student interviewed or talked with parents, administrators, elementary school students, or high school students; when would these people become participants?

ISSUE

Keeping a secret and making information public are often at odds with each other. Sometimes research participants want information to remain private, while other research participants are interested in knowing the outcome of the research. Is there a priority between preserving confidentiality and reporting findings to participating participants?

Case 9

"So when are we going to get my report?" said Ann Nunn to Dr. Fiedler. Nunn was calling because Dr. Fiedler had promised the participants of the research study a copy of the research report as appreciation for their participation in a research study of teachers in a school starting a school-wide improvement project. The study included interviews with the teachers about the project as it developed, and related some of the very mixed feelings the teachers had about themselves, their colleagues, and the value of the reform effort. It focused on a particular conflict over curriculum design that had erupted in the middle of the reform process, and how the teachers on both sides of the issue had felt about it. Nunn was one of the central characters in the conflict, and had always expressed a concern about whether her side of the issue would be fairly represented in the report. "Didn't you say you thought you'd have the study completed by now? What's holding things up?" Fiedler hesitated.

Discussion: Research participants deserve protection from the risks associated with participation in research. As far as possible, research should be designed to avoid any harm coming to them as a result of their participation. In many kinds of behavioral research, a substantial portion of the risks involved have to do with disclosing information that the research participants would otherwise have kept secret, and which might be used against them. **Standard 10** asserts the research participants' right to be anonymous or to have information remain confidential, and it also points out that there may be inherent limits in the researchers' ability to keep information from becoming public.

At the same time, one important way to show respect for research participants is to do something that recognizes the participants' awareness of the significance of the research activity. **Standard 9** reflects the idea that providing research participants with the findings of the research study is a symbolic expression of the researchers' understanding that the research participants can appreciate the significance of the research study in which they participated. It also shows that the research participants care about what the researchers may have found.

QUESTIONS

1. Should the researchers have promised the research participants confidentiality in the first place? Research participants in studies that include the study of a particular site, by virtue of their direct and long-standing familiarity with that site, find it difficult to keep from identifying other participants in a study if they receive a report of it. While it suggests good intentions on the part of the researchers to promise a research report, such researchers must know that the readers will be able to identify other participants.

2. If the researchers needed to promise to do their best to keep the information confidential, should they have refused to provide a research report in which study participants were likely to be able to identify each other? When they write up the research for publication, will they pull together stories from several different sites, so that individual participants are harder to identify?

ISSUE

Research participants sometimes want confidentiality because researchers may discover that the participants are a threat to others. Does the researcher then have a duty to warn others of the danger they have uncovered? Are researchers obliged to report illegal or dangerous behavior discovered in their research, even if they have promised the research participants confidentiality?

Case 10

Frank Lee stared at the letter in his hand, and his mind raced over the events of the last two months. It was all falling into place. He was now sure that Sal Allenbach, one of the drama teachers participating in a research study of coaching, was having a sexual relationship with one of the high school students doing set design for a student dramatic production. Bits of conversations, observations of comings and goings, the relationship between Allenbach and the student, and now a letter. This evasive letter came from a former employer about the circumstances under which Allenbach had left his last job.

What should he do now?, Frank asked himself. He was a public school teacher participating in a research project as part of a graduate degree requirement. He knew that as a teacher employed by the state he was required by law to report any case of suspected child abuse. Because the student was a minor, this situation met the standards for child abuse. Under ordinary circumstances, although he wouldn't be happy about the controversy he knew would erupt as soon as he reported it, the seriousness of the teacher's misconduct would have compelled him to report it.

But the research situation introduced additional complications. The principal investigator had promised confidentiality to the participating teachers because he wanted them to speak candidly about working long hours after school with these students. The research team had received a certificate of confidentiality to protect them from being forced to testify about what they were told by the teachers. Of course, the certificate of confidentiality only meant that Frank couldn't be forced to say anything, not that he couldn't voluntarily decide to make information public. But the principal investigator had gone beyond that in explaining the research project to the participants when he obtained their consent: He'd emphatically said they wouldn't reveal any information that could damage someone's reputation or allow anyone to identify who the information was about. One thing was for sure: if he reported it, the research project would come to a sudden halt, and Frank's hopes for a master's degree by the end of next year were gone.

Discussion: The reason for promising confidentiality to people is they have important information that they do not want to make public. To obtain that information for research purposes, researchers secure research participants' cooperation by promising that they will use the information only for research purposes.

Standard 10 addresses research participants' right to anonymity or confidentiality to the degree that this is practically possible. If researchers routinely violated their own promises, even for legitimate purposes, this would weaken the public's trust in such promises. Researchers would not gain access to the information if they did not promise confidentiality, and whatever valuable findings might have been obtained will never be discovered. This is particularly true in research activities concerning issues that frequently involve sensitive information. In this case, for example, it would be difficult to find out the conditions under which these relationships developed between students and teachers without promises of confidentiality.

At the same time, it is not reasonable to assume that research ideals automatically justify rising above the practical exigencies of any situation. The interests of research are not absolute, and there are circumstances where other interests should prevail. It would be better if this dilemma were not to arise, and researchers can take steps to limit their occurrence. For example, researchers may attach certain qualifications to their promises of confidentiality, in which they identify the information which they would be compelled to report. Of course this creates a constraint in the dampening effect it might have on what the research participants would reveal. But if this is what the researcher is committed to do, saying so would preclude the researchers' having to violate the research participants' trust.

It should also be noted that this case appears to differ from **Case 14** in several ways. First, if Sal Allenbach is guilty of having sex with a student, there is current harm, not merely the abstract possibility of harm. Second, while the evidence in this case is circumstantial and not conclusive, it is not speculative and based on uninvestigated hearsay. Third, it is not clear that the evidence that has come to Frank Lee's attention was obtained and linked to the research procedures.

QUESTIONS

1. Is Lee bound by the research team leader's promise not to violate the confidentiality of the research participants?

2. If Lee, as a state government employee, is legally required to report suspected child abuse to state authorities, does this legal requirement overrule his obligation to respect the confidentiality of the information he has?

3. Do the differences between this case and previous **Case 14** warrant a different conclusion?

INTELLECTUAL
OWNERSHIP

The Preamble, the Standards, and Their Rationale

Preamble

Intellectual ownership is predominantly a function of creative contribution.

Intellectual ownership is not predominantly a function of effort expended.

STANDARDS

1   Authorship should be determined based on the following guidelines, which are not intended to stifle collaboration, but rather to clarify the credit appropriately due for various contributions to research.

   a)   All those, regardless of status, who have made substantive creative contribution to the generation of an intellectual product are entitled to be listed as authors of that product.

   b)   First authorship and order of authorship should be the consequence of relative creative leadership and creative contribution. Examples of creative contributions are: writing first drafts or substantial portions; significant rewriting or substantive editing; and contributing generative ideas or basic conceptual schemes or analytic categories, collecting data which require significant interpretation or judgment, and interpreting data.

   c)   Clerical or mechanical contributions to an intellectual product are not grounds for ascribing authorship. Examples of such technical contributions are: typing, routine data collection or analysis, routine editing, and participation in staff meetings.

   d)   Authorship and first authorship are not warranted by legal or contractual responsibility for or authority over the project or process that generates an intellectual product. It is improper to enter into contractual arrangements that preclude the proper assignment of authorship.

   e)   Anyone listed as an author must have given his/her consent to be so listed.

   f)   The work of those who have contributed to the production of an intellectual product in ways short of these requirements for authorship should be appropriately acknowledged within the product.

   g)   Acknowledgment of other work significantly relied on in the development of an intellectual product is required. However, so long as such work is not plagiarized or otherwise inappropriately used, such reliance is not ground for authorship or ownership.

   h)   It is improper to use positions of authority to appropriate the work of others or claim credit for it. In hierarchical relationships, educational researchers should take care to ensure that those in subordinate positions receive fair and appropriate authorship credit.

   i)   Theses and dissertations are special cases in which authorship is not determined strictly by the criteria elaborated in these standards. Authorship in the publication of work arising from theses and dissertations is determined by creative intellectual contributions as in other cases.

   j)   Authors should disclose the publication history of articles they submit for publication; that is, if the present article is substantially similar in content and form to one previously published, that fact should be noted and the place of publication cited.

2   While under suitable circumstances, ideas and other intellectual products may be viewed as commodities, arrangements concerning the production or distribution of ideas or other intellectual products must be consistent with academic freedom and the appropriate availability of intellectual products to scholars, students, and the public. Moreover, when a conflict between the academic and scholarly purposes of intellectual production and profit from such production arise, preference should be given to the academic and scholarly purposes.

3   *Ownership of intellectual products should be based upon the following guidelines:*

a)   *Individuals are entitled to profit from the sale or disposition of those intellectual products they create. They may therefore enter into contracts or other arrangements for the publication or disposition of intellectual products, and profit financially from these arrangements.*

b)   *Arrangements for the publication or disposition of intellectual products should be consistent with their appropriate public availability and with academic freedom. Such arrangements should emphasize the academic functions of publication over the maximization of profit.*

c)   *Individuals or groups who fund or otherwise provide resources for the development of intellectual products are entitled to assert claims to a fair share of the royalties or other profits from the sale or disposition of those products. As such claims are likely to be contentious, funding institutions and authors should agree on policies for the disposition of profits at the outset of the research or development project.*

d)   *Authors should not use positions of authority over other individuals to compel them to purchase an intellectual product from which the authors benefit. This standard is not meant to prohibit use of an author's own textbook in a class, but copies should be made available on library reserve so that students are not forced to purchase it.*

RATIONALE

Part III divides intellectual ownership into concerns about authorship and concerns about research products as commodities. In the first case, the essential issue is the proper assignment of credit for intellectual work. In the second, there is concern for the entitlement to the profits that may be generated from research products. Academic freedom and the responsibility to ensure the efficient dissemination of ideas and research findings are also issues to be addressed especially in this second context.

The essential message of the **Preamble** is that creative contribution is the most important factor, but not the sole factor, in determining both of these intellectual ownership forms, and that creative contribution is not to be confused with mere effort. Ownership is not contingent on simply doing work on a piece of research so much as it is contingent on the kind of work done. The leading ethical principle at work here appears to be a principle of justice, which will be called the "Principle of Authorial Entitlement": **All and only those who create the intellectual substance of a work, either in collaboration with others or without collaborators, are entitled to be identified as its authors.**

The insight behind this principle is that to have authorship is to have a claim to the intellectual substance of a work that makes it worth publishing. A claim of this kind can only be grounded in one's having created that intellectual substance, in whole or in part, through one's own creative efforts. Some philosophers (John Locke, for example) have argued that property is created by *mixing one's labor* with some product.

A view of this sort seems to be at work here. But if so, then we must also argue that it is the creative process, not mere effort, that counts as the significant labor in creating an intellectual product. That is why the principle of justice above holds that the ownership is of the intellectual substance of the work.

Moreover, the kind of ownership involved in a claim to authorship may differ from that involved in ownership of a research product viewed as a commodity. If a researcher produces a work under contract, he or she will be the author, but the product may belong to whomever contracted for it. Concerns such as these may account for why the **Preamble** does not claim that creative contribution is the sole factor in ownership.

These comments suggest a number of issues. First, the **Preamble** says that intellectual ownership is predominantly a function of creative contribution and is not predominantly a function of effort. This leaves open the possibility that effort can carry some weight in determining intellectual ownership, and it also leaves open the possibility that other factors may play roles. Thus it may be that there is a balance struck between creative contribution, effort, and other factors in assigning ownership.

A second issue is how the distinction between creative contribution and effort is drawn. Conceiving a theory is clearly a creative contribution while typing is not. There are other cases that are less clear.

A final issue concerns when creative contribution counts toward ownership. It should be apparent that if the claim of the **Preamble** is interpreted too broadly, its consequences can be bizarre. All scholars work within an intellectual tradition. Their work depends on ideas and methods developed by those who have gone before. But we cannot credit everyone whose ideas have been formative for the development of a field with authorship of the subsequent work in that field, even if such work is heavily influenced by this formative work.

Also, sometimes ideas for research come out of seminars or are suggested by the writings of others. Sometimes colleagues contribute to work through discussion or criticism. But we do not usually regard these contributions as entitling seminar participants, helpful colleagues or other writers to authorship even if their influence is direct and crucial. These are rather viewed as reasons for citing their work or acknowledging their influence.

Similarly, before an article is published, reviewers and editors normally make comments on it. Sometimes these inputs result in a significant rethinking of the work. Often they make a significant contribution. But we do not usually see such input as creating an entitlement to authorship on the part of editors or reviewers.

Thus, while creative contribution is important to intellectual ownership, it cannot be sufficient for it. This is why the principle of justice previously noted emphasizes collaboration in the production of a work, not just influence on it, as crucial to ownership.

Here it seems important that the standards of **Part III** should be interpreted in the light of the problem they were intended to solve. The problem to be solved may be one of determining who among those who collaborate in the production of an intellectual product are entitled to authorship of it and in what order of authorship. Collaborators in the production of a work may include those who frame its questions and research strategies, graduate students who collect data, technical specialists who help with statistical analysis, and those who type, edit, or proof read text. Work done by graduate students for their theses, which is also associated with the work of their advisors, can be especially perplexing. **Part III** seems directed toward sorting out the relations between such collaborators more than worrying about the relations of collaborators to editors or seminar participants.

This distinction between collaborators and others who may influence a work is not merely a matter of convention. When intellectual collaborations are formed, the parties to the collaboration enter into a mutual agreement to work together and make a commitment to each other and to the project they are to work on together. That mutually recognized commitment is what makes them members of the collaborative team, and makes it reasonable for other members of the team to expect them to do creative work on the project. Anyone who is expected to do creative work on a project and accepts that burden becomes a party to the collaboration and a presumptive author.

Interpretation of the Standards: Issues, Cases, and Discussions

ISSUE

The following cases illustrate the application of the principle of authorial entitlement.

Case 1

- Professor Smock is hired by a project officer of the State Education Department, Patricia Cummings, to conduct a study of educational expenditures and achievement mandated by state law. Patricia Cummings' role is to monitor the project for contract compliance and to conduct a final review of the research. She claims that because she has contractual responsibility for the work she must be given authorship of the study. She also argues that her role in conducting the final review constitutes a creative contribution.

- Joan Goodman, a wealthy celebrity, attempts to hire an educational researcher, Sandra Coleridge, to undertake the entire work of writing a book on charter schools. Her instructions to Coleridge are that the book is to take a favorable view of charter schools because it should be clear to everyone that they are the best hope of revitalizing education in America. The contract with Coleridge stipulates that Joan Goodman be given sole or joint authorship.

Discussion: In the first example, only Professor Smock is entitled to authorship. He is the only person who has made the creative contribution that **Standard 1a** requires for authorship. **Standards 1a** and **1d** make it clear that neither Patricia Cummings nor Joan Goodman are entitled to authorship. Patricia Cummings, the project officer, has no claim to be listed as author simply because she has legal and contractual responsibility for the project and provides the necessary funds and authority to obtain data. Unless she takes on some of the intellectual work of the study itself and makes a creative contribution to it, she has no claim to authorship.

Normally, reviewing the final report would not count as creative work even if it was concerned with the substantive adequacy of the research. Even if her review resulted in significant changes in the final report along the lines she suggested, that would not entitle her to authorship. She is playing a role more analogous to that of journal editor than author. If her review resulted in significant collaboration between herself and Professor Smock in reworking the report, authorship would be warranted.

Joan Goodman cannot ethically obtain authorship in this way. The researcher cannot ethically enter into this contract, whatever the financial inducements may be, since **Standard 1d** goes on to say that: *It is improper to enter into contractual arrangements that preclude the proper assignment of authorship.* (We note that these standards are more restrictive than copyright law on this point because the latter allows authorship to be alienated and obtained through contract.)

It may be that the celebrity has contributed decisively to the creation of the book through the offer of a lucrative contract to a suitable author, but this does not constitute a *substantive creative contribution to the generation of an intellectual product,* by the lights of **Standards**

1a and **1d.** Nor does the fact that Joan Goodman dictated the topic and the main conclusion of the book entitle Sandra Coleridge to grant Joan Goodman authorship, because these stipulations do not constitute creative contributions.

Case 2

Andrew Hanover, a teacher in the Claredon Schools system, engages in a participant-observer research project in a pair of schools in the district at the request and under the supervision of a team of researchers from a local university. He provides the research team with the records of his personal observations regarding the peer-mediation systems in those schools. Those records are used as data by the research team that actually writes up the study.

In addition, Hanover drafts a related section of the article in which the study of peer-mediation is reported. The research team claims that Hanover is not entitled to authorship because he is not a member of the research team. Hence he has not been a collaborator in the research.

Discussion: This case provides a clear illustration of a creative contribution as required by **Standard 1b.** Although drafting the related section of the article makes the researcher's creative contribution even more substantial, the researcher would have made a substantial contribution and be entitled to authorship even without that contribution.

Standard 1b states that *collecting data which require significant interpretation or judgment* constitutes in itself a creative contribution sufficient for authorship. (We take this to mean that collecting the data requires interpretation or judgment, and not that the collected data requires further interpretation.) By this measure, the data collection would seem to warrant authorship. Finally, because Andrew Hanover was not a member of the university research team does not mean that he was not a collaborator in the research.

In contrast, under federal copyright law, Hanover's data collection would not generate any claim of copyright ownership, because such ownership is considered to require "copyrightable expression." Ideas and facts per se are not copyrightable no matter how much effort it takes to develop or discover them. It is only the original expression of an idea that is copyrightable. Given the presumption in academic publishing that authorship entails an initial transferable claim of copyright ownership, this means that the standards in **Part III** give protection, which copyright law does not, to researchers who play diverse roles in research teams.

Case 3

The head of a research team, Janice Leander, identifies the problem to be investigated and works out the general design of the investigation that is undertaken. Other members of the team complete the literature search, work out the details of the investigation and carry it out, and write up the study after its results are reviewed by Ms. Leander. Her role on the project is limited to designing it and reviewing its results.

Discussion: Under **Standard 1b,** Ms. Leander clearly deserves authorship, given the "generative" role played in this case by the creative intellectual work involved in identifying the problem and figuring out how to investigate it. That her role in executing the project is minimal is not a reason for denying authorship.

Case 4

Alice Stark, a novice researcher, is trained by Roger Parks, the principal investigator, in the protocols for conducting interviews. Working with these protocols, which require judgment to execute, she conducts one third of the interviews for the project. Another member of the team, Joanne Wood, is in charge of collecting recommendations regarding how the data set should be "cleaned up," e.g., which categories ought to be compressed into a single category to yield a sufficient number of data points in the cells. It takes her months of work to get the data set in usable form. When the research report is completed, Parks denies authorship to both Alice Stark and Joanne Wood.

Discussion: The case of Alice Stark is harder than the previous cases, because there is indeterminacy in the idea of data collection requiring *significant interpretation or judgment* in **Standard 1b.** If the kind of judgment involved in executing the interview protocols is not expert judgment, but rather a kind of judgment requiring only common sense and brief training, Parks might justifiably categorize this as a non-creative contribution.

Similarly, the case of Joanne Wood is another possible but unclear case of entitlement to authorship. It differs from that of Alice Stark because it involves not only uncertainties about how significantly creative the data interpretation is, but also uncertainties about how much weight should be given to the time and effort expended. If Wood's results could have been produced more quickly with only modest creative judgment by a statistician (if hired as a consultant), then it would be fair to decide that her creative contribution did not warrant authorship. Yet the team's decision was to have Wood do the work, possibly knowing that what would be a routine or modestly creative intellectual exercise for a statistician would require more creative effort and time for the team member to achieve a comparable result. One might conclude in these circumstances that the large amount of work or effort put in by the team member warrants the judgment that a substantive creative contribution had been made, even though that effort produced only modestly creative results. The standards do not compel this conclusion, but neither do they rule it out.

ISSUE

A primary concern of these standards is to clarify the conditions under which a person is entitled to claim and receive authorship, and so must be assigned authorship if she or he desires it. However, the principle of authorial entitlement does not compel those who are entitled to authorship to accept it, nor does it license the assignment of authorship without the consent of the person who is to receive it.

This does not mean that one can ethically refuse one's consent on just any grounds. However, these standards must be read in light of **Standard 2** of **Part I,** which states that *educational researchers must not fabricate, falsify, or misrepresent authorship, evidence, data, findings, or conclusions.* This identifies an obligation of truthfulness in reporting authorship, which has not been abandoned in **Standard 1** of **Part III,** though it is not mentioned in it. To knowingly or negligently claim or assign authorship to someone who does not satisfy whatever conditions define authorship would breach this obligation. Additionally, to refuse authorship when one believed or should have known that someone satisfies those conditions would be a violation of it. In either case, a misrepresentation of authorship has occurred, and misrepresentations are identified by these standards as unethical.

This obligation of truthfulness does not entail, however, that anyone who has made a creative contribution to an intellectual project must be listed as author or accept authorship. **Standard 1e** of **Part III** holds that *anyone listed as author must have given his/her consent to be so listed.* When someone is listed as an author, at least two conditions should be met: the person made a substantial creative contribution and he or she consented to be listed as an author.

This raises the question of whether it is possible to improperly withhold one's consent to be listed as an author.

Case 5

The Creative Results Project has had a team researching a new civics curriculum. They have recently completed a paper describing their results. Peter Sally, a member of the research team responsible for the technical editing of this paper, concludes that his efforts did not yield a substantial creative contribution and refuses to be listed as an author. Diane G'Sell, another member of the research team, concludes that although she did have significant input in the project, the project as a whole lacks substantial creative merit and does not wish to have her name associated with it.

> *Discussion:* In both of these instances there is no impermissible misrepresentation of authorship involved in exercising the option, established by **Standard 1e,** to withhold consent to being listed as an author. Technical editing is not a creative contribution. Peter Sally did not make a creative contribution and is not entitled to authorship. It should not have been offered. In the case of Diane G'Sell, one might argue that there is nothing of substance to claim credit for (assuming her judgment is correct). There is no inaccuracy involved in her not being listed as author. If, however, the paper is published, it might be claimed that the readers of the journal in which it is published are entitled to know the full list of those who are responsible for the work. This argument assumes that one purpose of **Standard 1a** is to inform the readership about contributors to a work. **Standard 1a** may be intended to protect an interest of readers as well as an interest of authors. Even so (as we explain more fully in the following **Case 6**), we conclude that **Standard 1e** overrules **Standard 1a.** People cannot be compelled to take credit for work of which they disapprove. (See also **Hard Case 1.**)

Case 6

Dr. Carmine Gonzales put great effort into the evaluation of the On Overdrive project. She was part of a team with five researchers who produced the final report. Her roles included some input into the design of the evaluation as well as interpretation of qualitative data. Despite her enthusiasm for On Overdrive, she saw little in the evidence that suggested the project had achieved any of its goals.

Her colleagues saw it differently. They noted that there was considerable support for the program among the students involved in it and the teachers who taught it. Dr. Gonzales, however, was more impressed that, although students in the project did appear to be learning, there was little evidence that the project contributed to that learning. She and the rest of the team have had numerous arguments about how to interpret the results. In the end, they have agreed to disagree, and the other members of the team have written a report from which Dr. Gonzales substantially dissents. Despite the fact that there is much in the report that she does agree with, and she is responsible for, she has decided she does not want her name on the report.

> *Discussion:* This is the kind of case that **Standard 1e** probably best accommodates. Dr. Gonzales has met the requirements for authorship, but has withdrawn her name and approval of the report because she is unable to persuade her collaborators that some aspect of it is intolerable or untrue. It falls short of her researcher's standards, but not those of the rest of the team.
>
> The evident intent of **Standard 1e** is to give someone in these circumstances an ethical escape hatch. No such escape hatch would exist if creative contribution were all that defined authorship, and the principle of authorial entitlement and an obligation of truthfulness were the only ethical principles at work in these standards pertaining to assignment of authorship.
>
> The most straightforward way to account for **Standard 1e** is to regard it as embodying the proposition that being an author of a work involves endorsing or authorizing its content. In

works of sole authorship, one will presumably choose not to publish, nor endorse or authorize a work that one is not satisfied with. But when a work is jointly produced, one's only option may be to withhold one's authorization or authorship. One is part of a team that is jointly responsible for the work, and one may see merit in it, but also defects, yet lack the authority or influence within the team to block publication or secure agreement on the changes one wants. One is left with the alternative of refusing responsibility for and refusing to endorse what one finds unacceptable and cannot control. In recognizing that this is ethically appropriate, we accept the idea that there is no impropriety in withholding one's consent to being named an author if one does not endorse or approve of the work content. We recognize endorsement of the contents as an aspect of authorship.

Case 7

John Marshall is the advisor of Paul Flexner. He regards Flexner as one of the more talented students he has had. It has been Marshall's practice to encourage all of his students to develop publications while they are graduate students. Not only is this good professional experience, it is important in getting an academic position after completing the degree. Marshall is not only Flexner's advisor, but has also employed him as a research assistant. They have developed a number of jointly authored publications. Marshall is worried that a set of publications authored by Marshall and Flexner will create the erroneous impression that Paul is unable to do quality work on his own. To avoid this misconception, he arranges with Paul to have two papers published with only Flexner's name listed as author.

Discussion: John Marshall has gone too far in trying to help his student. Because he has made substantive contributions to the two papers in question, Marshall breaches his obligation of truthfulness in declining authorship. Benevolence does not warrant deception. Note that nothing in **Standards 1a–1e** directly forbids the charitable bestowal of unearned authorship. However, it is inconsistent with the values of honesty and accuracy that are presupposed.

Case 8

Fred Osbourne has had little luck in drawing attention to his work. Recently, he had a conversation about his work with one of the most visible scholars in his field, Emily Provine. The next time he submitted a paper he listed Dr. Provine as co-author despite the fact that she had not been involved in its preparation. He sent the paper to Dr. Provine calling her attention to their conversation and claiming that it was helpful in developing the paper. Emily Provine finds this implausible, but she allows Osbourne to list her as co-author.

Discussion: This is an unethical way of procuring attention for one's work because it misrepresents authorship. Emily Provine is obliged to refuse her consent to authorship because she did not work on the project and made no significant contribution to it. This is true, even if she believes it is a good work, and that its association with her name would be good for the research in that area.

ISSUE

A variety of people may have helped to bring to final form a piece of intellectual property. There are dissertation sponsors, employees of the principal investigator, referees, journal editors, friends, and students. These people often contribute advice and direction to others who produce an intellectual product. A question posed is whether, and under what circumstances, these people might have a claim to authorship.

Case 9

Professor Carolyn Henley, a dissertation advisor, provides her student, John Denton, with the central ideas used in his dissertation. A fellow student who is working on a related project under Professor Henley also makes a substantive creative contribution to Denton's thesis work by developing a survey instrument and using it to gather data which they all share. The work of both students is part of a larger project conceived of and overseen by Professor Henley as principal investigator. John Denton also publishes the results of the dissertation as an article.

Discussion: Does the creative contribution of Professor Henley entitle her to be listed as a co-author on the dissertation? What about the fellow student's contribution? Henley has contributed a *generative idea,* to use the language of **Standard 1b,** and the fellow student has done creative data collection, but **Standard 1i** identifies the thesis as a special case. However, since **Standard 1i** is framed negatively, stating that entitlement to authorship of the dissertation is not determined strictly by creative contribution, it does not provide express guidance on how authorship of dissertations is determined and whether co-authorship of dissertations is permissible. Presumably, if dissertations are single-authored documents by convention, and advisor's names conventionally appear on them to acknowledge the expert guidance provided by the advisor, then it is reasonable to suppose that the intent of **Standard 1i** is to note that the standards enumerated in **Part III** are not intended to overturn those conventions. What we should presumably state is that the advisor and fellow student are not entitled to co-authorship.

The fellow student and dissertation writer will belong to the same research team headed by their advisor for the purposes of published research, given the facts of the case. In publishing the dissertation work in an article, Denton is obliged to list Professor Henley **and** his fellow student as co-authors.

ISSUE

Do employees who are hired to do creative work on an intellectual product have a claim to be listed as authors?

Case 10

• Professor Yoder hires a research assistant, Keshana Roberts, who makes a creative contribution to his project but is not listed as an author on the published report because her contract specifically waived any claims she might have to authorship.

• Professor Tender is brought onto a research team working over the summer with the offer of either a consultant's fee or co-authorship, but not both. His contribution to the work of this team is substantive. This option is justified to him with the argument that other members of the research team are not being paid for their summer work on this project. It is unfair for Tender to be paid and to receive authorship.

Discussion: **Standard 1a** and the **principle of authorial entitlement** make these clear cases of wrongly denying authorship. There is no basis in the case description for denying that Keshana Roberts is a member of the collaborative team whose creative contribution should warrant authorship, despite the terms of her contract. Indeed, since **Standard 1d** says that *it is improper to enter into contractual arrangements that preclude the proper assignment of authorship,* we conclude that the contract she was employed under is ethically void.

Similarly, in Professor Tender's case, it is understandable that researchers who conduct research not funded by sources providing summer salary replacement or other financial remuneration to themselves may think it is unfair to their team to recruit someone who will receive both monetary rewards and co-authorship. Nevertheless, if the presumption is that the person brought onto the team as a consultant will make substantive creative contributions, then it is not ethically acceptable to offer the option of financial compensation with no possibility of authorship.

One could offer co-authorship alone, or a fee plus co-authorship on the presumption that the consultant's creative contribution will warrant it. Also, one could offer a fee alone, with the understanding that the consultant would offer advice or analysis that is expert, but "routine" or noncreative within the consultant's sphere of expertise. For instance, hiring a statistician to do routine statistical analysis for a fee would be perfectly acceptable, but the statistician should be offered the fee alone, and not the option of authorship.

Case 11

Alice Amachi, a school teacher, gets involved in collaborative classroom research when her school becomes the site for an intervention study led by a pair of university researchers. She contributes important ideas that significantly influence the course of the research, but she is never considered a potential co-author and does not receive authorship credit when the study is published. The professors claim that she was never a member of their team and, under the **principle of authorial entitlement** is not entitled to authorship.

> *Discussion:* The university researchers may operate from professional prejudice. They may fail to properly reassess their initial presumption that they are the researchers and that teachers in cooperating schools are not. They may also feel entitled to claim authorship for themselves on the grounds that their livelihood depends upon doing research, whereas the teacher's does not. Whatever the cause of their oversight may be, the standards do not provide them any grounds for withholding authorship from the teacher. They are ethically obliged to offer it to her. Moreover, the interpretation of the principle of authorial entitlement cannot plausibly be interpreted to exclude Alice Amachi. Although she may not be a member of the research team, she is clearly a collaborator in the research.

> **Standard 1h,** which prohibits the *improper . . . use* [of] *positions of authority to appropriate the work of others or claim credit for it,* puts a special burden of care on the university researchers in such cases as this. They need *to ensure that those in subordinate positions receive fair and appropriate authorship credit.*

Each of these last three cases illustrate the intent of **Standard 1a,** stating that creative contribution to an intellectual product entitles all parties to the collaboration to authorship, **regardless of status.** Being a student, a practitioner, or a paid consultant is irrelevant to entitlement to authorship. Many other forms of status, such as age, sex, and race, are so obviously irrelevant that we needn't even consider them as possible scenarios.

ISSUE

Once the authors of an intellectual product have been identified, one faces the question of how to apportion relative authorial credit. The convention of listing authors in descending order of importance is the only widely used method available for indicating relative credit, so what is found in the standards are guidelines for how the order of authorship is determined. **Standard 1b** states that *first authorship and order of authorship should be the consequence of relative creative leadership and creative contribution.* **Standard 1d** adds that *first authorship* [is] *not warranted by legal or contractual responsibility for or authority over the project or process that generates an intellectual product.*

Finally, the obligation, identified in **Standard 1h,** to *take care to ensure that those in subordinate positions receive fair and appropriate authorship credit,* applies as much to assigning order of authorship as to determining who is an author. However, it will often be difficult to determine what the correct sequence of authors should be, and the variety of different forms of creative leadership and contribution introduces a great deal of indeterminacy.

Case 12

- Saul Conners contributes the conceptual framework for a study, while Norman Crane develops the data base and performs the statistical analysis. Both work on interpreting the results of the analysis.
- Deana Timms conceives of the basic idea of the critical experiment, while Thomas Ellison solves crucial methodological problems in the execution of the experiment.
- Alex Tonnies conducts extensive delicate interviews for the study, while Ted Reed devotes comparable time and creative energy to doing an extensive review of the literature.

Discussion: In the first two of these examples, Saul Conners and Deana Timms might be construed as having shown greater creative leadership, through providing the framework of the study. They have **taken the lead** in an obvious sense, and they display creativity that is arguably, though not indisputably, more rare. This might provide some basis for identifying them as first author, but the standards are not unequivocal on this point.

In the third example, we see different kinds of creative contributions which the standards provide us no way to rank, because neither author displays conspicuous creative leadership, and creative leadership is the only creative contribution singled out for specific mention.

The guidance that the standards provide in determining order of authorship is rather minimal, but this does not mean that we cannot easily imagine clear violations. We can all too easily. Faced with more subtle cases, collaborators in educational research should make good faith efforts to arrive at and apply reasonable collective judgments about the relative importance of their creative leadership and contributions to their collective work. Allowing these decisions to be made collectively is one way that principal investigators can, according to **Standard 1h,** *take care to ensure that those in subordinate positions receive fair and appropriate authorship credit.* (Also see **Hard Case 2.**)

ISSUE

According to **Standard 1f** contributors to intellectual products who do not make contributions that earn entitlements to authorship are nevertheless entitled to some appropriate recognition. This may include not only those who provide the *clerical or mechanical* contributions referred to in **Standard 1c.** It may also include those whose assistance was relied on in writing a dissertation, and the colleagues, referees, editors, and others who may offer assistance but do not qualify for authorship.

Furthermore, there is no reason to assume that it does not also include sponsors, administrators, and practitioners who provide financial resources, administrative services, access to data or classrooms, and other necessities of research. Many different forms of work may contribute and be necessary to the production of a given intellectual product, and **Standard 1f** states such work should be acknowledged.

This seems quite straightforward, but there is one puzzling case, and one obvious abuse worth noting. First, does this obligation to acknowledge all those whose contributions fall short of the requirements of authorship include someone who makes a significant creative contribution to a project but withholds consent to be listed as an author? Or should it be assumed that acknowledgments should be contingent upon consent, just as assignments of authorship are?

Case 13

Norman Crane and Thomas Ellison are responsible for the statistical analysis involved in a study. Well into their work they are unable to resolve disagreements, with the result that Thomas Ellison withdraws from the project and refuses authorship. Should Norman Crane (1) not acknowledge the contributions of Thomas Ellison at all, or (2) acknowledge his contributions in a way that suggests approval of the analysis as it was eventually performed.

> ***Discussion:*** Our sense of the intentions of the standards suggests that option 1 may not be appropriate if work completed by Thomas Ellison with which he was satisfied, is relied upon without acknowledgment. His refusal of authorship does not mean that he is not satisfied with the work he completed. Option 2 also seems clearly unethical, even if Thomas Ellison has not specifically asked that no acknowledgment be given, and it would seem all the more unethical if he has.
>
> Inaccurate acknowledgment involves a form of abuse similar to one considered in the previous section on refusal of authorship. Just as authors may try to draw attention to their work by padding the author list with prominent researchers who have little connection to the work, they may also try to lend credibility to it through acknowledgments that misrepresent the contributions of others without imputing authorship to them. For instance, they may insinuate close scrutiny and approval of the work by people whose attention would be flattering and judgment would be widely trusted.
>
> While **Standard 2** in **Part I** forbids misrepresentation of authorship and other aspects of research, it does not mention misrepresentation of contributions which do not warrant authorship. **Standard 1f** of **Part III** does not state that only those whose work has contributed to the project should be acknowledged. Despite this absence of explicit attention to the problem, one must assume that acknowledgments that misrepresent nonauthorial contributions are unethical.
>
> With regard to consent, although the standards do not specifically address requests that one's work on a project not be acknowledged, it is natural to assume that the principles here would be similar to those spelled out for consent to authorship. Consent is clearly not required for acknowledgment of all forms of contribution to research, since **Standard 5** in **Part V** limits educational researchers' obligations to *disclose the aims and sponsorship of their research,* only to the extent required to protect confidentiality and anonymity, and to allow sponsors to disclaim endorsement of the conclusions reached. Sponsors and financial support must be acknowledged.

ISSUE

Standard 1g requires *acknowledgment of other work significantly relied on.* However, it also indicates that *such reliance is not ground for authorship or ownership.* What is meant by significant reliance on the work of others is shown in the following examples:

Case 14

• Dr. Mona Dean develops a study of language acquisition designed to test certain implications of the theory of Vygotsky.

- Arthur Marx attends an AERA symposium at which he hears a speaker make a comment, resulting from her previous work on child psychology, that leads the professor to redesign his own project.

- Candice Eng offers, in the course of a seminar, a highly original and trenchant criticism of a piece of research that the seminar instructor, Fred Tobias, must discuss in an article. Tobias uses Eng's argument in the article with no acknowledgment of its source.

- Fred Tobias hears the same comment as in the previous case, but later expands upon and changes Eng's original idea. The resulting idea is different from Eng's, but Tobias would not have arrived at it without her starting point.

Discussion: Few would doubt that Professor Dean would be in violation of **Standard 1g** if she did not acknowledge her use of the Vygotskian perspective and cite the publications of Vygotsky presenting that perspective. The relevant publications of Vygotsky are work in the sense intended by **Standard 1g,** as is the theory itself. This is because it is a product of intellectual labor no less than the works in which it is presented. The professor has also *significantly relied on* this work of Vygotsky in developing her own project, because the whole conception of her study is built directly on the theory.

The boundaries of the concepts of "work" and "relying" on the work of others are not entirely well defined, as the second example suggests.

Does the speaker's comment heard by Arthur Marx constitute "other work?" There are reasonable grounds to say that it does, if it is not only a product of the speaker's past work, as we are told, but is also substantially original. The use made of it by Arthur Marx suggests that it is significantly original. Suppose, however, that we modify the case somewhat, and say that the speaker's comment is a spontaneous flash of insight that is not an obvious product of her previous work. We are then hard-pressed to categorize the comment as "work," and would have to conclude that it does not fall within the letter of **Standard 1g.** Does this mean that the professor has no obligation to acknowledge the comment? We certainly cannot conclude that he does not. It would clearly be in the spirit of the standards to say that he should acknowledge the comment, and that in general the ethical thing to do is acknowledge reliance on any substantially original ideas obtained from others, either in their work or through other communication.

In the first of the two Fred Tobias examples, it strains moral common sense as well as the spirit of these standards to suggest that his use of Candice Eng's comments is permissible because **Standard 1g** refers only to *other work significantly relied on.* It is more difficult in the last example to say whether the professor relies on the comment in a way that calls for acknowledgment. The comment was a starting point that Tobias used in developing his own ideas. There is a sense in which he relies on it, but it is not clear that this is the right sense. On the other hand, because he has worked his way to a view that he presumably finds more adequate, he may no longer rely on it in the sense of asserting, assuming, or drawing conclusions from it. If he does not acknowledge her comment, he is not appropriating her idea and presenting it as his own. He is instead failing to recount a path of discovery where he discarded an idea he had found useful but no longer needs or endorses.

ISSUE

Standard 1g qualifies its treatment of acknowledgment by forbidding plagiarism or other inappropriate use of the work of others. What is forbidden here?

Case 15

Professor Compton assembles an anthology of articles, carefully acknowledging the author and original place of publication of each selection, but does not obtain permission to republish them.

Discussion: Compton has acknowledged the works relied on in developing his own intellectual product. Since he does not represent the work of others as his own, this is not a case of plagiarism. However, in failing to gain permission to use someone else's intellectual property, he makes inappropriate use of these materials. Theft of intellectual property is a serious offense that is not mitigated by acknowledgment. The authors will have grounds for preventing the copying and distribution of the anthology and contesting his ownership of any advance payments or royalties it may have generated.

ISSUE

Standard 1j states that *authors should disclose the publication history of articles they submit for publication; that is, if the present article is substantially similar in content and form to one previously published, that fact should be noted and the place of publication cited.* The scope of the duty in this standard can be explored by examining the following cases.

Case 16

At one time or another Professor Redfern has done the following:

- He has submitted for publication without disclosure the same article that had previously been published under a different title in another journal;
- He has submitted for publication an article where only the central portion had been previously published in the same form. In this more recent version of the document, the introduction and conclusions are different;
- He has taken whole sections of previously published articles, woven them together with transitional materials, and sought publication without acknowledgment of the previous record of publication.
- He has taken a document that has been published previously, thoroughly rewritten it without changing the argument or conclusions, and submitted the resulting new document for publication without reference to the old one.

Discussion: Fully reprinting an article without acknowledgment would seem to be a paradigmatic example of a violation of **Standard 1j.** This is in contrast to a document that is wholly new in both form and content, because it is not even partly new. **Standard 1j** does not forbid submission of this document, but it does require full and timely disclosure of its prior publication. Unless Redfern retained copyright at the time of the original publication, he would also have to obtain the permission of the publisher to whom copyright was transferred, or have a copyright violation.

In contrast, a thoroughly reworked article shares only its content with its predecessor, so under **Standard 1j** it is considered a new work that does not have any publication history that needs disclosure or reporting at the time of submission. The terms *form* and *content* are not defined by the standards, but it is reasonable to assume that a thorough rewriting of a document will give it a new form. Having that new form, the new document will also have the substantial originality (original expression) required for it to be copyrightable under copyright law, even though it is a "derivative" work. Nevertheless, even if it is permissible to redraft a work and resubmit it, it is also appropriate and desirable, if not required, to inform those to whom one submits later versions of its relationship to prior work.

Whether it is not only permissible for the author to rewrite and submit this work, but also a good thing to do, will depend on further considerations, including the provisions of **Part I.** Here **Standard 5** of **Part I** appears to be particularly relevant, because it calls upon educational researchers to make efforts to *report their findings to all relevant stakeholders.* Given the variety of consumers of educational research, reporting one's findings to all relevant stakeholders might well require writing different versions of a paper suitable for different audiences.

The middle cases above are harder. The documents in both of these cases replicate a great deal of the content of previous work, and although their forms are different from those of previous works, they have one or more substantial parts whose forms replicate those of their counterparts in prior publications. Is either document *substantially similar in content and form to one previously published?* We are not given any simple way to decide this. To make any headway with this, we must ask what problem or problems this provision is a response to, and try to identify its intentions. Whom does it aim to protect? First, it presumably aims to protect publishers whose space is limited and goal is to devote that space to work of the greatest originality and significance.

This goal is strongly related to protecting the interests of consumers of research, including educational researchers themselves, who rely on publishers to bring them work of high quality and originality. To the extent that published work turns out not to be substantially original, it is a waste of publication capacity, a waste of readers' time, and a barrier to efficient searches for what one needs to know and consider in pursuing individual research and educational practice. It would serve the legitimate interests of publishers and consumers of educational research, including educational researchers, for authors to make full disclosures of any substantial duplication of content, together with an explanation of why the work may have enough originality to be worth publishing.

The legitimate interests of educational researchers would be protected by such disclosure, not only in their role as consumers of educational research, but also as authors, to the extent that the pool of submissions is inflated and duplicate work is mistaken for original work in the absence of disclosure. Finally, to the extent that the well-being of educational research depends upon the employment of those who do high-quality work, one might argue that adequate disclosure would benefit educational research indirectly. This is because personnel decisions made on the strength of publication productivity would be subject to less risk of undetected "double counting" of publications.

ISSUE

As we noted at the outset, **Part III** includes provisions pertaining to the treatment of intellectual products as commodities. **Ownership,** in the sense of entitlement to profits, is addressed in **Standards 3a, 3c,** and **3d.** The fundamental concern of the provisions of **Standard 3** is that although educational research, writing, and development work should be concerned above all with the pursuit of knowledge and the improvement of education, it is also permissible to seek financial profit from such work (see **Foreword**).

It should be noted that the ability of authors, publishers and others to profit by making intellectual products available may be an important condition of such works being freely available. Research contracts that forbid commercial use of research materials may result in the unavailability of valuable work or in unjustified control over availability by the research's sponsor. **Standard 3** may often serve the marketplace of ideas and academic freedom. When are people entitled to profit from an intellectual product?

Case 17

Professor Wright, a curriculum specialist, authors a book and secures a contract to publish it. The contract calls for her to receive some free copies of the book and royalties if sales exceed 500 copies. Later, she contracts to write an encyclopedia article on an educational topic in her area of expertise for a fixed fee of $300.

The research group she heads develops a new way of integrating inquiry skills into earth science instruction even later. In addition to publishing a series of articles in respected journals, they develop an instructional video, which they lease to school districts, and conduct training workshops for a fee.

> *Discussion:* The financial arrangements displayed by these examples would all clearly meet the approval of **Standard 3a.** There is nothing intrinsically wrong with seeking to profit from work, whether through sales, leasing, rental arrangements, or the collection of fees for performances or consultations.
>
> Beyond this fundamental point, **Standard 3a** states very little about exactly who will have entitlements to profits. It says that *individuals are entitled to profit from the sale or disposition of those intellectual products they create,* but it provides no guidance for determining who counts as having created an intellectual product. Perhaps it is enough to have collaborated on a project and made a substantive creative contribution, as it is defined in **Standards 1b** and **1c,** to be entitled to authorship. This possibility is suggested by the use of the word *authors* in **Standard 3c,** but there is no reference to either authorship or creative contribution in **Standard 3a** itself. Having made a substantive creative contribution to an intellectual product is not clearly asserted by this provision to be a sufficient condition for entitlement to profits.

Case 18

An editor, Charles Green, seeing the need for a collection of readings in an important emerging area of educational thought, takes the idea to an academic press, secures a contract, and gathers a team of prominent scholars to write original essays on the topics approved by the publisher. Money is never discussed, except in the editor's contract with the press, and the contributing scholars should not be surprised to discover that they will receive only a free copy of the book when it appears.

> *Discussion:* The prominent scholars in this case will make creative contributions to the project that will entitle them to authorship of their individual essays, but they have submitted their essays with no expectation of financial reward and will receive none. Does **Standard 3a** provide them any grounds for entitlement to a share of the royalties? We infer that it does not. What **Standard 3a** seems to do is give them a right to pursue opportunities to profit from their works, should such opportunities arise, and to collect any proceeds specified by the contracts they enter into. Creative contribution per se does not entitle one to a share of the financial rewards that a work one has contributed to may generate apart from such a contract. Moreover, it becomes obvious in **Standard 3c** that creative contribution is not a necessary qualification for entitlement to profits either.

ISSUE

Standard 3c claims that those who fund or provide resources for the development of intellectual property are entitled to a fair share of royalties or profits from the sale of these products. If so, might this not include a whole range of people and institutions that have made noncreative contributions? Not only funding institutions or corporate sponsors might be included, but also those who have provided various services for the project which have been relied on in producing its results. Nothing in the language of this provision excludes cooperating school districts, companies, or universities that have provided computers used in analyzing data or writing, or paid consultants or other employees who provide only routine services. All would apparently be *entitled to assert claims to a fair share*. So what does it mean to be entitled to assert claims to a fair share of the profits?

Case 19

Professor Judith Glen has been doing research in the Hanlin Schools. Hanlin has a policy that people who do research in its schools must provide it with a percentage of any royalties that result from such research in their schools. Dr. Glen has signed a contract with Hanlin entitling it to the specified share. While she is doing her research, she signs a contract with a book company to publish her research. She reluctantly concludes that she must share the proceeds with Hanlin. However, she is somewhat resentful about this because the money she will give the district is far greater than any costs it incurred in allowing her to do her work in its schools.

> **Discussion:** Just as in the case of those who have made creative contributions, the entitlement to assert a claim to profits is not the same as an entitlement to the profits themselves. It appears to be an entitlement to condition one's contribution on a share in profits. **Standard 3c** goes on to say that since claims to profits *are likely to be contentious,* the arrangements for distributing profits should be agreed upon at the outset of the work. What **Standards 3a** and **3c** seem to state is that all those who contribute to intellectual work in the educational domain have a prima facie right to the fruit of their labors and investments. They also have a right to participate in negotiations at the outset of the work to determine how profits will be distributed.
>
> Consultants and other employees who do routine work may bargain for royalties, or decline to work on the project, if they are not satisfied with an hourly or per-diem fee or stipend. Corporate and other institutional sponsors may negotiate for a share of profits, if they wish, as a condition of their sponsorship. Because universities now ask professors to sign patent agreements at the time of hire, the language of **Standard 3c** seems to allow that universities that provide resources for educational research can justifiably condition such resources on an agreed share of any profits that result.
>
> The principle behind **Standard 3c** is a principle of freedom of contract: a freedom to enter into contracts or arrangements through which one may earn financial returns on one's intellectual labor, products, and related investments. Dr. Glen has no reason to dispute Hanlin's entitlement to a share of her royalties. She has agreed to this without coercion.

ISSUE

When are contracts not free?

Case 20

Jason Fine, a senior professor, needs someone skilled in programming to write subroutines for a computer tutorial product, but has exhausted his current funds and does not wish to share his anticipated profits from licensing it to the armed services. Noting a junior colleague's expertise and vulnerability, he asks her to do the work as a favor after mentioning how valuable it is to have friends in the department when tenure time rolls around.

> **Discussion:** Professor Fine has put his junior colleague in a position in which she will quite possibly feel unable to decline his request or ask for compensation. His request is coercive

because she has a right to have her tenure case judged on its merits, and he has insinuated his own capacity to deny her tenure if she does not comply with his request. He does this to obtain her labor without the expense he would incur in procuring it, or comparable labor, without coercion. In other words, he uses his authority over her in a way that is exploitative and in violation of the freedom of contract protected by **Standards 1a** and **1c.**

ISSUE

Standard 3d is also concerned with coercion and entitlement to profits, but in a somewhat different way. Just as senior colleagues should not use their authority to compel junior colleagues to do work on projects without compensation, those who profit from the sale of books and other instructional materials should not abuse their authority over others. This is most obvious in the case of their students: it is wrong to induce purchases of materials that might otherwise not occur. Transactions at the point of sale must be free of coercion, just as transactions at the origination of the products must be. Otherwise, the profits have not been earned in an ethically justifiable manner.

Case 21

Professor Scribner has written what he believes to be the best psychology book in the field. He requires it for his educational psychology class. While he genuinely believes that this book is the best one for his students, he is not unhappy that he receives a 15% royalty on an expensive book that all 500 of his students must buy.

> *Discussion:* **Standard 3d** does not preclude Scribner from using his own book. At the same time, it recognizes that there is a conflict of interest involved that is especially acute if Scribner requires his students to buy his book. Scribner can reduce this conflict of interest by making it possible for students to use his book without buying it as **Standard 3d** requires.
>
> The conflict might be further reduced were Scribner to eliminate any financial benefit from his students' use of his book. He might, for example, contribute his royalties to a student organization. Although **Standard 3d** does not require this, merely allowing his students to use the book without buying it does not fully eliminate the conflict of interest involved. This is because most students are likely to buy his book and this gives him an incentive to use it regardless of whether it is the best book available.

ISSUE

Although **Standards 2** and **3b** contain the first explicit mention of academic freedom in the code, other concepts, to which academic freedom and the freedom of information are related, have been discussed. We have, for example, noted that a concern for the marketplace of ideas is implicit in **Part I,** where the obligation to equitably inform stakeholders of the results of research are required by **Standard 5** and intellectual honesty by **Standard 2.**

The marketplace of ideas is also the justification for academic freedom and the right to have access to information. Although **Standards 3a, 3b,** and **3c** rest on a principle of freedom of contract and permit profits from sales that are not coerced, **Standards 2** and **3b** identify ethical limitations to the freedom of contract. The limitations arise from academic freedom and a public and scholarly interest in the free flow of information. The assumptions of **Standards 2** and **3b** are that sometimes the freedom to contract can be inconsistent with academic freedom and the right to know. Furthermore, when this is the case, academic freedom and the right to know are the preeminent values.

Standard 3b essentially repeats the points made in **Standard 2.** Both say that the pursuit of financial rewards for intellectual work in the educational domain should be tempered by a conscientious effort to preserve academic freedom and to make findings widely available to those who have a stake in the advancement of educational inquiry. To understand this adequately, we need to be clear on the relevance of academic freedom, on what is meant by "appropriate availability" of intellectual products, and on the conflicts that may arise between maximization of profits and these ideals.

A revisiting of **Case 17** in which Professor Wright and her team of curriculum specialists profit from their instructional video and training workshops is a good start. **Standards 2** and **3b** are probably satisfied by the fact that the group published their work in articles from different journals before, or concurrently with, the development of their profitable spin-offs. In publishing their work in journals, they make it widely and easily available to scholars, students, and others with serious interests in educational development and policy.

Therefore, the fees charged for the related video and training workshops do not appear to unduly restrict the availability of their ideas or research findings. The progress of educational inquiry and the improvement of education are not significantly hampered. Nor is there any restriction of academic freedom, inasmuch as members of the group are not under any pressure or a covenant that restricts their ability to speak and write freely about their ideas and research findings.

The contrast between **Case 17** and the following case is apparent.

Case 22

Dr. Susan Green and Dr. Clarence Pratt make a very important discovery about how children learn to read, with potential for significantly reducing the number of children who finish elementary school without learning to read. They agree to keep their findings secret in order to maximize their earning potential, and seek out investors, marketing specialists, and others, in order to develop their ideas into an exclusive line of products and services.

> *Discussion:* This would seem to be a paradigmatic case of a violation of **Standards 2** and **3b.** Academic freedom is restricted by the agreement of secrecy that the researchers agree on, first between themselves and later within the burgeoning corporate structure they create. Their findings are not made appropriately available, since their research itself is never released to the academic community for scrutiny and replication, and to advance educational knowledge and practice. They have chosen to maximize their earning potential at the expense of academic freedom and the advancement of educational inquiry, in violation of **Standards 2** and **3b.** (Note, however, the variation on this case in **Hard Case 5** that follows.)

Hard Cases

ISSUE

Can scholars, whose creative contribution to a work entitles them to authorship, prevent the publication of a multi-authored work if they dissent from its conclusions?

Case 1

Professor Iawo Nakamura is part of a team of 15 scholars who have been doing an analysis of the relationships between expenditures and achievement outcomes in the Metropolis City Schools. This project is a multifaceted examination of productivity in Metropolis. The project involves both quantitative and qualitative analysis of what makes a difference in Metropolis. Dr. Nakamura is an economist. He has long taken the position that districts that wish to increase achievement should invest more money on in-service teacher education. His role in the project has been to design most of the quantitative studies, especially on teacher effectiveness.

During the writing of the report, a dispute has ensued concerning the interpretation of some of the results. One part of the study team looked at the consequences on mathematics achievement of an in-service program designed to help elementary teachers teach fractions. The results suggest that the program had no significant effects on student achievement. The project director and the rest of the team want to use this research to recommend that the district spend less on in-service training and put the money into other projects. Dr. Nakamura, however, argues that the implementation of the program was flawed, and that similar programs have been successful in other places. He interprets the data as an argument for a redesign of the program.

Dr. Nakamura and the other members of the team are unable to agree on this. The team members take a vote and decide to go with the recommendations of the majority. Dr. Nakamura's response to this is to insist that his name not go on the report. However, he also insists that because his work has been central in the design and execution of the project and he is entitled to authorship, that the report cannot be published unless he is listed as an author. He claims that without his consent the report cannot be published at all.

> **Discussion:** This case arises because the standards dealing with authorship have two aspects that conflict. First, in **Standard 1a** they claim that creative contribution justifies an entitlement to be listed as author. Second, in **Standard 1e** they claim that no one can be listed as an author without his or her consent. If both of these rights are absolute, a consequence might be that anyone who is entitled to be listed as the author of a work can prevent its publication by refusing to be listed as an author.
>
> One solution to this dilemma is to argue that neither right is absolute. Consider the purposes of these provisions. **Standard 1a** might be viewed as serving two functions. First, **Standard 1a** provides that credit is properly assigned, and second, readers are accurately informed about the source of the views expressed in the work. The latter function goes beyond a concern for appropriate credit. Knowing whose views are being expressed is sometimes important to assessing them. **Standard 1e** protects authors from having views ascribed to them that they do not endorse.
>
> In this case, these purposes could be adequately served by a note explaining that Dr. Nakamura made significant contributions to the work, but is not listed as an author because he dissents from certain of its conclusions. This serves the purposes of **Standards 1a** and **1e** adequately. We should also note that the other members of Dr. Nakamura's team and the public have an interest in having this work published. Although Dr. Nakamura has a right to have his contribution acknowledged and a right to not have views attributed to him that he does not hold, he has no right to a veto over the publication of work substantially created by others as well as himself.

QUESTIONS

1. Suppose that the work in question is a book and Dr. Nakamura was the sole author of one chapter. Can the book be published, including his chapter, without his consent?

2. Sometimes authors of multi-authored works agree to be listed among the authors of a work despite the fact that they do not wholly agree with it. Should they?

3. We have claimed that the public has interests in the publication of scholarly work. What are these interests?

ISSUE

How should first authorship be dealt with when two or more authors make an equal contribution?

Case 2

Professors Alpha and Omega have been collaborators for a long time on a research project concerned with teaching history. They have produced a series of papers over ten years that have achieved significant visibility. A few of these papers were also contributed to by others in their field. They view themselves as full and equal partners in this work. In many cases, it would be difficult to tell who made more substantial contributions to an article. They tried two ways of listing their names, first by listing Professor Alpha as first author on all of the papers. The reasoning behind this was that the operating assumption when authors are listed alphabetically is that each author deserves equal credit.

However, Professor Omega, who had always been uncomfortable with this, became even more uncomfortable when he was humorously introduced as Professor et al. at a conference at which one of the multi-authored papers was discussed. This and a number of other events suggested to him that Professor Alpha was widely perceived as the dominant figure on their work and was receiving the most benefit from it. When he presented this concern to Professor Alpha, Alpha agreed, and he proposed that henceforth they alternate first authorship. This worked fine until they produced a paper where it was Professor Omega's turn to be first author, but where Professor Alpha clearly provided most of the creative input.

> **Discussion:** What makes this case hard is the ambiguity of the conventions and common understandings about authorship. If the authorship of a paper is listed as Omega and Alpha, most people will assume that Omega is listed first because he has made the largest contribution to the work. However, if the authors are listed as Alpha and Omega, then the interpretation is less clear. It may be that Alpha has made the more important contribution, but it may also be that Alpha and Omega are coequals. There is no easy way to deal with this, and **Standards 1a–1j** provides no clear guidance. One reasonable response is this: neither alphabetical listing nor rotation of first authorship appears to violate the standards. Hence Professors Alpha and Omega may do as they wish so long as they are in agreement. Another position is that both procedures violate the standards, since both are misleading about relative creative contribution. We are inclined to think that the first view is preferable since the second makes it almost impossible to follow the standards in cases such as this. However, the standards do seem to forbid Alpha and Omega from rotating authorship when that results in one of them being listed as first author of an article when the contribution of the other to that article is clearly the greater.

QUESTIONS

1. There are some things that Alpha and Omega can do to mitigate this dilemma. For example they might attach a note in each article indicating the basis of first authorship. Are there other such strategies? What are the weaknesses of this one? (Consider that such a note would not be carried through into any citations of the work.)

2. Suppose someone were to argue that the level of concern shown for this topic is itself a problem. The purposes of research and scholarship are to increase knowledge and benefit humankind. Ideas should belong to everyone. We should not think in terms of ownership of them or of credit for them. Why do people care about authorship and first authorship? Are legitimate interests served by caring about such things?

ISSUE

What counts as plagiarism?

Case 3

Professor Corel had a system for digesting articles. He wrote a summary of an article's argument on blue cards, any comments he had on the substance of the article on white cards, and quotations on yellow cards. He wrote the source on the other side of the card. He also had his research assistant use this system. One day his office was out of yellow cards. To deal with this, both he and his assistant put a number of quotations on white cards intending to transfer them to yellow cards later. This was never done. A year later when Professor Corel was writing up his research, he found a number of comments on white cards that he found especially useful. Some of these *white card* comments went directly into his articles with no modification. Others were only slightly rewritten. Since he assumed that the ideas on these cards were his, he did not cite the reference on the back of the card.

Discussion: Plagiarism consists in treating other people's work as one's own. Theft of intellectual property consists in using the work of others without the owner's permission. Professor Corel has committed plagiarism. It is also likely that he has stolen intellectual property. It may be that, properly cited, the quotations that appeared in his work would have fallen within the Fair Use Doctrine that permits limited quotation of other's work for the purposes of scholarly discussion and argument, but he has not properly cited this work. Although he appears to have done these things through negligence, that does not change the fact that plagiarism and theft have occurred, but it might be a mitigating factor in determining a penalty should the plagiarism be discovered.

QUESTIONS

1. In some cases, because he did not realize that material he was using consisted of quotations, Professor Corel rewrote some of the passages. Is this still plagiarism or intellectual theft?
2. Most universities view plagiarism by their faculty as a very serious offense. They may find it grounds for terminating a faculty member or expelling a student. What should the penalties be for plagiarism through negligence?

ISSUE

When do others have a claim on the proceeds of one's work?

Case 4

Professor Salvador Marino had a grant from the Davis Foundation to study the teaching of phonics. He duly spent the money, did the research, and provided Davis with a final report. After this he wrote a few articles for scholarly journals. Several years later, as a result of this activity, he became involved with a project to develop a series of reading texts. He received a pleasantly substantial advance for this project and set to work. He was surprised when several months later he received a letter from a lawyer representing Davis calling his attention to paragraph 6.2 of the contract he had signed for the research with them. The paragraph reads: "Recipients of grants from Davis agree that any products developed under this grant are the property of Davis and that Davis will be entitled to 50% of the proceeds from any further discoveries or products resulting in whole or in part from research done under this grant."

The letter suggested that the connection between the research Davis had funded and his current work on the reading series was clear and invited him to contact Davis to arrange for the transfer of 50% of whatever royalties were involved. Dr. Marino was stunned. He had no recollection of this paragraph. After all when he signed the contract, he had no plans to do a reading series. He was just going to do the research and publish a few articles. He was more than happy to share the nonexistent returns from these publications. While it was true that the reading series did draw on the principles he developed in his research for Davis, he had also learned a few more things since he completed that work. Moreover, Davis' reading of paragraph 6.2 was so broad that it looked like they might want 50% of almost any work he did in his field forever.

> *Discussion:* Professor Marino probably owes Davis 50% of his proceeds from the reading series since it seems clear that it relies on the discoveries made through the research funded by Davis. It may be that Davis has a legitimate claim on any future income that seems to be connected to the ideas developed from this funded work. The crucial principle here is freedom to contract. Dr. Marino freely agreed to Davis's provisions. That he now finds them onerous does not change this fact.

QUESTIONS

1. How do the contracts researchers enter into provide incentives to make their work available? Are there some contracts that researchers should avoid?
2. Does Professor Marino have an incentive to switch his area of research simply to avoid further claims from Davis?

ISSUE

Standards 2 and **3b** assume that the freedom to contract can be inconsistent with academic freedom and the right to know. However, it may also be the case that refusing to allow scholars to profit from their work can restrict its availability.

Case 5

Dr. Susan Green and Dr. Clarence Pratt (who appeared previously in **Case 22**) make a very important discovery about how children learn to read, with the potential for significantly reducing the number of children who finish elementary school without learning to read. They made this discovery while doing research funded by the Spre Foundation. Spre has had a longstanding concern to achieve a wide dissemination of the results of its scholars. One consequence of this is that Spre has, as a part of its standard contract, a provision that permits researchers funded by them to publish their findings in scholarly journals, but forbids them from granting an exclusive copyright for any commercial use of products resulting from work done under their sponsorship. Dr. Green and Dr. Pratt have published their findings in scholarly journals. However, they also wish to develop a series of reading texts for use in elementary schools. Also, they have begun a college textbook based on their research.

They find, however, that they are unable to interest a commercial publisher in their reading program. Moreover, the only publisher who is willing to publish their college textbook is a university press known for expensive hardcover books and small circulation. The reasons given by commercial publishers for their disinterest is that the contract Green and Pratt have signed with Spre prevents publishers from having an exclusive right to profit from publication of their work. Were they to sink money into an expensive development project, they would not only run the risk of undermining the sales of their current texts, but other publishers would quickly imitate them. They would need to spend a great deal of money to secure a brief and fragile commercial advantage. Moreover, they could easily have the scholars who had developed their current books modify them to take into account the work of Green and Pratt. There is, then, little need to develop a new series.

Discussion: In our society the vast majority of textbooks and the majority of academic books are produced under arrangements that allow both their authors and their publishers to profit. Such arrangements may sometimes generate secrecy and constrain the availability of ideas. However, the ability to make a profit is part of the incentive authors have to write and publishers to publish. If this incentive is removed, this may also reduce the availability of materials. The fact that the desire to profit contains within it incentives that work both for and against the availability of the products of research may be why **Standards 2b** and **3** do not offer a clear rule of conduct. These standards rather suggest that when there is conflict, researchers are to resolve it in favor of academic freedom and the widest availability of intellectual products.

QUESTIONS

1. As noted previously, universities often make claims on patents on research that they have helped fund. However, it is rare that they make similar claims on royalties from publications. Are there principled reasons for this? Are the incentives different?

2. Some government agencies have insisted that research they fund must go into the public domain. Is this a good idea? Does it limit availability of research?

3. The Internet may pose significant questions about the availability of intellectual work. One issue is that much of what may be available on the Internet will not go through any referral process. Is this a good thing or not?

PART IV

GUIDING STANDARDS:

EDITING, REVIEWING, AND APPRAISING RESEARCH

The Preamble, the Standards, and Their Rationale

Preamble

Editors and reviewers have a responsibility to recognize a wide variety of theoretical and methodological perspectives and, at the same time, to ensure that manuscripts meet the highest standards as defined in the various perspectives.

STANDARDS

1   AERA journals should handle refereed articles in a manner consistent with the following principles:

   a)   Fairness requires a review process that evaluates submitted works solely on the basis of merit. Merit shall be understood to include both the competence with which the argument is conducted and the significance of the results achieved.

   b)   Although each AERA journal may concentrate on a particular field or type of research, the set of journals as a whole should be open to all disciplines and perspectives currently represented in the membership and which support a tradition of responsible educational scholarship. This standard is not incompatible with giving serious consideration to innovative work and should not be used to discourage perspectives not yet fully established in traditional scholarship.

   c)   Blind review, with multiple readers, should be used for each submission, except where explicitly waived. (See #3.)

   d)   Judgments of the adequacy of an inquiry should be made by reviewers who are competent to read the work submitted to them. Editors should strive to select reviewers who are familiar with the research paradigm and who are not so unsympathetic as to preclude a disinterested judgment of the merit of the inquiry.

   e)   Editors should insist that even unfavorable reviews be dispassionate and constructive. Authors have the right to know the grounds for rejection of their work.

2   AERA journals should have written, published policies for refereeing articles.

3   AERA journals should have a written, published policy stating when solicited and nonrefereed publications are permissible.

4   AERA journals should publish statements indicating any special emphases expected to characterize articles submitted for review.

5   In addition to enforcing standing strictures against sexist and racist language, editors should reject articles that contain ad hominem attacks on individuals or groups or insist that such language or attacks be removed prior to publication.

6   AERA journals and AERA members who serve as editors of journals should require authors to disclose the full publication history of material substantially similar in content and form to that submitted to their journals.

RATIONALE

Part IV enumerates standards governing the activities of editing, reviewing, and evaluating educational research and the documents that report and embody it. These standards apply explicitly to AERA journals—those journals published by AERA itself. The language of the **Preamble,** however, suggests that the standards may also apply to AERA members who serve other publications in which educational writings appear. In this regard, it may be important to distinguish between those standards of **Part IV** that should apply to all journals regardless of whether they are published by AERA and those that apply solely to AERA journals. Most of the standards assert principles that should apply to any journal. All journals should avoid racist and sexist language and personal attacks, for example. If AERA members are associated with non-AERA journals that fail to meet these standards, they should give consideration to ending their association.

Other standards, **Standard 3** perhaps, serve important ethical goals; however, it may be that theses goals can be accomplished in other ways and that it is unreasonable to conclude that a journal is ethically deficient because it does not satisfy them. In such cases, the responsibility of an AERA member may be to consider whether the point of the standard is adequately met. Also, as noted below in the discussion of the standards of **Part V** (see **Cases 5, 9,** and **Hard Case 3**), AERA's commitment to intellectual openness and the marketplace of ideas does not preclude AERA members from participating in research projects that support the agendas of advocacy groups. Neither, then, is it reasonable to claim that **Standard 1a** of **Part IV** should preclude AERA members from associating with journals that support particular agendas as long as they do so in responsible ways.

Two important concerns of **Part IV** of the **Standards** are to ensure fair treatment of those who submit manuscripts for publication and to promote the advancement of educational research through attention to the quality of research and the preservation of the robust methodological pluralism of educational inquiry. These concerns are displayed in provisions regarding honesty and fair warning in announcing a journal's policies, including the work it is open to publishing; competence, objectivity, and timeliness in the judgment of submitted work; dispassionate, informative, and constructive reports to authors of the reviewer's and editor's judgments; the judgment of work solely on its merits; and the necessity for AERA journals to be open to all responsible disciplinary and methodological approaches to educational inquiry.

The **Preamble** to **Part IV** recognizes editors and reviewers as having an obligation, as AERA members and as individuals in positions with authority and influence over the health and progress of educational research, to accept the existence of diverse theoretical and methodological approaches to educational research, and to safeguard the excellence of educational research. This dual obligation to the quality and diversity of educational research entails duties to educational researchers who submit their work for publication. This obligation can be understood in two ways. It can be understood as a consequence of a commitment, announced in the **Preamble** of **Part I,** that *educational researchers continually evaluate the criteria of adequacy by which research is judged* and in **Standard 1** of **Part I** that they *not jeopardize future research, the public standing of the field, or the discipline's research results.* It can also be understood as deriving from more basic obligations of collegiality and integrity. We consider these underlying rationales in turn.

It is clear enough why an obligation to the present and future well-being of educational research would compel a commitment to *ensur*[ing] *that manuscripts meet the highest standards.* The success of educational inquiry, as a pursuit of knowledge and improvement in educational practice, requires both methodological care and robust results. Methodological excellence and significant results are also required in order to secure a favorable external reputation for educational research. The enjoyment of such a reputation is itself important to the capacity of educational research to sustain itself and to make a difference to educational policy and practice.

But why would a duty to accept the diversity of educational research, and to hold work to *the highest standards as defined in the various perspectives,* follow from a general obligation to promote the well-being of educational research? Why should editors and referees not act on views they may have regarding the significance or soundness of different traditions or paradigms of educational research? Are there no neutral, pre-theoretic, or trans-paradigmatic standards of adequacy in educational research to which they would be permitted, indeed compelled, to hold research? These questions are perhaps impossible to answer without entering into controversies in the philosophy of science and epistemology which members of AERA are in varying degrees aware of, and disagree about vigorously. Nevertheless, we are compelled to address them in order to make sense of these standards, as they have been adopted by the membership of AERA.

First, there are reasonably compelling grounds for claiming there is a principled basis for methodological pluralism in educational research, no less than in the social sciences generally. Educational researchers address themselves and their inquiries, quite reasonably, to a range of different questions about education. No one method of research is suited to answering all of these questions. This is an important reason why different methods of research have emerged and established themselves. These various methods and traditions of research should not be presumed, then, to be in competition with one another, just because there are many of them and they all investigate educational matters. Some diversity of research methods is required if all the significant questions about education are to be addressed and answered.

What about those instances in which different methods and theoretical perspectives do struggle with the same questions and seem in competition? The question that becomes important in these instances is what the proper role of editors and referees should be. Will it best serve the progress of educational research for editors and referees to attempt to predict the eventual outcomes of these contests of methods and traditions? Should it allow those predictions to guide their policies for considering papers, and guide their judgments of the papers they do consider? Or should they follow their own convictions? Arguably, it is best for educational research if they avoid making and acting on such predictions or on their own views. The possibility of error in making these judgments is significant, and the risk in acting on them is that what may eventually have proven to be the best way to advance knowledge in a given domain may be foreclosed.

The values of the marketplace of ideas require that methodological and paradigm disputes be resolved by argument and debate. Such debates cannot occur if reviewers and editors reject all approaches other than the ones that they favor as having potential merit. Editors and referees have good reasons to accept the existing and emerging variety of approaches to educational research and to judge papers on their individual merits within the context of these diverse approaches. At the same time, the commitment to theoretical and methodological pluralism is not to be viewed as rooted in relativism (which, if true, would suggest that some theoretical and methodological disagreements cannot be resolved by argument). The commitment cannot be understood as inconsistent with applying rigorous standards to the evaluation of research.

The merit of a piece of research is inevitably determined in part, but only in part, by the requirements of the research type it exemplifies. The **Preamble** does not say this, but it is both true and clearly implied by the standards of **Part IV.** Research methods and traditions are not self-justifying. If they were, the **Preamble** to **Part I** would not urge researchers to *continually evaluate the criteria of adequacy by which research is judged.*

Methods of research are justified to the extent that they yield significant understanding, knowledge, and practical results. These goals, which are a dominant concern of the standards (see the final paragraph of the **Foreword**), provide a larger framework for judging the adequacy of the methods of research, and the significance of individual pieces of research. Within this larger framework, the methods of various disciplines and traditions have established themselves securely as effective paths to knowledge and better practice. They have established special (albeit evolving) requirements for the competence of research conducted under their aegis. These requirements of competence are quite properly the ones that editors and referees should have principally in mind in judging individual pieces of work. They should judge the methodological adequacy of a piece of work in accordance with the methodological requirements of its type. They should also judge the significance of its results in the context of the problems internal to its own tradition, and not the requirements and aspirations of types to which it does not belong.

However, this does not mean that editors and referees do not face further questions that are somewhat independent of the methodological idiosyncrasies of different research traditions. Whatever tradition or style of work that the piece exemplifies, the editor and referees must ask whether it accomplishes what it sets out to do—whether it is well argued, whether its results contribute significantly to educational inquiry generally, and whether it can be improved in any way. They can legitimately judge whether a paper successfully applies the methods of a research tradition to the particular question addressed. They can do this while neither judging the research tradition as a whole, nor being entirely limited to what is distinctive in that particular tradition's conception of methodological adequacy.

The preceding discussion is a statement of a first rationale for accepting the diversity of educational research, resting in a general obligation to promote the present and future well-being of educational research. The second rationale is based on obligations of collegiality and integrity and can be put more simply. AERA is an organization made up of members who *come from many disciplines, embrace several competing theoretical frameworks, and use a variety of research methodologies* as the **Foreword** to the **Standards** says in its opening sentence. What do obligations of collegiality demand in such a setting? The view of the membership itself, which is expressed by its adoption of the **Standards,** is that as colleagues, we owe each other mutual acceptance of our disparate approaches to educational inquiry and progress, even in our capacities as editors and referees. This does not compel us to accept the soundness of any approach without good reason, nor refrain from offering reasons in opposition, but it does compel us to allow each other's ideas and arguments a respectful hearing.

The ideal of collegiality makes an individual virtue of what is arguably best for the progress of educational research itself, and the same can be said of the ideal of integrity. What does it mean to be an editor or referee with integrity? The concept of integrity is invoked in the **Preamble** to **Part I** of these **Standards,** in the phrase *the integrity of research.* We take it that the integrity of research and of those responsible for producing it, consists in a constancy of concern for the goals inherent in research, namely truth, understanding, knowledge, good judgment, and the good that may come from them. The excellence of research is an important condition for the attainment of those goals, so just as collegiality compels mutual respect and acceptance of diversity, integrity compels a commitment to high standards of excellence in research.

Interpretation of the Standards:
Issues, Cases, and Discussions

ISSUE

Standard 1a states that work submitted for publication must be judged solely on the basis of merit. This should be regarded not only as an obligation of fairness to authors, but as a consequence of the responsibility which editors and referees have for the quality and progress of educational research. We have provided some background for understanding the distinction between quality of argument and significance of results in our discussion of the **Preamble** to this part of the **Standards,** but a few words of further clarification are in order.

The most important and general measure of the significance of results is the extent to which a piece of work answers, or takes a step toward answering, a basic question about education. One such question might be, "What factors most determine the success or failure of teaching and learning?" Others might be, "What is success? How do we decide what success is?" "How do we determine when success has been achieved, or measure the extent to which it has been achieved?"

We find ourselves already in difficult terrain in trying to say whether any of these questions might be more or less basic than the others, but it is from such questions as these that educational research begins, and from which subsidiary questions spring. What judgments of significance seem to require is a rough sense of which questions are relatively basic and central ones, and which are subsidiary. The answers to these questions may be contextual. Results that are significant in one set of circumstances may not be significant in others. Social circumstances or intellectual contexts may change and, with them, the nature of what is to be considered significant.

Results differ in how large a step they take toward answering a basic question, and also in the degree of certainty with which the step has been taken. The strength or certainty of a result may figure in the determination of how significant it is, but whether certainty is considered in this way or in connection with *the competence with which the argument is conducted,* may depend on the research in question. In any case, the competence of the argument for a paper's conclusion has everything to do with whether the conclusion is adequately established. What it means to adequately establish a conclusion varies greatly from one discipline and form of research to another. In every case, however, the point of the methods of argument and forms of evidence and investigation is to identify a significant conclusion and establish it with whatever certainty is possible in that domain, in the present epistemic circumstances.

Case 1

- Elizabeth Pastel submits a paper to AERA *Journal W.* This paper discusses the way in which the legal system of ancient Athens influenced the education of young men for public life. The editor of *Journal W* sends the paper to four referees who are knowledgeable about ancient Athens. While three referees recommend that the paper be accepted, one referee notes that Elizabeth Pastel seems unaware of some recent work on ancient Athens that undermines her argument. The editor rejects the paper for that reason.

- Elizabeth Pastel submits the same paper to AERA *Journal X.* The editor of *Journal X,* while believing that the paper was well argued, rejects the paper because it lacks relevance for the educational system of the United States.

- Elizabeth Pastel submits a different paper to AERA *Journal Y.* This paper is a philosophical and legal critique of a current emphasis in educational reform. It argues that while the reform is not illegal, it is inconsistent with the values that underlie certain constitutional rights. The paper is rejected because the editor of *Journal Y* believes that such papers make implementing a reform she favors more difficult and harms the process of educational reform.

- Elizabeth Pastel submits the same paper to AERA *Journal Z.* The editor of *Journal Z* rejects the paper arguing that the only rational way to assess the merits of an educational reform is to discover its effects on achievement.

Discussion: **Standard 1a** requires that papers submitted to AERA journals be judged solely on their merits. Merit is understood to include both the competence of the argument and the significance of the results. The first of the four examples clearly judges the paper on the basis of its merits. One of the referees has persuaded the editor that the paper is seriously flawed by its failure to consider relevant evidence. Even though the other referees did not identify this flaw, once the editor of *Journal W* is persuaded of its existence, the editor is entitled to reject the paper.

The second case is somewhat more difficult. Elizabeth Pastel might argue that understanding the relationship between any society's legal system and its educational practices is a significant result. However, the editor of *Journal X* has elected to understand the notion of significance, in part, in terms of relevance to the U.S. educational system. Here we should note the following. First, results are not simply significant or trivial. They are significant or trivial in relation to some context or some set of interests. The editor of *Journal X* must have some view of the context in which significance is to be understood if such judgments are to be made at all. Second, **Standard 1a** makes no attempt to define the concept of significance. We conclude that the judgment that this paper is not significant, even if controversial, is a legitimate editorial judgment.

In the third case, the grounds for the rejection of Elizabeth Pastel's paper are inconsistent with **Standard 1a.** The editorial judgment reflects neither the merits of the argument nor the significance of the results. Rather it reflects the editor's own assessments of the direction that reform should take and the belief that reform is made more difficult by debate. The editor's views are inconsistent with the values of the marketplace of ideas.

The grounds for the rejection of Elisabeth Pastel's paper by *Journal Z* are also inconsistent with **Standard 1a.** The editor may argue that the decision was based on an assessment of what counts as a competent argument for the worth of an educational reform. If so, the editor's view of the nature of competent arguments is so narrow as to constitute a violation of **Standard 1b.** Philosophy and law are broadly recognized as legitimate approaches to educational issues. Rejecting such approaches in favor of an exclusively empirical approach to the issues is inconsistent with the openness to different disciplines required by **Standard 1b.**

Case 2

Phillip Parker received a rejection from AERA *Journal Q* that read in part: "The reviewers, after considerable struggle, found that the argument of this paper is both convincing and important; however, the paper is so badly written that we must question whether the average reader of this journal will be able to discover this. We certainly think that they should not be required to suffer through your mangled prose in order to do so."

Discussion: **Standard 1a** does not explicitly warrant competent writing as a legitimate criterion for accepting or rejecting a paper. However, it is also the case, that it is worded so as to suggest that merit and significance may not exhaust the criteria. While the use of additional criteria should be done with caution to safeguard the central values of scholarship and the marketplace of ideas, readability is a criterion that can be justified in judging articles for publication. If, however, the argument of the paper is convincing and the conclusion important, the editor should suggest that the paper be rewritten and resubmitted. It also may be that the phrase "your mangled prose" violates **Standard 1e.** A more dispassionate way of making the point should be employed.

ISSUE

Standard 1a requires works submitted to AERA journals to be judged solely on the basis of merit. **Standard 2** requires AERA journals to have written, published policies for refereeing journals.

We have suggested previously that **Standard 2** should be consistent with **Standard 1a–1e.** To what extent do AERA journals have an obligation to have written published policies about the conception of merit that will be used to evaluate submitted articles?

Case 3

Andrew Stuart had written a paper that was based on detailed interviews and observations of a single student. He submitted this paper to AERA *Journal Z.* After review *Journal Z* rejected the paper. The editor provided two reasons. First, the editor argued that because the author focused on only one student, the results could not be generalized. Second, the editor argued that it appeared that the methodological considerations appropriate to ethnographical research were neither followed nor documented.

Stuart is considering protesting this decision to AERA's President. He argues that he was not doing ethnography, he was doing biography and that the standards appropriate to ethnography do not apply to biography. He also argues that **Standard 3** requires AERA Journals to explicitly note that they do not publish work of the kind he does. Finally, he claims that **Standards 1a** and **2** in conjunction require that AERA journals publish a statement of the methodological requirements for publishable work. He also notes that nowhere is there any indication that the results of research must be generalizable or that they must conform to any particular methodological requirements.

> **Discussion:** The kind of specificity Andrew Stuart wants is very likely both impossible and objectionable. It is impossible because what can be said about the character of intellectual standards of judgment in a policy statement that must necessarily be brief, is necessarily platitudinous and vacuous. Conclusions must be rooted in relevant evidence or conclusions drawn should follow from the premises adduced which, in turn, should be true. However, apart from more detail about what counts as relevant evidence or how we know when conclusions follow from premises, comments like this are unhelpful to those wishing to know what they must do to get their work published. Any attempt to specify such matters in detail runs into the difficulty that there are a great many ways in which evidence can be relevant or irrelevant and there are many different standards for judging whether conclusions follow from premises. An attempt to state the meaning of such ideas would need to do so for the variety of approaches that are appropriate to educational phenomena and would, of necessity, be both inadequate and contentious.
>
> An attempt to be explicit in a detailed way about standards of judgment would also be objectionable. It would put at risk the methodological pluralism that is implicit in **Standard 1b.** Moreover, it would tend to rigidify standards of judgment in a way that would make AERA journals less open to innovation again in violation of **Standard 1b.**
>
> Stuart also argues that the standards that apply to ethnography do not apply to biography, and that AERA journals need to make it explicit if they are not open to his kind of biographical research. However, so long as the methodological pluralism required by **Standard 1b** is not compromised, the decision of the character of the standards appropriate to evaluating a given work are appropriately the prerogative of editors and referees. As we suggest in **Hard Case 2,** that is part of the meaning of academic freedom and the autonomy of intellectual professions. Finally, if *Journal Z* were genuinely unwilling to publish work of a given genre while recognizing that genre as legitimate, it would need to publish a statement to that effect, and AERA would need to assure itself that other journals were open to that genre.
>
> At the same time, work cannot be isolated from criticism by claiming that it is of a genre to which those standards presupposed by the criticism do not apply. In this case, it seems unlikely that *Journal Z* is open to ethnography, but not biography. Rather it is more likely that

Andrew Stuart has attempted to represent his work as belonging to a unique genre in order to deflect criticism. We do not believe that he has a reasonable case. His protest does raise the question of how we are to distinguish between work that fails to meet current standards and work that belongs to a distinct genre to which certain standards may not apply. (See also **Hard Cases 1** and **2.**)

ISSUE

Standard 1a states that referees are obligated to judge submitted works on the basis of merit alone, understanding this as largely a combination of the quality of the argument and the significance of the result. Therefore, editors, for their part, must supervise the review process in a way that exercises care to ensure that submissions are judged on this basis. **Standards 1c** and **1d** make the editor's proper role in this more specific.

Standard 1c requires editors of AERA journals to make arrangements for blind, multiple review of all refereed manuscripts. The requirement of multiple readers demands a minimum of two referees, and the requirement of blind review demands that reasonable precautions be taken to conceal the author's identity from the referees. This means not only that the author's name should not appear anywhere on the manuscript, but also that references to the author's own work should be blacked out to the extent necessary to prevent identification. The following case illustrates this requirement.

Case 4

The text of a manuscript submitted to AERA *Journal Y* by authors Alpha & Beta includes the sentence, "As we have shown in previous studies (Alpha, 1988; Beta & Alpha, 1992), the epistemological beliefs of children are not organized in stages or levels."

Discussion: The editor should black out the parenthetical references to the authors' previous work, since these references would permit immediate identification of the authors. With this style of citation, it would ordinarily not be necessary to black out the bibliographic entries for these works where they appear in a list of works cited at the end of the article. In fact, to do so might make identification easier, since it would identify the approximate alphabetical position of the lead author's name on each article cited. On the other hand, the form of citation used in the humanities, in which cited works appear in footnotes or endnotes and nowhere else, would require blacking out the entire bibliographic entries. Knowing that the authors of the work under review are the same as the authors of published works that are notable in one way or another might be enough to compromise a referee's objectivity. This is true even if the editor has blacked out the names of the authors of the published works and the referee cannot recall who they are.

It might be argued that a knowledgeable referee may well infer who the authors are from what remains of the sentence in this case, even if the parenthetical citations are blacked out. That may be, but the editor should not black out the whole sentence. The editor's rule of thumb here must be that, while external references are fair game in the effort to conceal identity, the substance of the text of the work must not be diminished. The editor does all that can be reasonably done to conceal identity in blacking out the parenthetical citations. He or she has prevented immediate identifications of the authors, insofar as the referees would have to infer who the authors are from whatever independent knowledge they have of the research literature.

The point of requiring blind review and review by multiple readers is to improve the chances that submissions will be judged on their merits alone, and that all of their significant merits and defects will be identified. These efforts are required by the larger goals of promoting excellence in educational research, and treating authors fairly. Without blind review, referees may be influenced not only by the reputation(s) or previous work of the author(s), but also in some instances by personal ties of which the referees would not have been aware if the identity of the author(s) had been concealed. Their judgments are less likely, in those instances, to reflect the merits of the work alone, as **Standard 1a** and the publication of work meeting *the highest standards* require (see the **Preamble**).

Similarly, without multiple review it is less likely that all of a work's merits and defects will be accurately identified. Different referees may not only form different judgments of the features of manuscripts that they all notice, but will often notice and attach significance to somewhat different features of manuscripts. With multiple review an editor can not only make a better informed decision about whether to accept or reject a submission, but can also provide authors with better guidance for improving their work. Ensuring that manuscripts meet the highest standards requires that editors provide such guidance.

ISSUE

Standard 1d is intended to guide an AERA journal editor's selection of the two or more referees required by **Standard 1c.** The editor must choose referees who are competent to judge the work, which requires that they be familiar with the kind of research it involves and capable of rendering a disinterested judgment of the work's merit. Both of these qualifications for referees require some comment, though the groundwork for understanding them has already been laid in the commentary on the preamble and **Standards 1a** and **1b.**

A referee cannot be a competent judge of a piece of work without familiarity with that kind of work, and without strong research skills of a broadly relevant kind and a reasonable knowledge of the domain of study. This much is clear, but editors will often have to make judgments of whether even this is enough. The following case is an example.

Case 5
- A paper on the history of educational research since 1900 is submitted to AERA *Journal Q,* which publishes work from a wide range of disciplines.
- A paper on the history of legal education in the last quarter of the nineteenth century is submitted to *Journal Q.*

  Discussion: In the first of these two cases it may be good enough to pick referees who are familiar with historical research, but whose expertise is in other forms of educational research. Their general knowledge of the topic, namely educational research itself, will compensate at least somewhat for the difficulty they may have in judging whether it is a methodologically strong piece of research. To ensure that the piece is competently judged, the editor would do well to choose a historian as one of the referees. In the second case this is clearly necessary, since the time period and topic takes it further beyond the working knowledge of educational researchers generally.

ISSUE

The requirement that editors find referees *who are not so unsympathetic as to preclude a disinterested judgment of the merit of the inquiry* bears much of the brunt of the editor's obligation to give fair consideration to diverse forms of educational research. The idea is not that editors can't pick referees who have known misgivings about some or much of the work in a given research tradition. Rather, they must try to find referees whose feelings or commitment to their own preferred tradition will not make them partisans of their own tradition in their judgments of the work. The editor and referees alike must concern themselves with the advancement of educational research itself, and not with who will prevail in the contests among its traditions. In working with referees, an editor will develop a sense of who will be evenhanded and judicious in judging work on its merit, and not on the reputation of the tradition or type where it belongs.

Case 6

- A paper on curriculum in the tradition of critical social psychology is submitted to AERA *Journal X,* whose announced policy is to accept sociological and psychological research. The editor is unsympathetic and picks as referees, two empirical sociologists with evident contempt for critical theory.

- The same paper is submitted to *Journal X,* but the editor finds referees who do both philosophical and sociological research and who have a reasonably good understanding of the critical theory tradition. The editor has worked with them and regards them as evenhanded and fair referees.

- The same paper is submitted to *Journal X,* but the editor finds referees who do both philosophical and sociological research and who have a reasonably good understanding of the critical theory tradition. The editor has worked with them and regards them as evenhanded and fair referees. In addition the editor selects, as a referee, an empirical sociologist who has been critical of some work in critical theory, but who also has a reputation as someone who can appreciate good work in traditions not her own.

Discussion: The first of these examples provides an example in which the editor has done less than could be expected to ensure that the submission is judged on its merits. Knowing no more than this, there is reason to suspect that the referees will not be evenhanded in their judgment of the work.

The second example provides an instance in which the editor probably has done all that **Standard 1d** requires. The editor has reason to think they will judge the work fairly. Since critical theory bridges sociology and philosophy, the combined expertise of these referees provides a better match to the profile of the work than in the previous case. This may let them do a better job of identifying the paper's strengths and weaknesses.

The third example is also consistent with **Standard 1d.** It may be the best of the options. The purpose of **Standard 1d** is to protect authors from unfair criticism. This does not require that works be reviewed only by those who are predisposed to agree with them. Moreover, criticism from an open-minded reviewer from outside of the author's tradition may be beneficial.

ISSUE

Referees' reports not only provide editors with the basis for informed judgments on the merit of submitted work and the desirability of publishing it but they also give authors the basis for decisions about their work and information that may be useful in improving it or making choices about which lines of research to pursue. **Standard 1e** requires that referee's reports be both informative and appropriate in tone.

Case 7

Janice Saunders submitted a paper to AERA *Journal Y.* The single comment from reviewer A said "This paper is incompetent. The author should be encouraged to find another profession." The comments from Reviewer B said only, "This paper has some promise, but it does not provide an argument sufficient to justify its conclusions."

Discussion: In submitting their work for publication, authors open themselves and their work to the possibility of criticism. That criticism, and the rejection that will frequently accompany it, can be painful and discouraging. **Standard 1e** asks that editors and referees should be mindful of this, and avoid using their authority, and the importance of unflinching judgments of merit, as excuses for causing authors distress and discouragement. **Standard 1e** instructs editors and reviewers to give their reviews a calm and constructive tone.

Whatever feelings of annoyance, indignation, or contempt they may experience in noting the defects in a piece of work, they should make sure the remarks they transmit to the author do not express contempt, or any other such attitude. The comments of reviewer A are not only unhelpful, but are insulting to a degree that clearly violates **Standard 1e.** Reviewers and editors should provide authors with observations and judgments that will be helpful in improving the work, whether or not it is accepted for publication, if it stands in need of improvement and has potential. This is required not only as a courtesy to the author, but as an obligation to the progress of educational research.

Editors and referees are also required by **Standard 1e** to inform authors of their grounds for rejecting any articles. Authors are said to have a *right to know the grounds for rejection of their work,* and we can assume that this right is conferred on authors by AERA's adoption of these standards. Presumably, this right requires grounds that are informative, an expectation that is not met by comments that say only that the work is not competent or that its conclusions are not adequately argued.

One could defend the establishment of this authorial right, not only as an appropriate expression of collegial respect for one another, but on other grounds as well.

First, the requirement of a written statement of the grounds for rejection serves as a useful safeguard that helps ensure that referees and editors do have valid grounds for rejection. The attempt to formulate cogent judgments of the paper's deficiencies of merit that will be seen by the author, and potentially by others, creates a "paper trail" allowing external scrutiny of a decision. It provides referees with an exercise that can not only induce, but also facilitate, a review of their objections and concerns that may yield a more balanced judgment of the work. That is, it ensures that referees do not simply form holistic or impressionistic judgments of submissions, but instead think through their merits and deficiencies in a way that is disciplined by writing.

Second, it would be a waste of a referee's investment in the quality of educational research to form a well-considered judgment of the merits and deficiencies of a piece of work, and not transmit a summary of the basis for that judgment to the author. It is not the summary judgment itself that will be of use to the author in improving or rethinking the work, but the more specific observations and judgments on which that summary judgment is based.

ISSUE

Standards 2, 3, and **4** have in common the requirement that AERA journals have written and published policies dealing with a number of editorial practices. Collectively these policies inform prospective contributors on the requirements they must meet to publish in AERA journals, and inform readers of the circumstances under which manuscripts are accepted. By requiring written and published policies, they also, in effect, require AERA journals to make some decisions as a matter of policy.

Standard 2 requires that AERA journals publish written declarations of their policies regarding the submission and evaluation of refereed articles. By implication, these policies would necessarily conform to the principles enumerated in **Standards 1a–1e,** but might have other discretionary features.

Presumably, the stated policies would include requirements of format, style, length, number of copies to be submitted, and any other requirements for acceptable submission. These can be described as conditions for a submission's being accepted for review, and as part of a journal's policies for refereeing articles. The stated policies should also presumably include policies regarding the nature of arrangements for blind review, the expected length of time required to reach a decision to accept or reject, and the kind of referee's report an author can expect to receive. If **Standard 2** involves some discretionary matters, how shall we decide what is included?

Case 8

AERA *Journal X,* in consideration of **Standards 2, 3,** and **4,** routinely publishes a statement describing its policies for refereeing and publishing articles. This statement discusses the mechanics of submitting articles, states that at the discretion of the editor, solicited and non-refereed articles may be published when timeliness is critical, and describes the emphasis of *Journal X.*

Professor Roger Pancratz is in the fifth year of a six-year probationary period prior to his being reviewed for tenure. He has submitted a paper to *Journal X.* The editor of *Journal X* sent out the paper to four reviewers. One of them took seven months to return the review. Professor Pancratz's paper was accepted pending revisions. It took Professor Pancratz three months to complete the revisions, and *Journal X* several more months to finally accept the paper. It was scheduled for publication in the issue of *Journal X* that was to appear six months later.

In the interim, the editor of *Journal X* received what she viewed as a very significant and timely paper. This paper was rushed through review and was substituted for Professor Pancratz's article. Hence Pancratz' paper did not appear for another two issues. Thus, the article did not appear for about two years after it was first submitted and was not in final form in time to be considered for his tenure review.

>**Discussion:** **Standard 2** requires AERA journals to have written, published policies for refereeing submitted articles. It does not, however, specify the content of these policies. Therefore, it is not certain that this statement must include a policy concerning the timeline for reviewing and publishing articles, or that Professor Pancratz has been unfairly disadvantaged by the absence of a clear policy on timelines. However, several considerations suggest that *Journal X* should have a written, published policy concerning timelines for review and publication, and that this policy should be specific on how long it normally takes to review articles.
>
>First, **Standard 10** of **Part I** requires reviewers to decline to review work if they are not able to complete the task in a timely way. It is reasonable to suppose that this obligation of reviewers is based on the presumption that those who submit their work should have a timely review. Moreover, a specific and stated policy should inform reviewers on what counts as a timely review. This policy may provide some motivation for them to provide one.
>
>Second, the timeliness of reviews and publication is often important to authors, especially those beginning an academic career. It is reasonable to suppose that policies intended to inform potential authors of the conditions and requirements of submission and publication would take an author's needs into account.

These two points suggest two criteria that should govern the development of policy statements intended to conform to **Standards 2–4:** 1) the other standards that govern review, such as **Standard 10** of **Part I** and the other standards of **Part IV,** should provide guidance on the contents of such policy statements; and 2) the informational needs of authors should be taken into account. Both criteria suggest that policy statements written in conformity to **Standard 2** should include a specific policy on timeliness.

ISSUE

Standard 3 requires AERA journals to have some policy on *when solicited and nonrefereed publications are permissible,* and it requires them to publish a written declaration of that policy. However, **Standard 3** does not take any position on the proportion of articles in AERA journals that may solicited or nonrefereed. What purposes does this requirement serve?

Case 9

AERA *Journal X* frequently solicits articles on what its editors regard as timely topics from prominent scholars known to be working on these topics. Occasionally, a mix of solicited and regularly submitted articles are bundled into special issues or topical symposia. While the editor monitors the quality of the solicited articles obtained, and has rejected a few because of their quality, the articles are not sent to external reviewers. It is not always apparent which articles are solicited and nonrefereed.

There is no stated policy indicating that solicited and nonrefereed articles are commonly published by *Journal X.* Yet these articles may take up to 50% of some issues. Moreover, *Journal X* has a high rejection rate. Many articles of sufficient quality to be published in *Journal X* must be rejected solely because of space limitations. The editor of *Journal X* argues that this practice improves the quality and influence of the journal both by publishing articles on important topics in a timely way and by obtaining the work of recognized scholars.

Anne Ziadong has submitted several articles to *Journal X.* In each case, reviewers have responded positively to her work and recommended its publication. However, in each case, the editor rejected her papers on grounds of space.

> **Discussion:** **Standards 2, 3,** and **4** require that the standards and conditions for accepting or rejecting articles submitted to AERA journals be made public. One purpose of these provisions is to provide fair notice to authors of the terms of submission and review. Information about policies on the successful preparation of a manuscript, and on the choice of which journal to submit work to, should be equally available to all potential authors. This is to ensure fairness, as well as to promote an efficient use of editorial resources. Also, **Standards 2, 3,** and **4** make publication policies clear to readers by letting them know that some work may not have been refereed. This may be important to reader assessment of the work.
>
> In this case, **Standard 3** is clearly violated. It requires a stated policy concerning solicited and nonrefereed publications, and no such statement exists. The absence of a stated policy inconveniences and misleads authors like Anne Ziadong by denying them a realistic assessment of the chances of publishing their work. It also wastes editorial resources.
>
> *Journal X* is required by **Standard 3** to make clear and public its policy concerning solicited and nonrefereed articles. Ideally, policies complying with **Standard 2, 3,** and **4** should be published regularly in the journal itself. While **Standard 2, 3,** and **4** do not seem to require that *Journal X* announce special issues and topical symposia in advance, doing so when possible would enable authors to submit their work for these forums and would serve other purposes

of these standards. (This matter is more fully explored in **Hard Case 3.**) Without this information, authors will sometimes submit papers with no realistic chance of them being accepted. They will also be denied the opportunity to submit their work to relevant special issues and topical symposia.

ISSUE

Standard 4, like **Standards 2** and **3,** rests, in part, on the obligation to give potential authors fair warning of any restrictions or preferences concerning the content, disciplinary character, or methodological orientation of work submitted to any AERA journal for publication. This requirement reflects an acceptance of the premise that at least some of AERA journals will continue to have distinctive profiles that make them unreceptive to some forms of educational research. However, this liberty is qualified by an insistence in **Standard 1b,** that the *set of [AERA] journals as a whole* be open to all forms of serious educational research.

Standard 1b identifies the basic strategy by which the burden of accepting diversity, announced in the **Preamble,** will be made concrete. It places a burden on the officers and voting membership of AERA to ensure that within its journals there is a place for every *responsible* form of traditional or emerging educational research practiced by its members. It also places a burden on editors and referees to ensure that their own journals are as inclusive as AERA's plan for the set of journals requires.

The notion of responsible educational scholarship calls for some clarification, as does **Standard 1b's** requirement that the notion of responsible scholarship not exclude innovative work or emergent perspectives. (See **Hard Cases 1** and **2** for further discussion.) These expressions signify an attempt to balance openness to diverse forms of research with a commitment to high standards. They acknowledge the need for further improvement of the methods of educational research, in light of the overarching goals by which educational inquiry must ultimately be measured. Research might be judged irresponsible either for failing to adopt methods of inquiry that are plausibly related to its goals, or for adopting inappropriate goals. Goals unrelated to education or hostile to advancing the understanding or improvement of it might be judged inappropriate. Methods which ignore and defy research know-how that is accepted as a matter of broad consensus among established researchers would count as irresponsible, but methods which reject the consensus position on cogent grounds would not. It is on the strength of such cogent grounds, and a demonstration of significant results of an appropriate kind, that a novel path of research justifiably can be called a worthy innovation. There is nothing else that worthiness of respect could rest on in this context, except the achievement of a cogently established significant result or finding.

Case 10

- AERA *Journal Y* has no announced special preferences on the research it is open to publishing. However, its editorial board is dominated by scholars from one particular discipline, and the acceptance rate for submissions from a number of other disciplines is low.

- AERA *Journal Q* has the announced policy of being open to all forms of educational research. But it summarily rejects a submission that uses the methods of mathematical sociology to develop a formal model of the dynamics of academic labor markets. The reason given is that mathematical sociology is not an established research paradigm within educational studies.

Discussion: In the first of these cases it is fair to say that *Journal Y* exhibits a preference for work with a particular disciplinary profile. Even if there has been no conscious decision to expect articles to fit this profile as a matter of policy, the editor has an ethical burden to publicly acknowledge what has become a matter of fact (namely, that a decided preference does exist). The editor could also change the constitution of the editorial board to eliminate that preference. If the set of AERA journals as a whole requires as a matter of overall diversity that this journal be more receptive to other kinds of research, then the editor is ethically compelled to take the latter course.

The second case presents the *Journal Q* editor with a special difficulty, because the unusual character and technical demands of the work submitted may require making a special search to locate suitable referees. This is what seems to be required, however. Although the work does not belong to a tradition that is represented in the membership of AERA, the existence of a substantial body of such work within sociology itself should be brought to the editor's attention by the article's citations. This creates a reasonable presumption that the work is a worthy innovation. The editor should be open to the possibility of publishing it, and should find suitable referees for it.

ISSUE

Standard 5 requires editors to enforce appropriate and established standards of interpersonal respect and scholarly relevance in academic writing. The *standing strictures against sexist and racist language* referred to here are not identified anywhere in the standards themselves.

The policy of AERA is to follow the guidelines for avoiding sexist and racist language promulgated in the *Publication Manual of the American Psychological Association*.[1] In general, these APA guidelines promote respect and nondiscrimination by distinguishing acceptable and unacceptable uses of personal pronouns, other gender forms of reference, nouns referring to racial and ethnic groups, and other aspects of reference to race and ethnicity. We will review some important features of these guidelines in what follows, but members of AERA should not consider this a substitute for reading the guidelines in full for themselves.

The APA guidelines pertaining to gender discourage use of masculine pronouns to refer to both sexes, and provide alternatives, such as rephrasing (e.g., "When a teacher expects too little of his students, they will reward him with failure" to "A teacher who expects too little of students will be rewarded with failure"); using plural rather than singular forms (e.g., "When teachers expect too little of their students, they are rewarded with failure"); and use of articles instead of pronouns (e.g., "When a teacher expects too little of a student, the teacher will be rewarded with failure."). The use of "man" as a generic noun is discouraged, as well as the use of examples and forms of reference that exhibit discriminatory stereotypes.

Case 11

An author submits an article to AERA *Journal Y* that includes this sentence: "For a teacher to make a successful transition into administration, he must earn the confidence of his colleagues through demonstrated leadership." Examples are framed in such terms as, "In his capacity as Acting Assistant Principal, John establishes credibility with the social studies and English departments of his high school, by initiating discussions which lead to successful curricular integration."

Discussion: **Standard 5** calls upon the editor of *Journal Y* to require rewording that eliminates the use of "he" and "his" as they occur in the first sentence. The editor must also ensure that the net effect of the article's illustrating examples does not display a gender bias. One way of achieving this is to provide examples or cases displaying in a balanced way the variety of possible gender configurations that may occur. The illustrating example in this case is described as representative of the examples in the article as it is submitted, so the editor must require that many or all of them are modified.

ISSUE

Standard 5 prohibits racist as well as sexist language. It is clear that this prohibits the use of terms that are racial slurs (except where these terms are mentioned rather than used as discussed above and are required by the purposes of legitimate research). Some terms, however, are not obviously racist, but are not favored by those to whom they are applied. What view should be taken of these terms?

Case 12

Professor Smith writes and submits to AERA *Journal Z* a paper on race relations in newly desegregated schools in which he routinely refers to African Americans as Negroes. The paper also frequently draws a distinction between white and non-white students.

Discussion: The APA guidelines for avoiding racial and ethnic bias in academic writing identify two basic guidelines: researchers should use the designations preferred by the individuals they work with and groups they refer to, avoiding terms and stereotypes which are regarded as negative; they should also use narrower categories or more specific terms when possible, rather than broader categories and less specific terms. Researchers should be sensitive to the fact that preferences in these matters change from time to time and vary from one individual to another. Either "African American" or "Black" may be acceptable, depending on the person's preference. The term "Negro" has fallen out of use and should consequently be avoided.

Researchers should also recognize that potentially significant information is lost in classifying individuals under more general categories—for example, white and non-white. This pairing of categories has the added disadvantage of suggesting that the category "white" is normative or in some way more important. In addition, individuals often prefer more specific designations to more general ones—"Puerto Rican" rather than "Hispanic," or "Seneca" or "Mohawk" rather than "American Indian" or "Native American."

The underlying ethical ideas at work here are principles of equality and mutual respect. Forms of reference which presume or imply less than equal status not only offend, but can be perceived as, and amount to, attempts to assert dominance over others who have a fundamental moral claim to equal status. Forms of reference to ethnic and racial status which disregard the known preferences of individuals discussed have this character, as do terms of abuse and insinuations of inferiority.

ISSUE

Standard 5 also requires editors to prohibit *ad hominem* attacks. An *ad hominem* attack is an attack on a person or persons (individuals or groups) in the form of verbal criticism which may or may not be coded in terms that are inherently abusive (e.g., terms such as "stupid"). The use of inherently abusive terms is never warranted in academic writing, and verbal attacks on people, whether abusive or not, could have little legitimate role in academic writing about education. However, it is not clear whether criticism that is well-deserved, free of gratuitous abuse, and relevant to educational matters, is never warranted in educational writing, so it is not clear just where to draw the line.

The concern of this clause relating to *ad hominem* attacks is probably not just with abuse and personal attacks generally, however. An *ad hominem* attack typically means something more specific than a verbal attack on a person. The familiar form of an *argumentum ad hominem* consists of aiming one's criticism in a logically irrelevant way at the person making an argument, instead of at the quality of the argument itself. As such, there is a very strong presumption that *ad hominem* attacks have no legitimate place in academic discourse. They involve not just criticism, but criticism of colleagues that misdirects the attention of the scholarly community away from the evidence and argument on which assertions should be judged. They are damaging to the progress of educational inquiry, as well as to collegial relations.

Consider the following cases, the first taking the form of an abusive *ad hominem* and the second a more subtle circumstantial *ad hominem*.

Case 13

Dr. Kenneth Polk submits a book review to AERA *Journal S* that condemns the central argument of the book under review with the remark that: "An argument as feeble as this would be expected only of an ill-equipped sophomore, not of an established professional."

> *Discussion:* This seems a clear violation of **Standard 5**. The journal's editor should either simply refuse to publish the review with these remarks included, or should direct its author to address the argument on its merits, rather than impugning its source.

Case 14

Professor Burns argues in a paper submitted for publication that the flow of informational technology into classrooms, which is advocated by professors employed by a think tank, should be terminated. Burns claims that his research has exposed links between that think tank and the military which suggest that the professors' motives are not pure.

> *Discussion:* Impugning people's motives is a form of personal criticism that only has logical or evidential relevance if one is concerned with a person's credibility as a witness. If the role of the professors in their defense of educational technology is not that of witnesses testifying on the value of such technology, but of scholars who have found evidence and developed arguments for its value, then it is the arguments and evidence that should be addressed, not the motives the professors may have for giving them. In the case at hand, the editor of the journal to which the paper is submitted has the following options: reject the paper; publish the paper without that material if the author agrees and if the attack on the professors' motives is not central to the paper as a whole; or if the author can reformulate the argument in a way that gives the attack on the professors' motives obvious and substantial evidential relevance to a significant conclusion (which would be quite unlikely in the circumstances described in the case), publish it as reformulated.

ISSUE

Standard 6 places a burden on the editors of AERA journals and any AERA members who are editors of other journals, to require authors to disclose the publication history of any similar material which has been published, or is under review, elsewhere. What **Standard 6** requires of editors is that they should require authors to do essentially what **Standard 1j** in **Part III** expects them to do. This is to reveal the publication histories of any work which is substantially similar, in both content and form, to the work they are presently submitting for publication.

Two small but significant differences of wording between **Part III's Standard 1j** and **Standard 6** in **Part IV** must be noted. **Standard 6** requires disclosure of the *full publication history of material* *substantially similar* to that presently under submission, whereas **Standard 1j** of **Part III** requires disclosure when *an article is substantially similar in content and form to one previously published.* The reference to the publication history of work as opposed to work that has been previously published, makes **Standard 6** expressly relevant to work that is unpublished but committed to publication, and to simultaneous or nearly simultaneous submission of the same work to different journals.

Case 15

An author submits an article to AERA *Journal A.* While it is under review, the author gives it a new title, makes some cosmetic changes that do not substantially change its form or content, and submits it to AERA *Journal B,* without disclosing the earlier submission. The editor of *Journal B* does not require disclosure.

> **Discussion:** The editor in this case has failed to comply with the requirement established by **Standard 6.** Although **Standard 6** does not directly impose requirements on authors, and although **Standard 1j** of **Part III** is only expressly concerned with other versions of the work that have actually been published, the intent of the standards is obviously to require authors to make full disclosures in such cases. These are presumably more troubling cases than repeated submissions over a course of years since simultaneous multiple submissions would be more attractive to unscrupulous authors (given the value of timeliness in getting one's ideas before an audience) and harder to detect without disclosure.
>
> The reference in **Standard 6** to *material substantially similar in content and form,* rather than an *article substantially similar in content and form* also makes **Standard 6** a more demanding standard (on its face) than its counterpart in **Part III.** In **Part III** we considered a case in which an author takes whole sections of previously published articles, weaves them together with transitional materials, and seeks publication without acknowledgment of the previous record of publication. This was a difficult case for **Standard 1j** of **Part III** because, although sections of the derivative article have the same form and content as sections of previously published articles, the derivative article cannot itself be said to have the same form as any one previously published article. This is not a difficult case for **Standard 6,** however, for in submitting this article, the author does submit material having essentially the same content and form as material with publication histories in other journals. **Standard 6** requires in such cases that editors require authors to disclose the publication histories of the other works from which the sections of the present article are drawn. Thus, in its letter, **Standard 6** tells editors to require of authors what we inferred **Standard 1j** of **Part III** is probably intended to require of them.

Hard Cases

ISSUE

The **Preamble** to **Part IV** obligates editors, reviewers, and AERA to recognize a variety of perspectives, encourage innovative work and emergent perspectives, and ensure that manuscripts meet the highest standards. In some cases there may be tension among these aspirations. Although it is a debatable question whether all standards of evaluation are internal to research traditions, it does seem that new paradigms of scholarship may develop somewhat different notions of the goals of research and of ways of judging success in reaching those goals. Should a commitment to theoretical and methodological pluralism and openness to worthy innovations and emerging perspectives lead to generosity toward new ideas, letting the content they generate determine their worthiness? Or is the advancement of educational research better served by a conservative bias, placing the onus on a new approach to prove itself before securing representation in the leading journals? Also, when do the standards of **Part IV** apply to AERA members serving non-AERA journals?

Case 1

As Mike Hopkins read the paper before him for a second time, the furrows on his brow deepened. While purporting to be a piece of historical scholarship, the article made extensive counterfactual claims about what would have happened if certain crucial events in the history of American educational institutions had been different. The paper also introduced a cast of fictional characters whose experiences were said to be "representative" of their historical and social location. How was one to assess the truth of these claims, Mike wondered? As editor of *Educational History Review,* he was inclined to turn it down flat. But he had heard talk at a recent conference of "counterfactual history" and he knew some historians had argued that narrative "constructions" of fictional life histories can be illuminating. He could imagine the outrage of many readers: "Are historians becoming like shoddy journalists, not bothering to do the painstaking work of historical scholarship, preferring to make it up instead?" Yet the paper raised some interesting questions, even if in traditional terms it didn't answer them. If he were to send it out for review, where could he find someone prepared to give it a competent or sympathetic reading? If people wanted to do work as radical as this, maybe they should start their own journals. Mike sighed and stuck the paper in a file, resolving to return to it again another day.

> **Discussion:** This case raises two independent questions. One is the attitude AERA members acting as editors or reviewers should take towards new and innovative approaches. Should it be a conservative or a liberal one? The second is how or whether the **Preamble** of **Part IV** applies to Mike Hopkins, an AERA member editing a journal, the *Educational History Review,* that is not an AERA journal. Concerning this second question, while the individual standards of **Part IV** create duties for AERA journals, the **Preamble** seems to assert duties for AERA members who serve as editors and referees regardless of whether they serve on AERA publications. We do not know if this was intentional. However, it seems reasonable to take the view that, when the principles expressed in the **Preamble** and the standards of **Part IV** are general principles, ones that should govern the behavior of journals and those who serve them broadly, then AERA members should be guided by them regardless of whether the journal they serve is an AERA publication. However, as was noted in the **Rationale,** some of the standards may be viewed as expressing specific ways that AERA has chosen to implement more general principles. In such cases, the standards might bind AERA journals, but not AERA members who serve as editors or referees for non-AERA publications. Since the principles relevant to this case are those expressed in the **Preamble** it is likely that they should be viewed as applying to AERA members, not just to AERA publications.

As Mike Hopkins's ambivalence suggests, new research approaches can have a difficult time gaining a hearing. They are often suggestive and interesting, but also they do not conform to the expectations of current research practice. Qualitative research methodologies and feminist research perspectives are recent examples of innovations that many would think have proved worthy but were initially skeptically received. Innovators are likely to regard skepticism as mere prejudice against new ideas, or exercises of exclusionary power, while defenders of the established traditions may see themselves as the upholders of appropriate research standards. Both sides in these debates bear some responsibility—editors and reviewers for acknowledging pluralism and giving new ideas a respectful reading, and innovators for helping initiates from other traditions to understand their perspective.

It may also be that there is a balance to be struck. If AERA journals were to adopt a conservative attitude towards new approaches, it may be that some worthwhile new endeavors would die without an adequate hearing. However, it may also be that a more generous approach would commit valuable journal space to approaches that will eventually fail. Two suggestions may be helpful. One is that editors and reviewers need to give new approaches a very careful hearing and not reject them out of hand because they do not meet current expectations. A second is that new innovations may require time to make their case. An approach that is promising may not emerge in a highly articulate or polished form. Without forums of discussion, the needed opportunity to develop may be unavailable. This argument suggests that the values of the marketplace of ideas are best served by a generous approach.

QUESTIONS

1. We have said that some of the standards represent general principles that should apply to AERA members whenever they undertake to serve as editors or referees. Others represent specific practices that AERA has chosen to follow. These practices may express more general principles that could be served in other ways. Which standards might be of this second kind, and what principles do they express?

2. The next case (**Case 2**) provides some examples to which the "generosity" standard might be applied. Do they help in distinguishing between generosity and over-generosity? How are we to tell when we are being overly generous?

ISSUE

Standard 1b requires the set of AERA journals to be open to all forms of responsible educational scholarship as well as to innovative approaches. How do we know what counts as responsible scholarship or genuine innovation?

Case 2

Over the last year AERA journals have received, refereed, and rejected for publication the papers listed below, all of which were submitted to more than one journal.

- A paper arguing for teaching creationism based on doubts about carbon 14 dating, a discussion of the implications of the second law of thermodynamics, and an argument appealing to the notion of falsification in philosophy of science.
- A paper written from a post-modern perspective that argues for the importance of the category of paradox to educational administration.
- A paper written by an advocate of transcendental meditation (TM) arguing that TM is an important strategy for reducing school violence.
- A paper written by a lawyer arguing that the religion clauses of the First Amendment should be interpreted to require teaching scientific creationism if evolution is taught.
- A paper written by a philosopher who argues that justice requires the elimination of tracking.

In each case, excerpts from anonymous reviewers' comments were provided to authors. In each case, the authors found reason in these comments to think that their work was not rejected because of its quality, but because of the genre of scholarship it represented.

Discussion: **Standard 1b** requires that *the set of [AERA] journals as a whole should be open to all disciplines and perspectives currently represented in the membership and which support a tradition of responsible educational scholarship. This Standard is not incompatible with giving serious consideration to innovative work and should not be used to discourage perspectives not yet fully* *established in traditional scholarship.* The authors of these papers believe that their work was rejected because of the genre of work it represented. Let us suppose that they are right. That is, let us suppose that the set of AERA journals is not open to the scholarship represented in these papers because the editors of all AERA journals believe that there is not a tradition of responsible scholarship that underlies the work in question. Are they right, and how would we know that they are right? The wording of **Standard 1b** suggests that there are four questions to address. These are:

1. Is the scholarship educational scholarship?
2. Is there a tradition of such a scholarship?
3. Is this tradition responsible?
4. Is the scholarship a worthy innovation or an emergent perspective?

In each of the above cases, there seems no doubt that the work is educational scholarship. In each case some educational issues are addressed or educational recommendations made. That seems sufficient to justify the claim that the work is educational scholarship. Although the work is also rooted in other disciplines such as philosophy or law, this does not disqualify it as educational scholarship.

What does it mean to ask whether there is a tradition of such scholarship? This notion might mean that there are groups of scholars in academia who do work of this sort, that this work has developed for substantial reasons from earlier forms of inquiry, and that those who do this work form a recognizable community of individuals that think of themselves as doing a common form of work. This notion of a tradition of scholarship suggests that there is such a tradition that underlies several of the papers described previously. There seems no doubt that there are traditions of scholarship in philosophy and law. Therefore, if papers in these disciplines are unable to find a place in AERA journals because they are philosophy or law, **Standard 1b** is violated. This conclusion should also be drawn for the paper written from a post-modern perspective. Postmodernism is controversial among philosophers, some of whom find it irresponsible or irrational. However, that it is controversial is not a reason for excluding work of any genre. Indeed, the marketplace of ideas cannot be served unless controversial new approaches are given a hearing. That seems part of the point of the caveat that ends **Standard 1b:** *This Standard is not incompatible with giving serious consideration to innovative work and should not be used to discourage perspectives not yet fully established in traditional scholarship.* Only time and argument will allow us to decide what innovations are worthy. That an enterprise has emerged for reasons from traditions of scholarship and has found numerous practitioners in the academy means that it cannot be excluded because of its genre.

What are we to say of the creationist paper and the TM paper? It is less clear that they are rooted in traditions of scholarship. They are not significantly represented in mainstream universities. Perhaps this should not be decisive. Certainly each of these papers is rooted in a genre of work associated with a community of others who do similar work. Moreover, the caveat that ends **Standard 1b** suggests that we should exercise great caution in excluding a genre of work from publication because it is not currently well represented in mainstream scholarship. If there are reasons for excluding these genres of work, it must be that these genres are viewed as not being responsible traditions of scholarship. And if this is the case, we must also be able to distinguish between what is controversial and what is irresponsible. How would we know or decide this?

Here the best answer is that what is to count as a responsible tradition of scholarship is a judgment to be made by AERA (for its journals) through its representatives, i.e., journal editors and the reviewers they select, and that these judgments should be rendered for what seem to these individuals to be good and appropriate arguments. Two ideas are important here.

First, there is an issue of academic freedom. Academic freedom is different from free speech. Free speech secures the right of all speakers to have their say, free from government coercion, and regardless of the content or competence of their speech. Academic freedom, however, not only protects individual scholars from retribution for their ideas, but also secures the autonomy of intellectual professions to regulate their own intellectual life apart from governmental coercion. The autonomy of intellectual professions includes the freedom to make judgments concerning what work is worthy and what is not worthy of publication. Such judgments are not normally to be viewed as inconsistent with the academic freedom of individual scholars.

Second, those who exercise this authority on behalf of intellectual professions are expected to make judgments about the merits of intellectual work for good and appropriate reasons. These reasons should be broad enough to include genres of work that are not personally favored by those who make editorial judgments, and thus should reflect some collective judgment on the genres of work that are responsible. However, they cannot be so broad as to include every approach regardless of its merits. In short, AERA must promote a form of intellectual pluralism that does not fall into relativism.

Therefore, the force of **Standard 1b** might be viewed as this: AERA seeks to encourage the highest quality of educational scholarship. To this end, it seeks the most capable scholars to function as journal editors and reviewers, and it entitles them to make judgments on which articles are worthy of publication. At the same time, it expects that these editors will not use their positions to promote those views or genres of scholarship they personally favor over others that are viewed as responsible by the broad and diverse collectivity of educational scholars. Hence, editors must have a credible view of what views and genres of scholarship are responsible beyond those they personally favor. AERA recognizes that such judgments are difficult and fallible. However, when AERA finds capable persons and entrusts them with editorial responsibility, AERA also grants them the autonomy to do their work and does not interfere unless it believes that this authority is being abused.

QUESTIONS

1. While **Standard 1b** prohibits AERA journals, as a group, from excluding work rooted in a tradition of responsible scholarship, it does not appear to preclude editors, individually or as a group, from making a judgment that some forms of scholarship are more important than others. Should it?

2. The above discussion requires that responsible editors can distinguish between genres of work that they view as best, those that are responsible, and those that are not responsible. On what criteria are these distinctions made? Are there reasonable grounds for distinguishing among philosophy, postmodernism, TM, and creationism?

ISSUE

Does **Standard 3** require that all special issues or topical seminars be announced in advance?

Case 3

An AERA journal, *Journal X*, has the policy of rejecting any articles it does not need for its upcoming issues. It also sometimes devotes entire issues to articles on special topics, but not on any regular cycle with no announcement of this policy, the dates when special issues will appear, or their topics. In other cases, it devotes substantial portions of its space to special topical symposia. Such special issues and symposia are usually developed around a regularly submitted article that the journal editors believe is of particular significance. Occasionally, the editors will solicit an article from a prominent scholar known to be working on a topic they view as having special importance.

In developing these special issues and topics symposia, the editors' practice has been to develop a list of scholars who are known to have done research on the topic and to ask them to submit articles discussing the topic of the lead paper. Articles that are submitted as a result of this process are usually, but not always, refereed. Some are rejected on grounds of quality and others because of space limits.

However, since these special issues and special topics symposia are not announced in advance, there is no opportunity for scholars whose contribution is not solicited to submit their work. The editors justify their policy on the grounds that it is necessary if the journal is to respond in a timely way to work of special importance, to secure the work of prominent scholars who are likely to have a significant impact on their field, and to increase the influence of the journal. In addition, they argue that past practice makes it quite clear that it is their policy to generate such special topic issues and symposia. No regular reader of the journal could fail to notice that this is done. The most recent special symposium was concerned with the special problems faced by Muslim students in American public schools.

Anne Ziadong has submitted several articles to this journal. In each case, reviewers have responded positively to her work and recommended its publication. However, her papers were rejected by the editor on grounds of space in each case.

Holis Hassim had just finished his Ph.D and taken a position at a research university. His thesis concerned how public schools accommodate the religious interests of Muslim students and the First Amendment requirements for such accommodation. His article would have been appropriate for the special issue of the journal in question. However, since he was not known to the editors, he was unable to submit.

Discussion: As noted in the earlier variant of this case (**Case 9**), **Standards 2, 3,** and **4** require public statements of the standards and conditions according to which submitted articles will be accepted or rejected. These standards might serve several purposes. First, they provide authors such as Anne Ziadong an opportunity to learn what they must do to have their work published and the opportunity to judge the chances of having their work published in *Journal X*. Ziadong might learn that her chance of having her work accepted is considerably less than might be apparent to her because a significant amount of space is taken up with solicited work or unannounced special issues or topical symposia. Also, if the standards were interpreted to require the advance announcement of special issues or topical symposia, they might also provide the opportunity for authors such as Holis Hassim to submit his work to a symposium where it is appropriate.

These opportunities may be very important to young scholars. The time required for a journal to turn around a submitted article can often be significant. Young scholars who face time constraints associated with tenure may be significantly harmed if they must submit to several journals before securing publication of their work. In addition, good work may not be published on time. Moreover, scholars such as Holis Hassim will be denied the chance to have their work considered in a forum to which it is appropriate.

Second, the lack of transparency of a journal's publication policies may have an effect on the quality of the work the journal publishes. Journals have two basic mechanisms for ensuring their quality. The first is having articles refereed by competent scholars. The second is competition. Journals that are able to choose from among numerous submissions are often able to publish work of the very highest quality. Journals that solicit or do not referee a significant portion of their articles reduce the effectiveness of these mechanisms. For example, the paper that Hollis Hassim would have submitted might have been better than the work actually solicited and published for the symposium on Muslim students. However, the editors of *Journal X* have no way of knowing this.

Third, the absence of stated policies required by **Standard 3** means that readers are unable to know when an article has been refereed. This may be a significant factor in reader confidence in the work published by *Journal X* and in reader assessment of particular articles.

The requirements of **Standard 3** seem to fall short of what these underlying purposes require. They do not preclude the publication of solicited or nonrefereed articles, only publicly asserted policies on these matters. Moreover, nothing in **Standard 3** requires that the topics of special issues or topical symposia be announced in advance or opened to competition. There may be good reasons for this. These more stringent requirements would significantly reduce the capacity of journals to respond quickly to timely material or issues. Enforcement of these more stringent requirements would make one AERA publication, *The Review of Research in Education* (RRE), which consists entirely of solicited, state-of-the-art reviews by prominent scholars, virtually impossible to publish. (Since RRE is an annual hard backed volume it is unclear whether it is a journal.)

A ban on solicited articles might also make it difficult to get reviews of new and important books on time. Therefore, the concern that journal editors might have for timely work may justify avoiding a blanket prohibition against solicited and nonrefereed articles. Similarly, there may be reasonable grounds why all special issues and topical symposia should not or could not be announced in advance and open to competition.

Nevertheless, it might be a useful part of any public publication policy to indicate a presumption in favor of unsolicited and refereed articles. It might also be useful to favor open competition for special issues and topical symposia, along with some suggestion of the criteria to be employed in deciding when these presumptions might be waived.

QUESTIONS

1. Scholars with established reputations in their fields frequently receive numerous opportunities to publish their work in special editions or as book chapters. These invitations may be sufficiently numerous to relieve these scholars of the need to submit to refereed journals and undergo the normal scrutiny that the referee process involves. Is this fair to younger scholars who do not have such opportunities? Is it good for the quality of work of established scholars?

2. Book editors and journal editors may justify invitations to prominent scholars by arguing that their visibility is likely to promote more recognition and a larger readership for their publication. Is this a good argument?

ISSUE

Standard 5 requires editors to enforce *standing strictures against sexist and racist language.* How should editors deal with articles where such language is integral to the views being discussed?

Case 4

In writing about the pedagogical theories of Rousseau, Professor Guerra states: "Rousseau held in his *Emile* that in order to educate a boy both for himself and for society, one must preserve his natural freedom and goodness." Professor Guerra does not use sexist language except in reporting or displaying Rousseau's views, but does not, in any way, acknowledge that it is a sexist view or that Rousseau proposed a different kind of education for girls.

> *Discussion:* The distinction between using and mentioning or displaying sexist language presents editors and authors with decisions that are sometimes more difficult. This case illustrates that in the context of responsible scholarship, the truth may sometimes be distorted if an editor insists that all sexist language be removed.
>
> In saying, "Rousseau held that . . . ," Professor Guerra does not use or endorse the sexist language, but instead displays the sexist terms in which Rousseau's thought was formulated. It would misrepresent Rousseau's view to reformulate it in nonsexist terms. The editor should make an inquiry about whether the replacement of sexist language with nonsexist language here would be acceptable, but should be open to the argument that scholarly accuracy makes replacement unacceptable.
>
> On the other hand, the case presents a somewhat complicated context in which the sexist thought of Rousseau is displayed. Therefore, it may be appropriate for the editor to request that Professor Guerra note the sexist character of Rousseau's thought to foreclose the possibility of readers mistaking the display of sexist thought and language as its endorsement.

QUESTIONS

1. Suppose that the editor asked Professor Guerra to make changes taking note of Rousseau's sexist thought, but Professor Guerra declined arguing that the sexism of Rousseau was not at issue in the article and commenting on it would be distracting and gratuitous. Is there a question of academic freedom raised?

2. Would it make any difference if Professor Guerra agreed with Rousseau's views? Can **Standard 5** be read as permitting editors to reject articles if they believe the views expressed are racist or sexist?

SPONSORS, POLICYMAKERS, AND OTHER USERS OF RESEARCH

The Preamble, the Standards, and Their Rationale

Preamble

Researchers, research institutions, and sponsors of research jointly share responsibility for the ethical integrity of research, and should ensure that this integrity is not violated. While it is recognized that these parties may sometimes have conflicting legitimate aims, all those with responsibility for research should protect against compromising the standards of research, the community of researchers, the participants of research, and the users of research. They should support the widest possible dissemination and publication of research results. AERA should promote, as nearly as it can, conditions conducive to the preservation of research integrity.

STANDARDS

1   *The data and results of a research study belong to the researchers who designed and conducted the study, unless specific contractual arrangements have been made with respect to either or both the data and results, except as noted in II.B.4 (participants may withdraw at any stage).*

2   *Educational researchers are free to interpret and publish their findings without censorship or approval from individuals or organizations, including sponsors, funding agencies, participants, colleagues, supervisors, or administrators. This understanding should be conveyed to participants as part of the responsibility to secure informed consent.*

3   *Researchers conducting sponsored research retain the right to publish the findings under their own names.*

4   *Educational researchers should not agree to conduct research that conflicts with academic freedom, nor should they agree to undue or questionable influence by government or other funding agencies. Examples of such improper influence include endeavors to interfere with the conduct of research, the analysis of findings, or the reporting of interpretations. Researchers should report to AERA attempts by sponsors or funding agencies to use any questionable influence.*

5   *Educational researchers should fully disclose the aims and sponsorship of their research, except where such disclosure would violate the usual tenets of confidentiality and anonymity. Sponsors or funders have the right to have disclaimers included in research reports to differentiate their sponsorship from the conclusions of the research.*

6   *Educational researchers should not accept funds from sponsoring agencies that request multiple renderings of reports that would distort the results or mislead readers.*

7   *Educational researchers should fulfill their responsibilities to agencies funding research, which are entitled to an accounting of the use of their funds, and to a report of the procedures, findings, and implications of the funded research.*

8   *Educational researchers should make clear the bases and rationales, and the limits thereof, of their professionally rendered judgments in consultation with the public, government, or other institutions. When there are contrasting professional opinions to the one being offered, this should be made clear.*

9   *Educational researchers should disclose to appropriate parties all cases where they would stand to benefit financially from their research or cases where their affiliations might tend to bias their interpretation of their research or their professional judgments.*

RATIONALE

As the **Preamble** of **Part I** notes, research's potential to advance knowledge or improve the quality of education depends on the integrity of the research in question. That integrity, in turn, depends on whether the research activities and the conclusions, policies and practices drawn from them are well conducted and well warranted. The integrity of research can be usefully viewed as depending on two things. One is the competence and conscientiousness of the researcher. A second is the effectiveness of the institutionalization of the conduct and reporting of research. In this second case, the integrity of research is threatened when contrary interests are in a position to manipulate the conduct of research or to silence or distort the presentation of research projects, findings, and analyses.

The standards in this section focus primarily on the ways that institutional influences on research may serve to compromise research integrity. They seek to promote a research environment in which the values of academic freedom and the marketplace of ideas are respected. They also seek an environment in which conflicts of interest that might distort the conduct or reporting of research are avoided or their effects controlled, and a reporting process in which potential sources of bias are either removed or publicly acknowledged.

The **Preamble's** mention of obligations to the *standards of research, the community of researchers, the participants of research, and the users of research* implies that the appropriate institutionalization of research can be a complicated task. The obligations of these different factions may be in tension with one another. Moreover, their interests may include other objectives beside the pursuit of truth, creating additional potential conflicts. Since the ways in which research is carried out and used has an impact on the strength of public support for research, researchers who ignore other public interests in education and how the public receives and uses research violate **Standard 1** of **Part I.** This standard requires that researchers *not jeopardize future research, the public standing of the field, or the discipline's research results.* One purpose of the standards of **Part V** is to insist that the integrity that **Part I** expects of individual researchers should also characterize the institutional arrangements under which research is conducted and reported.

The **Preamble** of **Part V** assigns collective responsibility for the integrity of research to researchers, research institutions, and research sponsors. Responsibility for the integrity of research may be shared in several different ways. First, for a project in which several parties participate, specific responsibilities may be formally assigned to various parties, each only responsible for doing his or her own part. If one party fails to meet an assigned responsibility on which another party's responsibility is dependent, the second party may be excused from meeting his or her obligation. For example, if a university has promised resources for statistical analyses, or a school has promised to serve as a field site, and the promise is not kept, then researchers no longer are obligated to conduct a research project even if they had committed to doing one.

Second, some shared responsibilities concerning the integrity of research apply to the whole project. This obligation occurs when the parties' actions imply an unqualified commitment to attaining the research outcome, or if their roles in the project are so intertwined that it is difficult or impossible to untangle them. If a team of researchers has made a commitment to do a research project and one of them drops out, the commitment may mean the others are still responsible for seeing it through. Furthermore, they must either find a substitute for the person who dropped out or take over that person's assignments. Likewise, everyone on a research team may be responsible for ensuring that the research data collected for a project are accurately recorded and analyzed in unbiased fashion.

Between these two extremes lies the kind of responsibility for which people have responsibility that falls short of having to assume the entire responsibility when another party fails to meet their commitment. In such cases, there may be a responsibility to do something to address someone else's failure to meet their obligations, but not to carry out the entire project in its original form.

Besides this direct responsibility, researchers and others have certain indirect responsibilities for ensuring the integrity of research. By word and action, researchers and institutions contribute to the conditions that either encourage or discourage certain behavior on the part of others, and this affects the soundness and potential value of research. Through formal institutional policies and procedures or through the informal influences of attitudes and behavior, the research environment either fosters or stands in the way of good research practices. Even if someone else actually does something to thwart the integrity of research, the people who contribute to the research environment are partly responsible for the integrity of research carried out in that environment.

In some instances, a contract may serve to specify formally the assignment of responsibilities for a group project. In such cases, each party's responsibilities are spelled out, as well as the conditions under which someone's failure to meet their responsibilities release the others from their responsibilities. However, the idea of a contract is often contrasted with that of a **covenant**, when people pledge themselves to do something unconditionally. According to the idea of a covenant, parties are responsible for holding up their part of the agreement no matter what the others do, because of the overriding importance of the nature of the project.

Where researchers stand to gain financially or in some other significant and material way from their work, there may be a conflict of interest. One common solution for conflicts of interest is to ask for the party with the conflict to be excused from participating in the activity. For example, if a researcher is asked to review research grant applications and a submitted application includes provisions that result in financial gains for the reviewer, the reviewer has a conflict of interest and should withdraw from the review. Questions can be raised about other situations where researchers' financial interests or affiliations might affect their judgments, such as doing an evaluation of a curriculum that they own the rights to, or if they are called upon to judge the work of colleagues from their own institution. This is the focus of **Standard 9** that requires researchers to disclose financial interests or affiliations, which may bias their research or analyses. The presupposition of **Standard 9's** reference to affiliations may be that strong investment in an idea may itself be a source of conflict of interest or bias.

For issues concerning the use of data, the question is who owns the data? This is because the owners of data determine who may have access to the data, and when they may have access. Data are normally considered to be someone's property because someone has done the work of designing the study or collecting and organizing the data. There may also be some formal agreement among the parties about who has the right to decide who may use them. **Standard 1** identifies the intellectual products of research such as the data as the researchers' property, unless there is an explicit agreement to the contrary. (See **Part III** for discussion of issues of ownership.) Policies concerning the possession, use, and sharing of data should take into account the need to make it worthwhile for someone to invest the time and resources required to collect it. These policies should also consider the desirability of having the data used for various constructive purposes by as many people as possible. **Standard 1** may rest on the view that justice requires that those who produce a product are to be viewed as its owners, unless they voluntarily surrender their right. Furthermore, justice may also require the possibility that vesting ownership of research products in those who produce them is most likely to make them widely available.

Property considerations also have a bearing on who is entitled to research information, such as project descriptions and research findings. Accordingly, **Standards 3** and **7** both support the sharing of research information, rather than giving anyone exclusive rights over research results. **Standard 3** declares that researchers retain the right to make research findings available regardless of the wishes of the original sponsors of the research. Additionally, **Standard 7** entitles the sponsors to access to research information as a function of their sponsorship, even if the researchers have no desire to make that information available to the sponsors.

The integrity of research is enhanced by policies that promote the sharing and free exchange of ideas. The purpose of academic freedom is to allow people to offer their findings and conclusions to the research community or the public at large without fear or risk of harm from what they say or write. **Standard 2** affirms the academic freedom of researchers to share and interpret their findings, even if their ideas are not welcomed by sponsors, research institutions, or other members of the research community. The truth does not always please everyone. Institutions devoted to the pursuit of truth must develop ways to encourage the free expression of ideas and to protect people from unwarranted reprisals.

In education, where research findings often have implications for policy, academic freedom may be threatened by political power. Society at large, powerful factions within society, sponsoring institutions, or interested government entities may be more interested in preserving current beliefs, protecting special interests, or avoiding certain ideas than they are in supporting the open examination and discussion of research findings and ideas. **Standards 4, 5,** and **6** address this general concern about political influences silencing or distorting research information. **Standard 4** prohibits researchers from engaging in research activity that subverts academic freedom, or from participating in research in which the sponsors of research somehow curb the researchers' academic freedom. **Standard 6** forbids researchers from accepting funds from sponsors in exchange for their reporting in ways that misrepresent the relevant research. **Standard 5** seeks to balance the interest of academic freedom against two other related interests that are also considered legitimate. Although research sponsors are not permitted to stand in the way of researchers' rights to publish their findings, **Standard 5** permits them to insert disclaimers on research reports they sponsor so that the sponsoring entity is not required to endorse the researchers' findings. Researchers are also not free to violate promises of confidentiality or anonymity.

Within the academy, popular or established ideas may engender political efforts to thwart the fair consideration of contrary ideas and research work. **Standard 8** directs researchers to identify the limits and qualifying assumptions of their work and to recognize contrary points of view in the interests of an unbiased consideration of their work. Whether the opposition comes from within or outside the research community, the standards direct researchers and their supporting institutions to remember the importance of how their activities, attitudes, and policies affect the vitality of the exercise of academic freedom.

Interpretation of the Standards: Issues, Cases, and Discussions

ISSUE

Standard 1 claims that those who design and conduct research are the owners of the data and results produced. However, it permits an exception. Who owns the data for sponsored projects, what exceptions are allowed, and when should they be permitted?

Case 1

Professor Janet Roth-Jackson did a study on concept mapping funded by Concept Maps, Inc., a firm that creates and distributes software employing concept maps. However, the research did not support some of the rather sweeping claims made by Concept Maps, Inc. concerning the value of the technique. Concept Maps, Inc. demanded that the final report and all the data for the project be turned over to them and asserted that they have an exclusive right to determine their use.

> *Discussion:* **Standard 1** indicates that these materials belong to Janet Roth-Jackson. Hence, unless she has signed a contract giving the rights to her research to Concept Maps, Inc., she is free to use them and to publish the results without Concept Maps, Inc.'s permission. Moreover, it may be that **Standard 4** indicates that Professor Roth-Jackson should not sign a contract that gives Concept Maps, Inc. the control over the results of her project that they now seek to exercise. **Standard 1** may invest ownership of intellectual products in those who do the work rather than those who pay for it. This is because, in part, it is believed that they are more likely to use it in a way that is consistent with the values of the marketplace of ideas and academic freedom. **Standard 4** not only confirms this reading of **Standard 1** but also indicates that researchers are not free to contract away their work if academic freedom is threatened. Moreover, **Standard 1** may be viewed as in service to **Standard 2** that seeks to protect researchers from censorship from research sponsors.

ISSUE

Sometimes researchers collaborating in a research project separate before the end of the project. What happens to the data when a research team breaks up, and the parties all want the data?

Case 2

Dee Ross looked angrily at Gus Timms, who sat at the computer with his arms folded. The hard drive of that computer contained files with data from a two-year research study that she and Timms had designed and conducted with a federal grant from the U.S. Department of Education, and they were in the process of analyzing it. Ross had been turned down for tenure at Parker University and was leaving for a job at Trever College. She and Timms had done the data collection together, and she had done most of the work so far preparing the data for statistical analyses. Now she wanted to take the data files with her to Trever, where she hoped to publish their research findings. But Timms was refusing, because he had also worked on the data and because he hoped to analyze the data and publish the results himself. Ross and Timms had not worked well together on the project, and a long distance collaboration did not seem possible to either of them.

"Sorry, Dee," said Gus, "but I'm the principal investigator on this grant, and even though you've worked more than anyone else on this project, I am identified in the grant as the person who makes the decisions about staffing for the project. The data are mine. The university paid you for all the time you worked here, so you've been treated fairly. Sorry things didn't work out. I'll send you courtesy copies of the articles we publish when they come out in the research journals.

> *Discussion:* This is a case in which both the formal agreements about the property involved in this research and the work people put into the project should be taken into account. **Standard 1** states that in general the data belong to the individuals who designed and carried out the research, which in this case means both Dee Ross and Gus Timms. However, this standard also acknowledges the possibility of contractual stipulations, and in this case

such stipulations are likely to exist. Neither Ross nor Timms has full authority to decide what will happen to the data, because, under the federal grant, Parker University, not Timms or Ross, legally owns the data. Any decision to be made must be approved by an official representing Parker University, which presumably has policies regarding data sharing and researchers who leave the institution. **Standard 1** also makes it fairly clear that both Timms and Ross deserve more credit for their work than their paychecks, because they both made significant intellectual contributions to the design of the study. In addition, it suggests that in the absence of a contractual arrangement determining ownership, the data should be viewed as collectively owned by both Ross and Timms. Note, however, that **Standard 1** does not vest ownership merely on the basis of invested labor; instead, it vests ownership in those who designed and conducted the study. Here the intent is very likely to reflect the view of the standards of **Part III** where creative input is a key factor in determining authorship and ownership.

The conflict could have been prevented if Ross and Timms had foreseen this possibility, consulted relevant university policy, and reached an agreement before this event took place. Such agreements sometimes may need to be updated, but they are still often useful. In this case it seems as if they both deserve access to the data. Depending on the nature of the study, two options are possible. Either they both get copies of the data, and perform their analyses and report their findings independently, or if their work has progressed to the point where their contributions are inseparable, they must reach an agreement about how to complete the work, and share authorship.

ISSUE

Research sponsors often sponsor research not only because they are interested in an issue, but because they believe that a research project will produce research findings that will serve to support the sponsor's position on that issue. If the research project turns up different conclusions from those the sponsors expected, they may have little interest in making public the findings which cast doubt on their own position. Do sponsors have exclusive control over the research findings from projects they paid for?

Case 3

"If you think we're going to make this study public you are out of your mind!" shouted Ms. Inquist, glaring at Amanda Minor. Amanda had just handed in the research report she had done for the Horace Mann Foundation, in which she had compared high school student achievement of public and private school students. Her findings included better scores for the private school students, even after controlling for student socioeconomic status and parents' level of education. Ms. Inquist, the Foundation's program officer, was not happy about the findings, but she really got angry when Amanda informed Ms. Inquist of her intention to publish her findings. Ms. Inquist said that the study had been paid for by the Foundation, and that the report belonged to them. They could do what they wanted with this research, Inquist insisted, and in this instance what they wanted to do was lock it in a file cabinet and throw the key away.

Amanda Minor was not surprised that they weren't going to spend a lot of money to distribute the report widely, but she was taken aback by Ms. Inquist's instruction that she not publish the research findings either. Amanda had taken the job with the expectation that the research experience would strengthen her credentials, and without being able to publish or show anyone the findings, the year's experience was worthless. Had she done all that work for nothing?

Discussion: The Foundation's mission is to advance the cause of public education, and Ms. Inquist has both the right and the responsibility to support activities guided by that mission. If she believes that this report's findings are not consistent with the Foundation's interest in supporting public education, she may elect not to devote resources to publishing and distributing the report. But because its mission concerns the promotion of information relevant to the public's evaluation of public education, and it commissioned the research, Inquist is overstepping her role in support of public education by intending to suppress the report's findings. **Standard 2** declares that researchers have a right to publish and interpret the findings without interference from sponsoring entities. **Standard 3** also affirms their right to publish findings under their own names. These standards clearly indicate that if Amanda Minor believes that the research findings will make a significant contribution to knowledge in the field, she is entitled to use her own resources and time to get the research published.

Note that **Standard 3** not only serves the goals of **Standard 2,** academic freedom and the marketplace of ideas, but also reaffirms the standards of **Part III** concerning authorship. Authorship, according to **Part III,** depends on creative input. **Standard 3** of **Part V** indicates that while authors may contract away ownership of the products of research, it is unethical for such contracts to deny authors either the right to independent publication or the credit for their work.

ISSUE

Sponsoring organizations often sponsor research because they want answers to questions of particular interest to that organization. Sometimes they fund research because they believe that it will support preconceived ideas or agendas. Researchers seeking sponsorship don't always have those questions in mind, and propose projects designed to advance research knowledge in some other or broader way.

Of course researchers should not agree to carry out research that is deliberately designed to produce misleading results, just because a sponsoring agency is prepared to pay for it. This is not the same issue as when researchers propose a research project to a potential sponsor and that sponsor is only willing to support it if the research project design is modified to provide research information about a somewhat different question. May sponsors set conditions on the design of proposed research projects?

Case 4

Avery Stein's hand shook as he put down the phone. "Unbelievable!" he said, half to himself and half to Bert Quin, his co-principal investigator, who sat waiting to hear what had been said. "Those mindless government bureaucrats want us to alter the data collection on the Students Learn Citizenship research project we submitted for a grant! The intervention is supposed to last for two successive school years, and they want us to add another data collection point to our annual assessments in order to assess student achievement at the beginning and at the end of the summer in the middle of the project period. They also want us to collect background data on the race of the students, and to analyze the data for summer fade-out effects. We're proposing to look for cumulative program effects regardless of race, and they're trying to add this other issue." "That will cost more money," said Quin, alarmed. "Don't they realize that?"

"They do," said, Stein, "and they'll add that amount to the grant. They say we can hire another research assistant, and that there are enough graduate students here to get someone qualified. But they won't give us the grant at all if we refuse to make the revision in the research design.

This is Big Brother running roughshod over academic freedom! Who are they to tell us what to do in our study? I'd really like to do this research project, but I'm tempted to refuse on principle. It's blatant coercion! What do you say we tell them to go jump in the lake?"

Discussion: This case calls for the application of **Standard 4,** which affirms the principle of academic freedom and declares that researchers should not agree to *undue or questionable influence by government or other funding agencies* and requires researchers to report violations. However, while **Standard 4** gives examples of undue or questionable influence, it does not define the concept.

The overall context in the standards of **Part V** suggest two criteria. First, influence may be regarded as undue or questionable if it erodes the integrity of research. In this context, the integrity of research refers to its competence and quality. Does the research address a question of importance, and does it address it in such a way that the answers produced are well warranted? Second, influence is undue or questionable if researchers are expected to produce answers to the questions posed that are favored by the funding agency or to avoid finding answers that are disfavored by the funding agency.

These criteria suggest that it is legitimate for funding agencies to insist that researchers address the questions that are interesting to them, even if the researchers are interested in other and different questions, so long as the integrity of research is not threatened. If researchers and sponsors cannot agree on the questions they wish to answer, researchers may elect either not to accept funding or to agree to do what the sponsor wishes in order to get the contract. Moreover, mere disagreement about what questions are of interest is not reason to trigger the reporting clause: *Researchers should report to AERA attempts by sponsors or funding agencies to use any questionable influence.*

Researchers should, however, object to and report cases where sponsors or funders insist on conditions that unreasonably erode the quality of research or bias its results. In this case, it appears that the funding agency wishes answers to questions that are not of special interest to the researchers who have proposed the work, but that are not unreasonable or valueless questions. Moreover they have promised to provide the resources required to do the additional work required. Nothing in **Standard 4** precludes this.

Finally, **Standard 4** should not be understood so as to entitle researchers to object to requests for "quick and dirty" responses to questions that must be addressed in a timely fashion. Nor should they object to affordable research designs when better but more expensive designs are available so long as these constraints are reasonable under the circumstances and provide a reasonable possibility for research that is credible and useful.

ISSUE

Standard 5 requires researchers to disclose the aims and sponsorship of their work and gives sponsors the right to a disclaimer separating their views from those of the researchers whose work they fund. The purpose of the first of these provisions may be to permit the reader to understand potential sources of bias in the research. The second recognizes that, since sponsors must respect the academic freedom of researchers, they may not always agree with or support the conclusions researchers reach and publish. It is thus improper to attribute the views of researchers to those who fund their research.

Case 5

Professor John Cornelius accepted a contract from the Native American Rights League. The League has as its purpose "the conduct of research intended to further the educational rights of American Indians." The work Professor Cornelius was asked to do was intended to provide evidence that would justify the League's drive for greater autonomy for Native Americans in operating their own schools. Professor Cornelius intended to do a history of the educational policies of the Bureau of Indian Affairs. The League's intent was to use the research to document a history of oppressive policies on the part of the Bureau. Should Professor Cornelius accept a grant from an organization with these purposes, and what responsibilities does he have to report the purposes and sources of his funding?

Discussion: It should be carefully noted that the standards of **Part V** do not prohibit scholars from doing "adversarial" research or from accepting funds from sponsors with clear agendas. There are good reasons why they do not. Society recognizes that adversarial forums are appropriate ways to seek the truth. Courts are the best example of forums where truth is sought by a process in which representatives of different perspectives defend their own views in an impartial forum. Similarly adversarial groups play an important role in public debate. It is entirely appropriate for Professor Cornelius to lend his expertise to an advocacy organization whose cause he presumably supports.

However, the standards expect two things in such cases. First, it is expected that Professor Cornelius retain his independence and objectivity. The role of expert witness is a useful analogy. Expert witnesses generally are hired to give testimony by one of the parties in a litigation. They may occasionally do research in support of their testimony. Presumably they are hired because it is believed their views and research support the case of those who hire them, and they agree to testify for similar reasons. Nevertheless, it is expected that the testimony they give will be truthful, and the content of their testimony must be determined by what they believe is true, not by what is in the interest of those who pay them.

Similarly, researchers who do sponsored research for advocacy groups must do research guided by suitable intellectual standards and report results rooted in the evidence. They, too, may not distort their procedures or their findings to support the predetermined views of those who have sponsored the research.

Second, it is expected that Professor Cornelius will fully disclose the sources of his funding and the purposes it is intended to serve. Human nature being what it is, when research is funded in order to promote a given agenda, the possibility of bias exists. It exists even if researchers do their best to maintain their independence and their integrity. Disclosure protects consumers from bias by alerting them to the interests being served.

ISSUE

Just as sponsors may not impose their substantive views on researchers as a condition of providing funding, researchers may not attribute their findings to their sponsors. Indeed, sponsors have a right to have a disclaimer in research reports that differentiates their sponsorship from the conclusions of the research. Such disclaimers might not, however, appear in media reports of research. Researchers often complain that the media misrepresent their research findings. News stories are often said to sensationalize research, or to give a one-sided account, or to omit the qualifications of the findings identified by the researchers. Knowing this, researchers who agree to talk about research with reporters have reason to worry that what they say may be misrepresented. Media reports are especially likely to ignore the qualifications and disclaimers that researchers believe are important to the correct interpretation of their work or to the accurate understanding of the views of sponsors. In some cases such qualifications and disclaimers are required by **Standard 5.** Who is responsible for media misrepresentations of research findings?

Case 6

Sue Pervis slammed her copy of the *Big City Rag* down on her desk, and glared at Angela Deem. "Look at this story," she said. "Once again they've made us look like we're providing research evidence that contradicts the Administration's policy position. I told you this would happen."

Deem looked at the story, which described research findings taken from a U.S. Department of Education report about state education finance policies, and highlighted recommendations about how states should redistribute tax revenues for schools collected at the local district level. The *Rag* news story also described the irritated reaction of a White House official who was asked about the report. The official denied that the Administration was changing its position that this was an issue for states and localities to work out on their own without federal intrusion. Deem saw no mention of her report's disclaimer stating that the Report's contents did not represent the Department's policy position. She also remembered emphasizing this point to the *Rag* reporter when they had talked about it, and felt some consolation that she had made sure Pervis heard her say it to the reporter.

The phone rang, and Pervis picked it up. "The White House? About the State Financing Report story in the *Big City Rag*?" She glowered at Deem. "Sure I'll take it."

> **Discussion:** Pervis and Deem have both behaved responsibly, even though they knew that the report's findings would probably be misrepresented in the media. They believed that the report contained useful research information that the public should be able to see and so it was responsible for them to make the information available through the media.
>
> **Standard 5** permits sponsors to insist on the inclusion of disclaimers in reports they sponsor, and so they were certainly entitled to point this out emphatically to the reporter. They may well have doubted that the disclaimer would be mentioned in the reporters' story, but if the implied misattribution is unethical, then the reporter is to blame.

ISSUE

Researchers may produce more than one account of a research activity. Depending on the audience for the information, and the kind of research concerned, they may produce multiple reports, some of them shorter or less technical, or different ones focused on different aspects of the research. Questions arise, however, when different reports portray research findings in inconsistent ways. When does the editing of research reports for different audiences become misleading?

Case 7

"We want quantitative and qualitative data included in the report," said Cal Mann, "and we want it to capture every positive effect of the Golden Past History Program—student and teacher reports, assessment data, and surveys about changes in student engagement in the subject—everything that's available. The budget can be expanded if you don't find good stuff in the first round of investigation. Write up all the data collections and analyses for the internal report, so that we have a record of everything you did when we review your budget submissions. The formal report should only include the data that support findings that indicate positive effects. Let's make sure we show a complete picture of how good our program is. Nobody wants to read about data that are inconclusive."

Belle Bendix found it hard to suppress a smile. Mann was the director of World History of All (WHOA), the organization that had developed the Golden Past History program. WHOA had also helped the Demo City School District obtain a grant to implement the program, and the grant included both a budget for professional development and training and a requirement that the program's effects be evaluated. Bendix's Research Corporation had been asked to do the evaluation, which would be submitted to the grant institution, the Demo City school board, and WHOA's Board of Directors. Both reports would be entirely truthful. Mann wanted two different reports for two different audiences, and WHOA was willing to pay for Bendix to dig until she found the information they wanted. This project was a guaranteed winner for all concerned.

> *Discussion:* This research project will probably produce a distorted picture of the effects of the new history program. It violates the prohibition in **Standard 6** against multiple reports that distort and mislead. There is nothing unethical in the idea of designing research to ensure that any positive effects are detected, but that's not all Mann is asking Bendix to do. She is also being asked to provide Mann with both a private and a public report. The request to omit any findings from the public report that are not positive is highly problematic, because the result will be a report that does not give a balanced representation of the data collected and reported in the private report.
>
> A general audience may not want to read a lengthy account of insignificant relationships among numerous variables, but the public audience report could still include some summary information about the range and type of variables investigated and the lack of significant relations among them. Likewise, evaluation instruments designed to produce an exaggerated account of the program's positive effects also violate **Standard 6.** It is perfectly acceptable for Mann to ask for the more exhaustive report of all the data collections for budgetary reasons, but he has gone beyond that in asking Bendix to paint an overly optimistic picture of the program. His request may also violate **Standard 5** of **Part I,** which prohibits selective reporting of research findings to relevant stakeholders. (See **Part I, Case 6.**)

ISSUE

Sponsors' demands for information about their funded projects often cost researchers considerable time and effort responding. Sponsors are often interested in knowing the status of research that is underway, whether funds are being spent properly, and what information the researchers can provide about related research issues. Providing this information takes time and effort. What are the limits of researchers' responsibilities to their sponsors?

Case 8

"I'm sick and tired of doing these stupid progress reports," said Curt Mudgson to no one in particular. "What's the point? The sponsors don't publish them; they don't use them to terminate the funding; and they don't use them to inform their own research. I don't think they even read them—all they do is check their little lists to make sure they've been sent, and then they stick them in a file drawer. What makes me mad is that I don't have time for these things; every three months I have to interrupt my real research work to spend two days assembling all this garbage they say they want. They should give us the money and then get out of the way. That old saying should be changed to: 'Those who can, do, and those who can't, demand progress reports.'"

> *Discussion:* **Standard 7** clearly states that researchers are obliged to honor the conditions of their funding, including reporting requirements, even when they seem pointless. The sponsors may have a variety of legitimate reasons for such information, including obtaining information about project or program impact, documentation of compliance with funding requirements, and reporting to the sponsor's sponsors or constituents. Even if they

do not have good reasons for wanting the information they require, if researchers have agreed to provide the reports requested as part of their contract, they are obligated to keep their promises and provide the reports.

The burden of such reporting requirements should be minimized to avoid wasting anyone's time, and researchers should be informed at the outset what their reporting burden will involve. And, of course, researchers may raise questions or offer suggestions as to how they can give the sponsors the necessary information in the most timely and efficient manner. Still, researchers should not simply ignore the administrative requirements of sponsored projects.

ISSUE

Standard 8 deals with disclosure. In this case, researchers are expected to be forthcoming about two things when dealing with the public (and presumably other consumers of research) in the role of consultant. First, they must reveal the evidential basis of their judgments. Second, when there is division in the professional opinion available, they must acknowledge that reasonable people think otherwise. People don't often go out of their way to help their critics, and researchers are no exception, especially if they believe that their critics' claims are biased or unwarranted. Researchers are not inclined to devote substantial time and effort to airing such claims rather than presenting their own findings, recommendations, and supporting evidence. Of course, the integrity of research requires them to identify the weakness and limitations of their research, and researchers should not actively seek to silence their opponents. But what should researchers say about research findings contrary to their own?

Case 9

"To summarize, my research on tracking shows that tracking in any form is bad for students, especially disadvantaged ones. It slows their academic achievement, and it discourages them from pursuing further education. It perpetuates institutionalized racism. It is an anathema, and should be eliminated as soon as possible." Al Fenster was testifying to the State Board of Education about its review of student assignment policies, and he wanted them to hear his message loud and clear. "Not just my own research, but that of every researcher I respect shows the same thing. I urge the State school board to adopt a policy that will eliminate tracking in every school in the state."

Abe Grup, the Board member from Boone County, leaned over to the microphone. "I know, Dr. Fenster, that you are a leading researcher in this area, which is why we are so glad you have come to testify to this Board. And I have no doubt that you have faithfully represented the findings of your research. However, I also know that many of the teachers in this state believe in student assignment and curriculum modifications on the basis of student ability. What I ask is this: First, are you telling us that all of the available research shows that all forms of tracking are bad for the students involved? Second, how reliable is this research? Does it include controlled scientific experiments?"

Fenster did not hesitate: "All the research worth reading supports the elimination of tracking, period, and that research includes comparisons of tracked with untracked students. Run tracking out of your state, Mr. Grup."

Discussion: The research on tracking is complex and contentious. It is likely that Fenster has misrepresented his own work and highly likely that he has misrepresented the existing research in this area. Fenster may be absolutely convinced of the wisdom of his recommendations, and he is entitled to show how his and others' research work informs those recommendations. But he has violated **Standard 8** both because he has given a misleading answer about the technical design of the research work he has done and because his comments about contrasting professional opinions are unreasonable. He has also violated **Standard 4** of **Part I,** which calls for honest disclosures when providing professional opinions to the public, and **Standard 7** of **Part I,** which requires researchers to be careful not to mislead the public about practical or policy implications of their research. In sum, he has misrepresented the nature and the quality of the existing research in order to make the evidence appear more one-sided than it is.

What exactly does **Standard 8** require Fenster to do? It seems unlikely that the intent of **Standard 8** is to require consultants to provide their audiences either detailed methodological commentary or elaborate argumentation for their views. The requirement is that consultants disclose biases and rationales. The expectation is that consultants will provide an overview of what was done to produce the conclusions drawn and the degree to which their research procedures warrant these conclusions. These characterizations should be truthful and not misleading. Second, **Standard 8** does not require consultants to provide a detailed formulation of the views and arguments of those who hold other positions. They are not required, in effect, to occupy all sides in an argument. They must only acknowledge that there are responsibly held positions other than their own. Here, too, it goes without saying that these representations must be truthful. What purposes do these requirements express?

First, the standards of **Part V** seem intended to permit researchers to occupy the role of advocates for views conscientiously held within the bounds of truthfulness. Researchers may advance the views they have, but may not lie or distort evidence in the process. Second, the standards of **Part V** ask researchers to respect the marketplace of ideas and to respect the need of their audiences for independent judgment by acknowledging the basis of their views, their limits, and the fact that there are alternatives to be considered. In his testimony, Fenster is neither a responsible advocate nor respectful of the need of his audience for independent judgment.

ISSUE

Standard 9 requires researchers to disclose instances in which they have a financial conflict of interest. It views disclosure as the appropriate solution to such conflicts. But conflicts of interest are not always immediately and directly apparent. Do conflicts of interest extend beyond the financial interests of the involved individuals themselves? Moreover, sometimes withdrawing is a better solution to conflicts of interest than disclosure.

Case 10

"So now what do I do?" said Professor Rea Voulker, as she showed page 56 of the application to Maude Richardson, the chair of the review panel. "A colleague from another department at Benn University where I work is named as part of the evaluation team for one of the school systems which has agreed to serve as a research site in this research proposal. So some of the budget for this grant would go to Benn U. to pay for his time. But I don't know him, and you can be sure that I won't get a raise if Benn U. gets this grant money. You know I'm a professional, and that I'll score these proposals fairly without favoring Benn U. I'd be insulted if you suggested otherwise. I don't want to think I've wasted almost a whole day reviewing proposals only to find out that I can't participate as a proposal reviewer."

Maude Richardson shook her head, and said matter-of-factly: "I believe you, but if Benn U. is named as a recipient of support, you're history. Thanks for your help, but I'm afraid you're out of the review process."

Discussion: Maude Richardson is correct in stating that there is a conflict of interest here, and according to **Standard 9,** Rea Voulker was obliged to bring that fact to her attention. Conflicts of interest extend to the financial interest of the institutions where people work, and the reviewer's employer (Benn U.) clearly may benefit financially if the application is funded. (Similarly, conflicts of interest extend to other members of one's immediate family, including spouses and children.)

Regardless of whether the reviewer's judgment would be influenced by this factor, she has a conflict of interest and must say so, so that Maude Richardson can decide whether she should not participate in the review of proposals. **Part I, Standard 10's** prohibition against reviewing others' work might also be considered here, but it only applies *where strong conflicts of interest are involved,* which does not fit this case. The decision is up to Maude Richardson, depending on the procedural rules of the sponsoring organization conducting the reviews.

Note that **Standard 9** requires disclosure, not recusal. Researchers who find that they have conflicts of interest are asked to make this fact public rather than to immediately withdraw. There are good reasons for this action. Capable and successful researchers may be strongly associated with the positions they have advocated. They may be personally invested in advancing their views, their prestige and influence may be on the line, and they may even have financial interests in the advancement of their positions.

On the other hand, they may also have unparalleled expertise, and public debate would be poorer were they required to abstain from all consulting and advisory roles which dealt with matters with which they were identified. Here, disclosure seems a better policy than recusal. Similarly, researchers who function as reviewers may often be asked to review papers for possible publication that deal with issues in which they have an interest. Here, too, disclosure may be a better solution that recusal. There are, however cases in which recusal seems required. Suppose Rea Voulker were reviewing a set of proposals that contained one of her own. Here the conflict of interest is strong, and disclosure is not an adequate remedy. Conscientious researchers will occasionally need to make difficult choices between recusal and disclosure.

Hard Cases

ISSUE

Progress in research depends on both the collection and sharing of data. Often the individual interests of researchers to collect data are in tension with the community's interest in sharing those data. What are researchers' obligations to archive and share data for other researchers to analyze?

Case 1

"So when can I expect to receive the data, Dr. Ames?" asked Fred Cramer, senior research scientist for the Fast Findings Research Corporation. "I'd be happy to send over a messenger with a disk, if that will help. I'm really excited about the chance to look at your data."

Penny Ames bit her lip and looked at the calendar on her desk. She had been working on this research project for four years, collecting data for a longitudinal study of academic achievement and various student characteristics and school factors. She'd finished collecting the data last year, and had spent whatever time she had since then entering and cleaning the data. As a junior faculty member at Orem University, she had a fairly heavy teaching load and very little research assistance at this point in the project. She had spent enough time working with the data to know that it contained some interesting findings. Her presentation about the design of the study and preliminary findings had been well received at the last AERA meeting. But it was going to take her some time to do the analyses carefully, and to write up the findings for publication. Cleaning the data for a public release database had also taken time away from original analysis.

Now here was Fred Cramer, who had been at the presentation, and was requesting a copy of the database. She knew his resources were ample if he had a client, and that Fast Findings would surely produce a report with the most important findings well before she could do the analyses and get them published in a research journal. She might be able to get one article accepted, but her dreams of a series of related articles were quickly vanishing. Orem University had a data-sharing policy, and, in principle, Penny believed it was good to allow other researchers access to data. But from the standpoint of her career, this had every sign of being a disaster in the making. She sighed, and put a clean disk into the drive of her computer.

> *Discussion:* It is important to make data available for researchers to examine. Collecting data is an expensive, time-consuming process, and researchers should make every effort to maximize the use of collected data to generate research findings. In addition, sometimes other researchers have other perspectives or questions than those of the researchers who collected the data, and their analyses can serve to both check and extend the research analyses of the original researchers. For these reasons, data archiving serves an important and constructive purpose in research.

> At the same time, data sharing policies must also take into account the incentives for collecting research data in the first place. If researchers all have the same access to the data as its collectors, and professional credit is a function of the first publication of research findings, then the incentive for generating original data will be offset by a policy that requires immediate sharing of data. **Standard 1** gives the researchers who conducted the study ownership of data and results. That researchers own not only the data, but also the results, implies that those who conduct research are entitled to reasonable time to analyze and report findings before sharing their data with others. Similarly, the guidelines under **Standard 3** of **Part III** regarding ownership of intellectual products also imply that researchers are entitled to benefit from the work they do. Once the original researchers have analyzed and reported on collected data, the database should be made available to others to review and do secondary analyses, in the interest of promoting the kind of open inquiry reflected in **Standard 6** of **Part I.** The values of the marketplace of ideas warrant making data widely available; however, they need not be interpreted so as to undermine the rights of ownership or the benefits that properly accrue to those who conduct the research.

QUESTIONS

1. Should researchers have the right to first publication of research findings from data they have collected no matter how long they take to do it? Or should there be some limit to the time they have before the data should be released, in the interest of having the data made public? What is it reasonable for sponsors to require in this regard?

2. Who should pay for the time and effort required to create a public database that can be provided to others for analysis of the data? Is this a responsibility of researchers themselves, of the host institutions or sponsors of the research they do, or of the researchers who wish to obtain the data?

ISSUE

Researchers sometimes work for organizations whose primary mission is not the pursuit of knowledge. The priorities of such institutions sometimes change, altering the value of particular research projects to the organization. Given limited resources, the organization may opt to discontinue support for such projects. Are researchers entitled to seek alternate routes for publication of sponsored research findings that the sponsors choose not to publish? Do the employees of private research companies or government agencies have the same right to academic freedom as do university professors?

Case 2

Lucy Cannon's eyes went from the piece of paper in her hand to her boss, Sid Lentz, and back again. The publication order form in her hand said "CANCELLED" in big red letters across the page, right over the description of the research study she had completed for the state department of education where she worked. "I don't understand. The central office assigned this study to me, they reviewed and approved the study design and the findings, and there was money set aside for publishing it. Now it's going to be thrown out? What's the story?"

"Politics as usual" said Sid, as he took the editor's copy of the study report off Cannon's desk. We've got a new state superintendent, and a new agenda, and your findings don't fit into the agenda's priorities very well. So we're not going to waste state funds publishing a report whose findings are just going to cloud the picture. It's happened before, and it will happen again. I should be able to give you your next research assignment on Monday, when we've met with the new superintendent. Meanwhile, please throw out all your files on this study; we don't want them anymore."

Lucy's eyes flashed. "Now wait just a minute, Sid! I put a lot of work into this project, and I think the findings are important. Our state superintendent may not want to use them, but there are forty-nine other chief state school officers who might. I want to seek outside publication of this report, even if the department isn't going to publish it. Give me back that editor's copy!"

"It's not yours, Lucy, it belongs to the department. We paid you to do it, and we have the right to decide whether we want to publish it or not. And the answer is: Not." Sid backed quickly out the door, with the copy still in hand. Lucy opened her briefcase and checked to make sure that her second copy was still there.

> **Discussion:** In general, property owners have the right to dispose of their property as they see fit, so long as they do not violate the rights of others. This includes the right to keep and not use their property, such as books, or cars, or clothes, even if these goods would be beneficial to others if they were transferred to them. Products developed by employees on company time belong to the company, unless there is an agreement to the contrary. A research study may fit this description of a product owned by the company that paid its employee to perform it. **Standard 1** allows for the possibility that researchers working for organizations such as state departments of education may be contractually obliged to recognize the organization's ownership of any research data or results they produce at work.
>
> At the same time, **Standards 2** and **3** both assert researchers' rights to make their findings public, under the auspices of the principle of academic freedom. This obligation is derived from researchers' obligations to contribute to the common stock of knowledge by the research community, and from their obligations to apply knowledge that may benefit society. It appears that the study in question might serve one or both of these research purposes.

Moreover, **Standard 4** suggests that academic freedom should not be contractually waived. Although it is commonly acknowledged that university professors have a right to academic freedom, it is not similarly acknowledged that employees of private research corporations or of government agencies have a similar right. While the standards of **Part V** make no explicit distinction between university-based researchers and those employed by government agencies or the private sector, they are frequently worded to suggest that their intended application is to university-based researchers. The status of other researchers under these provisions is less clear.

QUESTIONS

1. Assuming that Cannon has the right to seek publication for the report on her own time, is she obliged to do so, or would it be ethical for her to simply drop the project?

2. What obligations does Cannon have to the organization, if she chooses to seek publication of the findings on her own time? Is she entitled to use her organizational affiliation, or would this effectively violate **Standard 5** which gives sponsoring agencies the right to a disclaimer?

ISSUE

Some organizations use their resources—including research information—to advance identified mission objectives in education reform. They may hire researchers to perform or report on research that supports the organization's objectives. While it is obvious that it would be unethical to assign researchers to report false information, it is not so obvious whether it is unethical to assign researchers to selectively report the truth. Are researchers permitted to accept assignments to identify only those research findings in which their employer has an interest?

Case 3

Dr. Spinner looked at the e-mail message again and sighed. "That's the trouble with research work at an advocacy organization, I guess. First you identify the conclusion, and then you find the evidence to support it," he said to himself. Indeed, that is exactly what his new assignment said: He was supposed to find all the research evidence available that supported the organization's position on gender-based differences in education. Any evidence to the contrary was not to be included in the report; his task was to make the strongest possible research-based case in favor of the position that the organization's president had taken that morning at a press conference. Dr. Spinner was vaguely familiar with the research in this area. He knew that there was some research that supported the president's views, and so he was confident that he could put together the report. He also knew that there was some research to the contrary, but apparently that was something he didn't have to worry about. There was one thing that bothered him. He got up from his desk and walked out of his office and down the hall to his supervisor's office. "Did you see this gender and education research report assignment?" Spinner asked. "Why didn't that new person get this—I thought it was right up her alley?"

His boss looked up. "Yes, so did I. But she quit when I gave it to her and told her not to include the contrary research evidence. Maybe she intends to write the counterpoint for the other side. It's all yours."

Discussion: **Standard 5** of **Part I** prohibits researchers from selectively communicating research findings, and **Standard 7** of **Part I** requires them to identify the limits of research evidence in public reports and not to misrepresent their practical implications. **Standard 4** of **Part V** declares that researchers should reject efforts from sponsoring agencies to distort research analyses or findings, and **Standard 6** directs researchers to resist sponsoring agencies who request distorted or misleading reports of research. Beyond that, **Standard 8** obliges researchers to note the existence of contrary professional opinions, where such opinions exist.

Researchers are supposed to be committed to the free and impartial reporting of research, and are not supposed to present a biased or distorted rendering of research findings relevant to a particular viewpoint. If a sponsoring organization asks them to distort research results, they are supposed to refuse. A request to present only the research evidence supporting one of several rival positions, when research to the contrary exists, seems to violate this obligation.

At the same time, it must be understood that some organizations exist and hire employees for the purpose of advocating specific policy positions and representing particular groups' interests. Normally there are other organizations representing alternative positions and constituencies. Moreover, as noted above, the standards of **Part V** seem formulated to countenance advocacy research and recognize that in some cases adversarial processes are a means to the pursuit of truth. Here it is reasonable to expect that if one organization presents the research evidence in favor of its views, that other organizations in adversarial relations with that organization will make the research case to the contrary. Consequently, someone working at one such institution may reasonably expect that they can put together the strongest possible research-based argument in favor of their organization's interests, and know that the other research will also be made available to the public. A one-sided presentation may not be a distorted one, if the other sides will also be available.

The particular mission of the organization may well be relevant here. If the organization openly identifies itself as advocating a particular position, then this may be taken as a clear and honest statement of the kind of information that organization makes public. Moreover, such an organization should not be expected to employ researchers who do not share its aims. Nor must researchers refuse employment by such organizations. An institution of higher learning may be in a different position, as its devotion to the advancement of knowledge might prohibit such one-sided presentations of the relevant research evidence, on the grounds that academic institutions should air all sides of the question. Nothing in the standards of **Part V**, however, permits researchers to lie or misrepresent evidence because they work for an advocacy organization.

QUESTIONS

1. If a researcher writing for an advocacy organization were to publish a report in which there is only a statement acknowledging the existence of opposing views, is this sufficient? Should specific references to the literature containing the opposing views be included? Should it be summarized? Analyzed?

2. The conventions of academia are such that researchers can expect that if they publish research making one side of the case on an issue, it is reasonably certain others will publish rebuttals. May researchers then assemble the research evidence on one side of a question and rely on academic colleagues to provide the arguments and evidence to the contrary? To put the question differently, it appears that the standards of **Part V** permit researchers to lend their services to causes and advocacy groups. This seems to suggest that in such contexts scholars need not provide their audiences with a balanced and questioning account of the evidence of a sort that might be appropriate in a seminar. However, because they are working in an adversarial context does not entitle them to lie or to mislead. Are these expectations simply inconsistent? If not, how can they to be balanced?

ISSUE

Practitioners do not always welcome research findings. They often complain that research findings are too narrow or complicated, and they also question the researchers' impartiality. For their part, researchers often express reservations about over-generalizing their findings. How should researchers present research findings in circumstances of practical decision-making?

Case 4

Connie Kirp stifled a yawn and tried to look attentive without making eye contact with fellow School Board member Diane Taylor, who had been speaking for about ten minutes. This was her first board meeting after winning election to the board last month, and she seemed to be taking her new role quite seriously. Taylor was a parent and an education researcher in the school of education at the local university, and had campaigned for the school board on the promise of using the latest research to improve the school system. The school board's first agenda item concerned a decision about the allocation of budget resources, and Taylor had said that she would like to familiarize the other board members with relevant research findings.

And that was what had Connie a little disappointed by what Taylor had been saying for the last few minutes. First of all, Connie thought, having had five children who had gone through the school system and ten years' experience on the board was sufficient background for understanding what the issues were. Besides, she didn't think what Taylor was saying was exactly to the point: The question Taylor had raised was a little different from the decision at hand, and it was difficult to understand some of the terms she was using. The findings she was talking about seemed more general than the question being put to the board, and she'd mentioned that those findings were more than ten years old. Didn't that make them out of date? Diane Taylor had spent the last five minutes qualifying the conclusions she'd drawn. On top of all that, Connie had the vague sense that for all her protestations of impartiality, Taylor had some very definite ideas about how this should all come out, and was twisting the findings around to convince the other board members. Connie started to doodle on her agenda.

Discussion: Researchers should not misrepresent or overstate the strength of research evidence having a bearing on practical matters in education. **Standards 2** and **7** in **Part I** and **Standard 8** in **Part V** all admonish researchers to carefully present an accurate picture of relevant research and its implications for educational practice. These standards require researchers to avoid misrepresenting data, identifying limits to inferences drawn from the data, and disclosing the existence of contrary views where appropriate. It is dishonest to knowingly misrepresent the practical implications of research findings, and such behavior could well result in decisions that did not hold any particular promise of improving education.

One of the central objectives of education research is to benefit educational practice, and this requires using research findings to inform practical decisions. The standards for the most desirable presentation of research findings to an audience of researchers are not the same as those for an audience of the public, educators, or other practical decision-makers. Researchers interested in finding ways to use research findings to improve educational practices need to tailor their presentation of research knowledge into a form that makes it accessible and useful to a practically oriented audience. This frequently means that researchers cannot present the relevant research findings persuasively and still meet research standards for precision and accuracy.

QUESTIONS

1. How far could Taylor go to simplify research findings for the others on the School Board? Is she entitled to rely on her own judgment in extrapolating research findings to the practical

questions at hand, or are such judgments something she is obliged to leave to the other Board members? Should Taylor routinely disclose her personal biases about education issues when presenting research findings to the other members of the Board?

2. In this case, Taylor is acting as a school board member. In this role is she still bound by AERA's **Standards**? Do the facts that she is a researcher or an AERA member create ethical obligations for her that differ from other board members?

ISSUE

Researchers sometimes are associated with education practices or research activities even though they have no financial interests in them. Their reputations may include being a public spokesperson for or against a particular educational practice, or they may have personal friendships or intellectual debts to researchers who designed or evaluated those practices. Even though they may not profit financially from the success or failure of those practices, they may not be neutral in the way they approach related research activities. Should researchers be disqualified from participation in research activities for other than financial conflicts of interest?

Case 5

A smile crossed Bea Hunter's face as she looked down at the report she had just finished. The state department of education had commissioned her to develop design recommendations for the new state assessment, which was to be created under a request for proposals that would be published in a few months. Hunter had been hired because of her expertise in the field, and because she never accepted offers to do any assessment development she had no financial interest in whatever contract was awarded as a result of the activity. Hunter thought she had done a good job on the report, and she was confident she knew who would get the contract.

It would be Belle Winter, her mentor at the university where Hunter had done her graduate work, who had just formed an independent company and was providing services to clients, including state departments of education. Bea Hunter had learned a lot from Belle Winter, and naturally many of Hunter's recommendations for the new assessment reflected Winter's views about designing valid, reliable, and sound tests. Winter's views were different from those of the other assessment development providers in the state, and the recommendations Hunter had put in the report, if accepted by the state, would effectively eliminate Winter's competition. That was fine with Hunter; she believed in Winter's approach. Student assessments in the state would provide better ways to understand and improve student learning across the state, and her former teacher and graduate school associates would have work in Winter's company.

There was a knock on the door, and before Hunter could move to open it, it opened and a head appeared around the door. "Dr. Hunter?" said the young woman who smiled as she stepped in. "They told me I could find you here. My name is Lonnie Dray, and I write for the *Capital Rag*. I cover news stories about education. I heard that you were submitting a report and recommendations about the new state tests, and that one of your old teachers from the university is planning to submit a proposal when the contract is offered.

"They told me over at the state department of education that you signed the financial conflict of interest form when you agreed to write the report. Some of the other test development companies in town are saying that this contract is going to be fixed so that Winter gets the job. I was just wondering if I could ask you a few questions about how well you got along with Dr. Winter, and whether you're still friendly. Do you mind?" Lonnie sat down in a chair, and took out a recorder. "Mind if I tape this? I never did learn to write fast enough in school, you know."

Discussion

Like everyone else, researchers often want certain things to happen even though they will have little or no impact on the researchers' personal financial status. In the law the term "conflict of interest" is usually used to refer to situations in which someone has a financial interest in the outcome of a decision-making process in which they play some role, but there are also other kinds of involvement. Philosophical preferences, the consequences for friends and associates, or the impact on one's professional reputation may all be affected by decisions about such things as the awarding of grants and contracts or decisions to publish papers. In some cases, even though the decision does not even appear to involve material gain, the outcome may be very important to the researcher. Researchers' beliefs are often the strongest concerning education issues with which they are especially familiar and most knowledgeable. **Standard 8** requires researchers to make clear to the public the limits of the bases for their professional judgments, and **Standard 9** requires them to disclose the potential bias of their affiliations as well as their financial interests. At the same time, it would seem foolish to exclude precisely those who know and care the most about the particular issue from participating in relevant decisions. And it is unrealistic to believe that there are always totally disinterested and impartial experts available to make such decisions.

QUESTIONS

1. Should those without a financial interest in a decision have complete discretion to decide what role they are able to perform when they have a nonfinancial interest in a research activity? How might the recommendations of interested rational experts be checked?

2. Should researchers be required to identify relevant philosophical preferences and collegial relationships as a condition of participating in a research decision-making process? Should Dr. Hunter have disclosed her prior association with Dr. Winter or her identification with her views? If a researcher is unwilling to make public their non-financial interests in a research activity, should he or she be excluded from the decision-making process?

ISSUE

Ethical standards exist to guide and encourage ethical behavior on the part of professional researchers. In addition to considering how standards apply to their own conduct, researchers may be aware of whether other researchers are observing standards of professional conduct. If violations of those standards occur, are researchers obliged to report research misconduct to professional societies like the AERA?

Case 6

"I'm not going to let Dr. Kantzer get away with it," said Jack Pyle. "What he did was wrong. You know it, and I know it, and he knows it, and he shouldn't be allowed to engage in such unethical conduct without being held responsible. He altered our conclusions because that bureaucrat from the state suggested that the commissioner wouldn't like them. Then he fudged our data to support what he thinks the commissioner wants to hear. I'm going to report it."

Seena Evans narrowed her eyes as she looked at Jack to judge how upset he was. "I hope you realize what you're doing. Dr. Kantzer is very popular at this institution, and nobody will be happy to hear about this even if it is true and you have the evidence. He brings in a lot of money. His ability to get all of those state contracts pays your salary. And Kantzer's mistakes had nothing to do with a federal grant either, so you can't go to the Feds. So to whom are you going to complain while you're making yourself the least popular man on campus?

Jack frowned, and then brightened. "I'll go to the AERA!" he said. "They have a set of ethical standards. I'm a graduate student member, and Kantzer belongs too. And AERA **Part V, Standard 4** specifically calls on people to report one kind of ethical violation of the code. Why wouldn't they pay attention to this one?" "Because it will cost the organization money to investigate, and if they find Kantzer guilty and try to punish him he'll probably sue them. Besides, AERA's **Standards** have a note saying they don't intend to enforce the code, they just mean it to be an educational device. And their *reporting clause* (**Standard 4** in **Part V**) only concerns undue influence by government agencies. But it was Kantzer who fudged our data, not the state. You'll need to find someone here to whom to report Kantzer's actions. Why don't you just put a copy of AERA's **Standards** in Kantzer's mailbox? Maybe he has a conscience you can access. Or you could save your career by forgetting the whole thing."

> **Discussion:** Whistle-blowing in research nearly always causes trouble, and the whistle-blower's bad news is not often particularly welcome. Whistle-blowing brings to light misconduct, threatens the reputations of individuals and institutions, provokes controversy, and triggers time-consuming and costly procedures. Whistle-blowers are sometimes mistaken or are unsure of whether anything wrong has been done, and are often suspected of having ulterior motives for their actions. Whistle-blowers have often had their careers suffer as a result of their actions, even when their allegations have proven to be well founded. It is often unclear who has the proper authority to investigate and adjudicate such allegations, and whether the investigating officials have a conflict of interest by virtue of their positions at an involved institution. In the published version of the standards, AERA noted that the **Standards** was intended to serve as *an educational document, to evoke voluntary compliance by moral persuasion. Accordingly, it is not the intention of the Association to monitor adherence to the Standards or to investigate allegations of violations to the code.*
>
> On the other hand, whistle-blowers can serve an important and valuable function for the welfare of the research community. Their actions can minimize damage done by the original unethical behavior and serve as a warning and a model to other researchers. **Standard 4** does call upon researchers to report to AERA sponsors or funding agencies that try to exercise questionable influences. (This is apparently the one standard that the AERA might be willing to investigate and take steps to enforce.) Moreover, **Standard 12** of **Part I** declares that good faith whistle-blowing about violations of the standards should be protected from reprisals.
>
> In this case Dr. Kantzer has clearly behaved unethically. He has violated **Part I, Standard 2.** He has done this in order to please his funding sources. It is less clear that the state official behaved unethically. His remarks about the commissioner's views may have been entirely innocent. Even if he made the remarks intending to influence Kantzer, it would be hard to prove misconduct. He has not asked Kantzer to change his conclusions or fudge his data. He may be relying on Kantzer for some self-censorship knowing that Kantzer knows that his "reliability" is one reason why he regularly gets state contracts. This conduct would surely be unethical, but the official has maintained plausible deniability.

QUESTIONS

1. Are researchers who observe violations of their professional ethical standards by others obliged to do anything? Are they obliged to confront those whom they have observed? To persuade

them to rectify their misconduct? To report them to an authority? Could one reasonably expect this of a powerless graduate student? Should there be a mechanism for anonymous whistle-blowing?

2. Who is responsible for enforcing the professional standards of education researchers?: the researchers themselves, their professional organization, the institution where they do their research, sponsoring organizations, or ordinary law enforcement officials?

3. Should this case be reported to the AERA? What might the AERA do about it? Might the AERA take this issue up with the state without accusing the state official or proving his guilt?

4. Why is **Standard 4** of **Part V** the only one with a reporting clause? Is there something especially important at stake here for the AERA?

VI

PART

GUIDING STANDARDS:
STUDENTS AND
STUDENT RESEARCHERS

The Preamble, the Standards, and Their Rationale

Preamble
Educational researchers have a responsibility to ensure the competence of those inducted into the field and to provide appropriate help and professional advice to novice researchers.

STANDARDS

1   *In relations with students and student researchers, educational researchers should be candid, fair, nonexploitative, and committed to their welfare and progress. They should conscientiously supervise, encourage, and support students and student researchers in their academic endeavors, and should appropriately assist them in securing research support or professional employment.*

2   *Students and student researchers should be selected based upon their competence and potential contributions to the field. Educational researchers should not discriminate among students and student researchers on the basis of gender, sexual orientation, marital status, color, social class, religion, ethnic background, national origin, or other irrelevant factors.*

3   *Educational researchers should inform students and student researchers concerning the ethical dimensions of research, encourage their practice of research consistent with ethical standards, and support their avoidance of questionable projects.*

4   *Educational researchers should realistically apprise students and student researchers with regard to career opportunities and implications associated with their participation in particular research projects or degree programs. Educational researchers should ensure that research assistantships be educative.*

5   *Educational researchers should be fair in the evaluation of research performance, and should communicate that evaluation fully and honestly to the student or student researcher. Researchers have an obligation to report honestly on the competence of assistants to other professionals who require such evaluations.*

6   *Educational researchers should not permit personal animosities or intellectual differences vis-à-vis colleagues to foreclose student and student researcher access to those colleagues, or to place the student or student researcher in an untenable position with those colleagues.*

RATIONALE

The standards of **Part VI** directly address the claims made in the code's **Foreword** that researchers should view themselves as educators as well as researchers and should be responsible for the competence of those they induct into the field. Indeed, the standards of **Part VI** may be read as expressing an expansive view of the role of educator since researchers are not only to care for their students' academic progress, but are also to provide encouragement and support and to care for their students' welfare. Ensuring competence in novice researchers requires careful selection, responsible instruction (ensuring that assistantships be educative, for example), conscientious supervision, candid evaluation, communication of ethical standards, and giving honest assessments of students' competence to others in the field.

The standards in **Part VI** couple the obligation to ensure competence with the responsibility of supporting and nurturing students and student researchers, including helping students advance their careers through providing appropriate professional advice and assisting them in obtaining research support and jobs. Finally, relationships with students and novice researchers must accord with relevant moral norms such as fairness, honesty, nonexploitation, and nondiscrimination.

The **Preamble** itself suggests that educational researchers have two broad obligations with respect to students and student researchers, presumably incorporating those noted previously. The first, the obligation to ensure that they are competent, involves providing proper training and supervision as well as making sound and candid decisions about whom to admit to training and practice. The second is an obligation to nurture novice researchers through commitment to their professional development. Whereas most of the standards discussed so far forbid various actions, the standards of **Part VI** also seem to require researchers to assume certain affirmative duties.

The six standards of **Part VI** emphasize the obligations associated with training future researchers and suggest that a fundamental responsibility of those who have advanced or specialized knowledge is to share that knowledge. Researchers have a general obligation to make their discoveries known through publication and other dissemination because only knowledge that is shared has value to others.

Researchers also, however, have a special obligation to share their knowledge with novices. This responsibility is quite clear in the case of typical faculty-student relationships in a classroom or other formal instructional setting but it extends to other expert-novice relationships such as those between advisor and advisee, principal investigator and research assistant, and experienced researcher and new colleague.

There are three principal bases for experts' responsibility to properly educate novices. First, experts have an obligation to the field of education and its consumers to ensure the competence of their students. The field, in general, suffers when poor students are sent out to struggle with the demands of research or continue on without any awareness of their deficiencies and errors.

Integrity, credibility, and potential impact are maintained in educational research only through high standards in the preparation of researchers and provision of adequate support for newcomers to meet those standards. **Part I** of the code, *Responsibilities to the Field*, cites the gatekeeping side of this obligation—enjoining researchers to hire and recommend only competent researchers. But since educational researchers have the primary responsibility for educating future researchers, the continued competence of the research community depends greatly on the quality and conscientiousness of their instruction.

Second, students and novices have a right to proper training and guidance from the expert researchers who are their teachers and supervisors. By definition, only experts have the specialized knowledge that novices need to develop into competent educational researchers. While the profession broadly has the responsibility to train new scholars, the standards do not explicitly state who has the educative responsibility with respect to any particular student or novice.

Certainly, not every researcher can have the duty to nurture every aspiring scholar. It is assumed that these obligations are generated within the context of particular relationships. In some cases, the responsibility follows on accepting certain roles in educational institutions, for example, when students take courses from the professors who agree to teach them. In other cases, graduate students may elect to work under the direction of a particular researcher who agrees to supervise the student's work.

Less clear from the **Standards** are the obligations of senior scholars to mentor newly credentialed researchers who work with them, or who are simply new faculty members in the same institution. While these novice researchers are no longer "students" in an official sense, they nevertheless have some claim to help from those who are more experienced, for the reasons described in this discussion.

Third, educational researchers' responsibility to novices rests in part on their own self-interest. This is clearly present in the case of principal investigators supervising the work of research assistants. The quality of investigators' own work depends on their conscientious supervision and instruction of their assistants. Further, if senior researchers' own contributions to research are used and extended, subsequent generations of researchers must be prepared to do that work. Senior researchers can never accomplish all the worthy projects that they can envision. They must ensure that their successors are competent to carry on the research traditions they have initiated.

Beyond the commitment to properly train novice researchers, senior researchers have a responsibility to ensure through conscientious gatekeeping that only competent researchers are inducted into the field. Here the standards recognize that one of the roles of educational researchers is to decide who is admitted to training to become an educational researcher, and who is to be credentialed and hired to do research after training. The **Preamble** tells us that only those who are competent are to be admitted to the field. Presumably, this includes both credentialing, usually through awarding advanced degrees, as well as hiring for research positions. This is an obligation that is owed largely to the field and to the consumers of educational research. It assumes that the social value of educational research depends on both the integrity and expertise of educational researchers and the credibility of the field (see **Part I**). It is also rooted in the assumption that judgments of the novice researcher's competence are professional judgments that can only be made by those who are competent in the field whose practitioners they are judging.

The **Preamble** tells us that the obligation to train and induct competent researchers is matched by an obligation to nurture novice researchers by providing appropriate help and professional guidance. Beyond the acquiring of research knowledge and skills, students are dependent on senior researchers for information on the process of educational research—getting funded, complying with human subjects requirements and meeting other ethical standards, working through the processes of manuscript or proposal submissions, and other processes. They also need to learn about the various norms, assumptions, and preferences that typically underlie educational researchers' work, and they need advice on strategies for career development and promising avenues for research. Only someone who has gone on ahead of the novice can help him or her along the path toward a life in educational research. Indeed, those who have succeeded have done so because of such help from others; they repay their obligation by helping their students.

The standards of **Part VI** view the training, nurturing, and evaluation of students as taking place within a complex set of relationships. As will be shown, these relationships involve multiple obligations such as competent evaluation, fair treatment, candor, concern for the student's welfare, nondiscrimination, nonexploitation, and competent and timely career advice. Some aspects of expert-novice relationships have been addressed in previous parts of the code and are not repeated in **Part VI. Standard 11** of **Part I** prohibits all forms of harassment of students and student researchers, including the coercion of *personal or sexual favors or economic or professional advantages.* **Standard 5** of **Part II** forbids researchers from requiring students to become participants in their research. And **Part III** covers fairness in acknowledging student contributions to any publications that result from research in which they have been involved.

Responsibility in the expert-novice relationship is not one-sided, however. Students also have responsibilities toward their teachers, work, research participants, colleagues, peers, and others. They must be held accountable for their behaviors. This responsibility implies a need for educational researchers to make sure that students understand what is ethically appropriate behavior in the conduct of research, in the relationships that support that research, or in other aspects of their work. It also implies that experts should foster novices' commitment to exhibiting appropriate behavior over time. Educational researchers are therefore responsible for communicating the ethical dimensions of research to their students.

It should be noted that the **Preamble** and the standards that follow do not address some questions that might have been appropriately addressed in **Part VI.** In some cases, answers to these questions are implicit in the standards, either in **Part VI** or elsewhere. In other cases, they are not.

For example, we have argued that the obligations to train, nurture, and evaluate students addressed in **Part VI** arise in the context of particular relationships between the researcher and the student. There are some sensitive issues concerning when these relationships can be undertaken and when they can be dissolved. The rationale for these standards views the relationship between those researchers who have responsibilities to train and credential students and their students as an expert-novice relationship and suggests that researchers have a duty not to enter into supervisory relationships with students whose work they are not competent to judge.

Also, some of the difficulties we have noted elsewhere concerning the standards' call for acceptance of multiple perspectives and standards for judging research become issues here. How is a researcher to relate with a graduate student when their views of an appropriate approach or appropriate standards differ? Do novice researchers have the same right as do mature scholars to have their approaches to research judged on their own terms? Although **Standard 6** enjoins researchers not to let their intellectual differences with colleagues limit their students' access to those colleagues, the standards say nothing about conflicts between researchers and their own students. Because students may have limited choice of faculty to work with within their areas of specialization in some departments and because graduate assistants may be assigned to work on faculty projects outside of their areas of expertise, intellectual differences between expert and novice are a real possibility.

The standards of **Part VI** indicate that the relationship between a novice and an expert must be conducted for the benefit of the student, and that the relationship must be fair, educative, and nonexploitive. However, the standards take only the briefest note of how this relationship is formed and how it might be dissolved when it is not going well.

Second, there is no standard that insists that the teaching relationship between expert and novice be exercised responsibly, despite the emphasis of the standards on the educational aspects of the relationship between experts and novices. Perhaps this is because not all researchers have a formal teaching relationship to their assistants or because these matters are assumed to be covered by other codes, such as the American Association of University Professors (AAUP) code for college and university faculty. Nevertheless, the importance of proper teaching to the development of competent researchers suggests an implicit commitment of the code to responsible and conscientious instruction, whether formal or informal.

Neither is there an explicit standard requiring that only those who have demonstrated competence be credentialed. **Part I, Standard 9** only requires researchers not to recommend those who are manifestly unfit. In **Part VI,** the **Preamble** insists that researchers have the responsibility to ensure the competence of those who are to be inducted into the field; **Standard 2** indicates that students and student researchers be selected on their competence and potential; and **Standard 5** requires researchers to supply honest evaluations of the competence of their assistants to those who need them. Therefore, it seems reasonable to assume the code implicitly subscribes to the notion that only those who have demonstrated their competence to do satisfactory research should be credentialed or hired.

Finally, the standards of **Part VI** hint that the obligations researchers have to their students go beyond the professional aspects of the mentor-student relationship, and involve broader obligations to care for students' welfare. The possibility of such obligations raises two issues. First, we need a view of how these obligations arise, of their content and scope, and of how they are to be distinguished from professionally rooted obligations. Second, we need some wisdom on how such further obligations are balanced against those duties that characterize the professional relationship between researcher and student. For example: what obligations do researchers have to be concerned about the personal lives of their students, and when and how might they accommodate students' personal needs when these interfere with their professional responsibilities? Note also that although the standards of **Part VI** hint of such obligations, it is possible to argue that, while it would be a good thing for researchers to care about their students' welfare in areas that go beyond their professional relationship, there can be no duties to do so. Taking on such responsibilities is optional.

There may be two reasons why these issues are not taken up in the standards of **Part VI.** One may be that the writers of the standards did not feel it appropriate to take up such issues. The other may be that it is difficult to deal with these matters in the language of a code of ethics. The reader will find that questions of the scope and nature of any duty to care for the welfare of students dominate in the cases that follow. Perhaps these matters require wisdom and judgment and are difficult to codify. Nevertheless, we are hopeful that they can be illuminated by a sensitive discussion of cases.

While **Part VI** does not address every ethical dimension of the expert-novice relationship, its general principles of developing and acknowledging competence, and of nurturing students in relationships conducted for their welfare, provide a framework with the rest of the standards for evaluating many of the situations that may arise. In some cases, however, standards governing particular situations need to be inferred or guidance needs to be sought elsewhere.

Interpretation of the Standards: Issues, Cases, and Discussions

ISSUE

The expectation that researchers will nurture new scholars best fits the relationship between primary investigators, their graduate assistants and their graduate student advisees. In the case of graduate assistants, training takes place primarily through the student's active engagement in a research project, hence, the requirement that the project be educative and that students receive proper support and supervision.

Part of the supervisory process for both assistants and advisees will involve honest feedback and evaluation that allows students to recognize their errors and make improvements. In these contexts, researchers will communicate ethical standards of research by obeying them themselves and by insisting that their students do the same. The overall obligation of the researcher to promote the welfare and progress of students clearly emphasizes the educative function of the expert-novice relationship, forbidding researchers from regarding students as merely a source of labor or from enforcing conditions of work that strongly interfere with students' academic pursuits.

Nurturing young scholars, however, is often more a matter of conscientiousness and good judgment than the following of rules and prescriptions. This fact is reflected in several of the cases that follow. For example, in the next case, exercising the conscientiousness expected by **Standard 1** means that advisors must find a reasonable balance between supervision and independence.

Case 1

TaShera spent many hours lying awake in the middle of the night, trying to figure out exactly what had gone wrong. When she started working as Professor Cain's research assistant, everything seemed great. At that point, the project had already been underway for two years. It involved on-site work in middle schools, where TaShera felt very comfortable because of her earlier teaching experience. She was excited to be working with Professor Cain, whose work she admired very much. She was flattered that Professor Cain had chosen her for the project and she wanted to do her best on it.

At first, TaShera and Professor Cain met twice a week to discuss the work, and Professor Cain accompanied her on every site visit. Over time, though, Professor Cain came to rely on TaShera more and more. Eventually she let TaShera take over all of the on-site work, and their conferences with each other dwindled to one a month. When Professor Cain got an invitation to spend four weeks at a university in China, she felt confident that TaShera could continue collecting data in her absence.

By this time, however, there was trouble brewing. In TaShera's eagerness to impress Professor Cain by collecting extremely detailed data, her regular visits to the middle school had become more and more disruptive to classroom routines. The three teachers involved expressed their concerns to TaShera in varying degrees of sternness. TaShera did not want Professor Cain to think that she couldn't handle the situation, so she did not tell her about the growing problems. By the time the teachers decided to express their complaints directly to Professor Cain, however, the professor was on her way to China. The teachers therefore requested a joint meeting with TaShera and told her very clearly what she would and would not be allowed to do in their classes from that point on.

TaShera felt caught between what she thought Professor Cain wanted in terms of data collection and the new conditions that the teachers imposed. What seemed worse to her, though, was that she had grown to hate the entire project. She no longer felt welcome or comfortable in the middle school, and she dreaded Professor Cain's return when she would have to take the blame for ruining the research project.

Discussion: Research assistant positions are one of the best means for graduate students to get hands-on experience doing research. Their educative potential is high, but as **Standard 1** points out, this potential can only be realized if the student receives conscientious supervision and support. While Professor Cain seems to have initially provided appropriate support, she appears to have overestimated TaShera's readiness for the degree of responsibility she now holds. It is never an easy matter to set the proper balance between constant supervision that inhibits a student's growth as an independent researcher and a hands-off approach that amounts to negligence. Furthermore, there is a potential for conflict between giving student researchers room to fail in the interest of their education and maintaining the integrity of the research. It may not be easy to decide when a senior researcher's mistakes in judgment amount to unethical behavior.

However, Professor Cain has so lost contact with this research site that, not only has TaShera's educational experience soured, but the research is now on shaky ethical grounds. **Part II** of the **Standards** requires researchers to be mindful of the potential disruptions to institutional life that may result from their research and counsels them to minimize negative impacts. TaShera's eagerness to collect the detailed data she believes Professor Cain wants appears to have had disruptive consequences, at least from the teachers' perspectives. Not only is Professor Cain not conveying the proper ethical standards to TaShera, as required by **Standard 3** of **Part VI ,** she may have put pressure on TaShera to behave in an unethical manner.

TaShera does not appear to be entirely blameless, however. While the code is silent on the responsibilities of students and student researchers, surely students have a responsibility to keep faculty supervisors informed about ongoing research, acknowledging that faculty members have the ultimate responsibility for the direction, procedures, and products of the research. Students are supposed to be governed by the same professional standards that govern the behavior of expert researchers. TaShera should have reported the teachers' concerns to Professor Cain as soon as she became aware of them. Nevertheless, the primary responsibility for ensuring that the research is being properly conducted belongs to Professor Cain. She should have made TaShera aware of the importance of keeping her informed and made sure that the lines of communication were open.

ISSUE

Standard 1 requires researchers to be both candid and fair to their students and student researchers, and also to encourage and support them. These two requirements may need to be balanced.

Case 2

Alice Brownsell was angry. She worked hard on the literature review for Professor Sharon Henderson, and she believed she did a good job. Professor Henderson thought otherwise. Her note to Alice began with the comment "Alice, this is entirely unacceptable." This was followed by a detailed critique of Alice's review. It ended with the line "If you're going to continue to work with me, you need to be more conscientious in your work. This reads like you dashed it off in your spare time over the weekend."

In fact, Alice spent almost two weeks doing the work. Maybe she didn't put every available minute into it, but she did put in every second of the fifteen hours a week her assistantship required and then some. As she read over Professor Henderson's comments, many seemed picky. Some seemed wrong. She decided to discuss the comments in detail with Professor Henderson and demand an accounting.

This proved not to be a good idea. While she had not intended to be confrontational, she did have to admit (with 20/20 hindsight) that she was a bit aggressive. Professor Henderson started out patiently, but eventually responded in kind. Words like "inept" and "incompetent" worked their way into the discussion with increasing regularity. By the end, Professor Henderson clearly was enjoying the drubbing she was handing out. Even worse, as the conversation wore on, it became increasingly clear to Alice that Professor Henderson was right. She didn't do a good job. She didn't have a clear idea of what was required. Alice finally saw both that Professor Henderson had a point and that being confrontational with the person who was responsible for her support was not a good idea. She rose and left quickly. She still recalled, with deep embarrassment, her parting shot. She had stood in the doorway and said, "Well you may be right, but you're not very affirming." She was not sure she could ever face Professor Henderson again.

Discussion: While Alice's last comment may have been unwise, it may also express some wisdom about this case. **Standard 1** can be understood as asking Professor Henderson to temper fair and accurate criticism with encouragement and kindness. However, her initial response to Alice's work appears to have been merely blunt and critical. Although it may have been accurate, it seems insensitive to Alice's need for some help and encouragement. A beginning remark, such as "Alice, I know you're new at this, so it's important for me to be clear that this is not what I expected from you," and a concluding comment like "Let's sit down and go over this so you'll understand what I need from you" might have encouraged Alice to enter into their meeting with a more constructive attitude.

Moreover, even if Alice's demeanor was provocative, Professor Henderson should have been mature enough not to respond in kind. A patient explanation of what was expected might have helped Alice to progress in her work. Professor Henderson should not be expected to accept substandard work or to refrain from criticizing it when she receives it. However, she should avoid sarcasm and disparagement. **Standard 1** suggests that she needs to find a better balance between candor and encouragement than she has here.

ISSUE

In addition to the responsibility to educate new scholars, the obligation to ensure the competence of those inducted into the field requires senior researchers to serve as gatekeepers. The standards require the gatekeepers' judgments to be based on the competence of those judged and to be fair, candid, and nondiscriminatory. **Standard 2** requires that students and student researchers be selected *based upon their competence and potential contributions to the field,* not on the basis of characteristics such as *gender, sexual orientation, marital status, color, social class, religion, ethnic background, national origin, or other irrelevant factors.* (Note: On comparing this standard with **Standard 8** of **Part I** on discrimination in hiring and retention, one finds that the categories listed are identical with the exception of the mention of *physical disability* in this standard but not **Part VI, Standard 2.** Because there is no apparent reason for prohibiting discrimination on the basis of physical disabilities in hiring and retention, but not in admission to graduate school, it can be assumed that disability is covered in **Standard 2** of **Part VI** under *other irrelevant factors.* Similarly, as in **Standard 8** of **Part I,** "irrelevant" means "irrelevant to" research competence.)

Case 3

Professor Assize had just finished reading the file of new applicants to his department's Ph.D. program. Some seemed promising, he thought, but he was troubled by the growing number of applicants from Russia. The two students previously admitted from Russia had not worked out. They were poorly prepared academically and were unable to read English well enough to keep up with the required reading. Although they had managed to complete their coursework, writing acceptable dissertations was impossible. They had both dropped out of the program. Professor Assize resolved to vote against the new applicants from Russia at the next faculty meeting.

Discussion: Professor Assize is discriminating against the new applicants from Russia since he is making his assessment based on their national origin rather than on the evidence presented in the application concerning their *competence and potential contributions* as **Standard 2** requires. Even if he had had negative experiences with many more than two students from Russia, the **Standards** still would require that he evaluate each applicant as an individual on the basis of his or her claim to competence.

ISSUE

Standard 2 may be violated not only in the overt way described in the previous case, but in more subtle ways.

Case 4

There seemed to be a pretty solid consensus in the department: if you wanted to get your career off to a flying start, you did your doctoral dissertation with Professor Warren. He demanded extraordinary effort and had very high standards, but if you made it through the program with him, he could open doors for you that most of his colleagues didn't even know existed.

Kim was very ambitious and hoped for a career in educational research. She worked extremely hard in Professor Warren's educational finance course in hopes of impressing him. Her undergraduate major in economics served her well, and she caught Professor Warren's attention. At the end of the course, he asked her if she would be interested in working with him on a research project on school-finance reform. She eagerly accepted his offer. Before long, Professor Warren was also Kim's academic advisor, and a part of the research project was taking shape as Kim's dissertation. True to his reputation, Professor Warren was generous with his ideas and advice and would accept nothing but hard work and excellence in return.

Kim was aware that most of Professor Warren's other advisees—and all of those who worked on his research projects, except herself—were men. She didn't think much about this, assuming that he tended to attract advisees from male-dominated fields such as economics, and she was used to being in the female minority in those fields.

After some time, however, she noticed that the other graduate assistants seemed to have a lot more firsthand knowledge about Professor Warren and his lifestyle than she did. It appeared that most of them had been guests in his home or had traveled to conferences where he had introduced them around. To be fair, Professor Warren once caught her as she was leaving an on-campus lecture given by a visiting colleague of his. He introduced her to the lecturer but then bustled away, leaving them to chat awkwardly.

Professor Warren's frequent international trips proved to be excellent opportunities for him to showcase his best student talent. Kim felt that her own particular project had its best audience in the United States, but she couldn't help wondering what tips and insights her graduate peers were getting on those long trips that she never seemed to get to go on.

Discussion: Professor Warren has made many opportunities available to Kim, but he has not treated her fairly in comparison with her male peers. Although he may be unaware of his own behavior, and may not intend to be discriminating on the basis of gender, he appears to be doing so. The example of Professor Warren points out that gatekeeping decisions, such as admission, credentialing, hiring, or retention, are not the only points where discrimination can take place. The sort of mentoring and sponsorship Kim's peers were receiving can make all the difference between professional mediocrity and success. **Standard 2** precludes more than discrimination in selection of students. It also indicates that researchers have an obligation to make career development opportunities available without regard to educationally irrelevant characteristics. (See also **Hard Case 3.**)

ISSUE

Standard 2 precludes discrimination on the basis of *other irrelevant factors.* In some cases, anti-discrimination laws require employers to accommodate handicaps. Moreover, reasonable and humane employers will try to accommodate their employees' special circumstances even if they are not required to do so by law. In work with graduate students, knowing what is reasonable in accommodating special circumstances may be more difficult than in other work settings. Understandings about how much work can be expected and when it is to be done are often informal. Even when institutions have guidelines or policies on the matter, sometimes the boundaries between the paid work a student does for a project and the work the student does on his or her own academic program are unclear.

Case 5

Margaret was walking home from an appointment with her advisor, Professor Douglas, a highly respected scholar, who had devoted her career to studying various aspects of early childhood. Margaret's fondness for children was part of her attraction to early childhood education as an area of study. Now she and her husband wanted children of their own, and having just married in their mid-thirties, they did not want to postpone a pregnancy. Unfortunately, they were obliged to go through the considerable stress of infertility treatments, and the frequent medical appointments were causing ongoing complications in the research laboratory's schedule. Professor Douglas finally called Margaret in and told her that unless she was willing to give the research project the undivided attention it deserved, she would be asked to leave the project.

Margaret was devastated to think that she might have to give up either her work on Professor Douglas's project or her hopes for a family.

> **Discussion:** It is clear that Professor Douglas cannot, in effect, make Margaret's continued childlessness a condition of her employment. Professor Douglas may have high expectations for Margaret's commitment to research, but she does not own all of Margaret's time or life. However, it is also clear that Professor Douglas does have a reasonable expectation that Margaret will fulfill her duties to the project. We are not told in this case whether Margaret is not doing her work adequately or whether she is merely asking Professor Douglas for some flexibility in when it is done. Ideally, in cases of this sort, Professor Douglas should be willing to accommodate Margaret's schedule so long as Margaret is able to do her work responsibly. If Margaret and Professor Douglas are not able to come to a workable agreement, they might consider using a mediator. Senior researchers' commitment to the welfare of students, and the mentoring relationships they form with them, may involve them in issues extending beyond the professional sphere. They are involved when their students' personal lives have ramifications for their professional lives. The standards do not clearly obligate researchers to offer help or support outside the professional sphere, presumably leaving the degree of involvement here to the judgment of the individual and the nature of the relationship. Nevertheless, the standards do not forbid sympathy, understanding, and attempts to accommodate special circumstances.

ISSUE

Standard 3 asks researchers to mentor their students concerning the ethical dimensions of research. This may mean more than researchers providing occasional comments on ethics or answering questions when they are asked. It may require them to be ethical role models even to the point of admitting their own mistakes.

Case 6

"This will look great on my curriculum vita!" thought Patrick excitedly as he drove home from a meeting with his advisor, Professor Yates. Yates was an eminent researcher who had just hired him to help with a major research project. Professor Yates had collected data through a nation-wide survey of high school principals, and although he had already begun to publish findings from the surveys, he wanted Patrick's help with the data analysis for further papers. Patrick's first task was to take care of a few coding errors in the data set by comparing certain data entries to responses on the original survey forms. In going through the surveys one by one, Patrick discovered a different problem. The survey had been sent out to three groups of principals whose schools had been involved in one of three new federal initiatives (A, B, or C). The last section of the survey was addressed only to the A and B principals, and the C principals were asked to skip that section. When Patrick joined the research project, Professor Yates had just published a manuscript, based on responses from that section, that showed significant differences between the A and B schools in student achievement, retention, and graduation rates.

While reviewing the survey forms, however, Patrick chanced upon a survey in which the last section was completed by a principal whose school participated in initiative C. He wondered how many other C principals might have made the same mistake. Doing some simple checks on the data, he discovered that nearly 34% of the respondents had misinterpreted the instructions that in retrospect seemed unclear and had either responded when they should not have or vice versa. The data-entry personnel had not caught the problem, and it appeared that Professor Yates had not caught it when he did the early analyses.

Patrick cleaned up the data set the best he could and then, out of curiosity, reran the statistics on which Professor Yates's recent publication was based. He found absolutely no statistically significant differences between the A and B principals: the previous significant finding had been due entirely to responses from C principals who were supposed to have skipped the survey's final section.

Patrick felt very uneasy as he knocked on his advisor's door, evidence in hand. When he explained what he had discovered, Professor Yates dismissed his concerns, attributing them to Patrick's relative inexperience in data analysis. Patrick left Professor Yates's office shaking his head. Three months later, however, the paper was retracted.

Discussion: Patrick appears to have uncovered a serious mistake in the data coding and analysis. **Part I** of the code makes it plain that researchers should not misrepresent data, findings, or conclusions and that they should not jeopardize future research or the discipline's research results through their work. While there is no evidence here of deliberate misrepresentation in the analysis or publication in question, once Professor Yates has been made aware of the problem, he should take steps to rectify the error. Apparently, he did so by retracting the previously published paper based on this work.

His treatment of Patrick, however, clearly fails to make plain to Patrick Professor Yates's support of appropriate research standards and the ethical dimensions of research as required by **Standard 3.** Perhaps initially he could be justified in thinking that the mistake was more likely to be Patrick's than his own. Nevertheless, he should have taken Patrick's concerns very seriously and given them his immediate attention. He also should have discussed with Patrick the import and implications of the new evidence to let him know that such problems cannot be handled lightly. Finally, after careful review of Patrick's analyses, he should have immediately taken steps to address the problem as an example to Patrick of how to take responsibility for errors. These steps would have honored Professor Yates's obligation to encourage and support Patrick in his academic work (**Standard 1**), as well as supporting Patrick's concern with competent and ethical research.

ISSUE

Standard 4 requires researchers to ensure that research assistantships are educative. Often, however, researchers who value their time are inclined to want to spend it on the more interesting and complex aspects of their research while assigning more routine tasks to research assistants.

Case 7

Andre Lumumba looked with some bemusement at the Castle and Moat adorning the sweatshirt he had gotten from the university's bookstore. "If this place had considered my assistantship," he thought, "the appropriate symbol would have been a doormat." Andre had spent most of his work time for the last few weeks in the library doing bibliographical research. When he had searched the educational databases using the keywords Professor Mercer had given him, he came up with a list of 357 papers. Professor Mercer had said that there were a few that he didn't need to know about. When he returned the list to Andre, he had reduced the list to 342, for each of which he wanted a one-paragraph synopsis. Andre had not encountered a new idea anywhere after article 25 and he was having difficulty staying awake. Moreover, it was plain from the papers' references, that only about a dozen of the papers on the list were important. But Professor Mercer wished to leave no stone unturned, and he had Andre to turn them. Andre sighed, and began to read article 59.

> **Discussion:** Professor Mercer has turned his assistant, Andre Lumumba, into a gopher. While the work Andre is doing may, in Professor Mercer's judgment, be necessary, it has ceased to be educative for Andre. Does **Standard 4** mean that it is unethical for Professor Mercer to assign this work to Andre? This is not clear. We should first consider that if the work is genuinely necessary, someone has to do it. If Andre is Professor Mercer's only assistant, the someone else may be Professor Mercer himself. While it might be thought that researchers should share the more onerous labor with their assistants equitably, it is also the case that one reason why research assistants are funded is to allow skilled researchers to spend their time on those tasks that are more productive or which demand the attention of people who are highly qualified and, quite likely, expensive. Thus, there are reasons why those members of research teams who are least experienced should be asked to do a disproportionate amount of the routine work. We should also note that, even if Andre has ceased to learn much from his reading, the work he is doing probably does require some skill, and he may well learn something more from further reading. We are thus not able to say that Professor Mercer has clearly violated **Standard 4.**

> However, there is more to say. Both Andre and Professor Mercer should be expected to look at Andre's work over his career and over the duration of his time on the project. **Standard 4** should not be understood to prevent Professor Mercer from assigning Andre some work that is routine and not especially educative, but he should ensure that this is not typical of the work that Andre does throughout his assistantship.

ISSUE

Standard 5 states that researchers *should be fair in the evaluation of research performance, and should . . . report honestly on the competence of assistants to other professionals who require such evaluations.* **Part I** of the code develops similar standards for hiring, retention, and advancement (see **Standard 8, Cases 8–13,** and for personnel recommendations see **Standard 9, Case 18**).

Thus it seems reasonable to suppose that the code implies that only the competent, or those who have the potential to develop appropriate competence, should be admitted to training and only the competent should be credentialed and hired. Ensuring competence is presumably the responsibility of the expert researchers who train, certify, and hire because only those who have the relevant expertise are qualified to judge whether others meet the appropriate standards. Proper exercise of the function requires both not admitting to the profession those who are manifestly incompetent and not unjustly excluding those who are competent.

Case 8

Professor Reed sighed and reached over to turn on her computer. There was no point in avoiding the day's task any longer. Normally she wouldn't mind writing recommendations for her own advisees, but today she didn't feel up to the challenge.

First there was Albert. She really couldn't have asked for a harder-working research assistant than Albert. He not only kept their collaborative project moving, but he took the initiative in pursuing all promising leads. He was reliable, conscientious, and cheerfully helpful. That said, she knew that his primary limitation was his inadequate academic background. He had gotten through his master's degree and into his doctoral program on the strength of the collaborative work he had done with his previous advisor on a project that had made the advisor quite famous. Just what Albert contributed to that project was never quite clear, although Professor Reed suspected that he was primarily responsible for the minutiae, at which he would have been very good. His writing skills were inadequate, his ability to conceptualize or generalize material was limited, and he struggled daily to rise to the challenge of doctoral level work.

Now he had asked Professor Reed for a recommendation for a postdoctoral fellowship. It would involve working with one of the most eminent scholars in the field, and Professor Reed knew that Albert just might get it if she wrote a glowing recommendation. Professor Reed cringed when she thought about what was likely to happen if Albert got the fellowship—he would be eaten alive in the high-intensity world of the eminent scholar's work.

But Albert wasn't the only problem. Professor Reed had also agreed to write a recommendation for Barry. Although Barry was not quite finished with his dissertation, he was applying for a position as a policy analyst in a federal agency. Barry's credentials, like Albert's, looked good on paper, but for a very different reason. Barry was extremely bright and had breezed through his ivy-league undergraduate years as well as his graduate work with very little effort. He just never put much into his work. He seemed to know how to allocate his effort to the most strategically important tasks to keep his career going, but Professor Reed had long ago given up trying to motivate him to anything beyond minimal effort or commitment.

Professor Reed knew personally the director of the federal program to which Barry was applying. She knew that the director expected hard work and long hours from her small staff. Professor Reed knew that if Barry got the job, the situation was likely to end in bitter disappointment all around.

> **Discussion:** The standards of **Part VI** require Professor Reed to be committed to her students' welfare and progress and to help them find research funding and jobs. On the other hand, they also demand that she report honestly on her students' competence to other professionals who request her evaluation. These two standards are not really in conflict here. She must give her honest evaluation of her students' ability to perform well in the positions they desire. She must also, however, share her concerns candidly with the students themselves to make them aware of what she perceives as potential problems, and to prepare them the best she can to address those problems. Indeed, insofar as these students' problems have been evident during their graduate careers, Professor Reed should have already shared these judgments with them as part of her obligation to communicate her evaluations of their research performance to them *fully and honestly* as **Standard 5** requires.

Should Professor Reed counsel Albert and Barry not to apply for these positions? Doing so could unjustly preclude her students from taking advantage of professionally superior opportunities. And no one can know for sure how a person will perform in a new environment. Not telling her students what she knows about the domains that they seek to enter, however, could compromise their own options to withdraw themselves as candidates for positions that might well prove disastrous.

Are these students competent to be inducted into the field of educational research? Professor Reed apparently does not raise this question. The question seems to be most pressing with respect to Albert. While Barry's work ethic may be lacking, he is not described as incompetent. But Professor Reed believes that Albert's writing skills and conceptual abilities are poor. He barely measures up to appropriate doctoral standards. Is Professor Reed behaving unethically in credentialing and recommending Albert? Deciding where the bar should be set for induction into the field of educational research is a difficult judgment.

However these questions are answered, it should be clear that the one option that is not open to Professor Reed is to mislead those to whom her letters are sent as to the qualifications and capacities of her students.

ISSUE

May educational researchers preclude their students from taking classes with colleagues whom they disrespect?

Case 9

Petra Imanez, a beginning graduate student, was shocked by her conversation with Dr. Huslander. Dr. Huslander was both Petra's chair and the supervisor of her assistantship. Dr. Huslander was one of the country's more prominent economists of education. Petra felt fortunate to work with him. However, when Petra had brought in her tentative course schedule for Dr. Huslander to sign, he had insisted that she drop the course she had wished to take in qualitative methods from Professor Fred Presser. "Qualitative research just isn't science," Huslander had said. "It produces nothing generalizable and of worth. I won't have my students wasting their time with this participant observer nonsense or with fools like Presser who promote it."

Discussion: This may seem a paradigmatic case of what **Standard 6** is intended to forbid. Dr. Huslander has forbidden Petra Imanez from taking a course from Dr. Presser apparently because he holds Dr. Presser's methodology in contempt and dislikes Presser himself. We believe that Professor Huslander has violated **Standard 6,** but we do not believe that this is self-evident. Some explanation is called for.

Consider that it is reasonable for advisors to take into account the competence of their colleagues or the relevance of their fields for their students' programs. Although advisers should certainly take pains to avoid gratuitous negative appraisals of colleagues, if they are aware that some colleague's course is badly done, it would also be irresponsible for them to ignore this in advising students. Additionally, suppose that Petra Imanez had been a third year student about to begin a thesis in which qualitative methods played no part. In this case, it might be reasonable to advise her that this course did not contribute to her thesis work.

However, these are not the reasons Dr. Huslander has given. He does not claim that Professor Presser is incompetent, and he does not argue that the timing of Presser's course does not fit into Petra's program. Instead, his grounds appear to be of two sorts. First, he does not value Professor Presser's methodology. Here we should note that although tolerance for methodological diversity is not mentioned in **Standard 6** or elsewhere in **Part VI,** it is a significant theme of the **Standards** occurring in the **Foreword,** the **Preamble** of **Part I,** and **Standard 1a** of **Part IV.** It is thus reasonable to conclude that AERA gives methodological pluralism considerable weight and that it is a principle that can be applied in graduate education. So long as an approach has legitimacy, it is improper for Professor Huslander to forbid a student from taking it for no reason other than that he opposes it. Second, Professor Huslander's distaste for Professor Presser's methodology seems to have become translated into a distaste for Professor Presser himself. This is clearly improper as a reason to exclude a student from one of Professor Presser's classes.

Hard Cases

ISSUE

The standards of **Part VI** hold senior researchers responsible for more than competent training and fair evaluation in their relationships with novices. The **Preamble** of **Part VI** assigns them the positive obligation to nurture students and student researchers through providing *appropriate help and professional advice.* This obligation entails commitment to the students' *welfare and progress* (**Standard 1**). Senior researchers are enjoined to *encourage and support students* in their academic programs and to *appropriately assist them in securing research support or professional employment* (**Standard 1**). They should *realistically apprise students and student researchers with regard to career opportunities and implications associated with their participation in particular research projects or degree programs* (**Standard 4**). Together, these standards imply a commitment to the career development of students, apprising them of the practices and mores, and making available the opportunities that lead to a productive career within the educational research community. Within the context of the other standards, it can be inferred that this help should be made available to all students on the basis of their competence. It should also not be distributed in ways that discriminate on the basis of irrelevant factors, such as those listed in **Standard 2**.

Why do senior researchers have these obligations? Successful practice as an educational researcher requires more than technical skill. Novices must acquire the tacit knowledge embedded in expert judgment, as well as practical knowledge of the norms, attitudes, and dispositions of the research community, if they are to be successful in the profession. Only someone already knowledgeable can show a newcomer the way. The same reasons that underlie the senior researchers' obligation to share their technical knowledge and expertise with students provide grounds for nurturing and mentoring them as well. The obligation is generated by a commitment to maintaining the integrity of the field of educational research by a commitment to seeing both one's own research agenda and that of the field furthered, and especially by the particular relationships one enters into with students.

Case 1

"Tina, are you okay?" her friend asked. "What was wrong with that guy, anyway? Was he born a jerk or did he just have it in for you?"

When Tina recovered her voice, she suggested that they find a quiet corner in the conference hotel where they could talk. When they sat down, the first thing she said was that she never expected her first conference presentation to be an occasion for such utter humiliation.

The paper that Tina presented was part of a major research study on which she, her advisor, and several others had been working for a couple of years. She was delighted when her advisor, Professor Bent, suggested that she take the lead authorship on this particular paper and present it on behalf of the group at a national conference. She prepared diligently, and the presentation itself went very well. When she finished, she sat down in relief to listen to the remaining presentations. She was not prepared for the discussant's comments that followed the last presentation. She had assumed that the discussant would summarize and integrate the findings from the session's four papers. Instead, the discussant launched a sharp and detailed critique of each paper. When he got to Tina's paper, he summoned his considerable dramatic skill in accusing her and her collaborators of fraudulent data handling.

It seems that the discussant was very familiar with the research team's earlier publications. One particular paper, based on data from 134 high schools, provided only tenuous support for its primary hypothesis. The discussant noted that Tina's paper, however, presented strong support for a very similar hypothesis and that this finding appeared to have been obtained by dropping from the analysis the high schools from the 27 economically poorest districts. He accused Tina of using unethical means to get statistically significant results.

Tina was aware of the earlier paper, which had been published before she joined the research team. She and her advisor actually had completely justifiable reasons for doing further analyses on a subset of the original data set, but under the pressure of the discussant's accusations and the audience's attention, she was unable to defend their approach in an articulate way. At the session's conclusion, most people left wondering just how appropriately Tina's group had handled their data.

Case 2

Ben Wong wished that he had never submitted the paper for publication. He knew at the time that it had some weaknesses, but he was not prepared for the reviewers' scathing comments. It was clear that they considered reading the manuscript a waste of time, given what one reviewer referred to as "the study's notable deficiencies of conceptual development, design, analysis, and presentation."

He took the setback very hard, because he felt that he had let down his advisor, Professor Kelly, who had been supportive. He had practically written the research-paper proposal for the regional conference where he first presented his results. After the conference, Professor Kelly helped him sort through and respond to the session critic's comments, many of which he dismissed as uninformed or petty. He had been extremely encouraging, as always, in urging Ben to submit the manuscript as soon as possible.

Now that the journal had summarily rejected Ben's paper, Professor Kelly was furious. Ben was startled and even a bit frightened to see Professor Kelly's reaction. He took the rejection personally, immediately phoned the journal's editor whom he knew well, and vented his anger for all on the sixth floor to hear. After slamming down the receiver, he composed himself the best he could. He then quickly drafted a cover letter for Ben to sign and send with the manuscript to another journal. Professor Kelly insisted that he do so that very afternoon.

Discussion: Together, the last two cases point out opposite ways of going wrong in assisting students' career development. While Professor Bent appeared too distant, Professor Kelly is overly involved.

Professor Bent may have failed to prepare Tina adequately to step into the professional arena of educational research. It is not enough for students to have mastered the subject matter of their field. They must also be coached in the arts and mores of professional life. Tina should have been aware that professional scrutiny often demands that researchers defend their work, sometimes on the spot. Preparing for such a defense requires thoughtful consideration of the work's weaknesses, its connection to the broader literature, and its ethical dimensions. Tina was not prepared to deal with any of these aspects of her research. She also did not know what to expect from the discussant and had neither experienced nor anticipated the kind of immediate, harsh, and public criticism that he presented.

Although her advisor helped Tina gain professional experience through making the opportunity to present a conference paper available to her, Professor Bent could have prepared her better for the experience by letting her know what to expect. Tina should not have been ignorant of the role the discussant might play. While the discussant may be faulted for both the severity and tone of his accusations, Tina's advisor could have equipped her better to address any such criticisms with cogency, integrity, and poise. One might also question whether Professor Bent has carefully thought through Tina's professional development. It would have been helpful to Tina to attend conferences prior to making a presentation. Because this was her first conference presentation, one might have expected the advisor to be present, perhaps as a co-presenter, to provide support in case situations such as this one arose.

Of course, advisors cannot be expected to protect students from all negative experiences; handling such setbacks is itself part of professional growth. Nurturing students requires judgment. It is not simply a matter of following a set of rules. Advisors will likely make mistakes, even given the best of intentions. Presumably the standards of **Part VI** here articulate a moral ideal of the expert-novice relationship, an ideal that will be realized to greater or lesser degrees given the humanity, skill, and resources of the senior researcher.

In contrast, and despite what may be good intentions on Professor Kelly's part, his intense personal reaction to Ben Wong's setback is inappropriate. It appears that in championing his career, he may have been less than candid in his assessment of Ben's work. He should have helped Ben to deal directly with the criticisms he received, even if he regarded them as mistakes. In taking Ben's problems personally, he did not give him the opportunity to learn from setbacks or to see his work stand on its own merits. Contrary to **Standard 6,** he may also have put Ben in an untenable position with the journal editor who will not soon forget his association with the overbearing professor.

QUESTIONS

1. Is there any reason to suppose that the respondent's treatment of Tina in her case was unethical? For example, the claim about unethical manipulation of data seems to have been presented as an accusation. Should it have been presented as a question?

2. When professors and students work closely together on projects over a significant period of time, they may become friends, and they may begin to feel a personal interest in one another's work and success. Professor Kelly's reaction to the rejection of Ben Wong's paper may suggest that he is genuinely concerned that Ben do well. Are there other ways in which relationships of care or friendship can go wrong? For example, can professors maintain their objectivity about the quality of work of their students when their students are also their friends? Should professors avoid a friendship with their students in order to maintain their objectivity?

3. Many of the standards of **Part VI** seem to suggest that the duties researchers have to assistants go beyond fair treatment and include such things as nurturance, consideration, and kindness. There is no doubt that these are good things. But should we regard them as duties or obligations? Could Professor Bent argue that the obligations we have constructed for him with respect to Tina's professional socialization are morally optional?

ISSUE

The code does not address whether the prohibition against discrimination in **Standard 2** is meant to forbid female senior researchers or minority senior researchers, for example, from taking special responsibility for nurturing and mentoring female students or minority students, especially when women or minorities are underrepresented in their fields. Beyond prohibiting discrimination, the code does not speak to the issue of affirmative action in admission, credentialing, hiring, or retention. Additionally, the code does not address the value of diversity in relationship to the health of the field or the improvement of society. (See **Cases 8–13** and **Hard Cases 5–7** in **Part I**).

Case 3

Professor Mary Reynolds is one of two female professors in a department of eight. Eight of twelve female graduate students in the department work with her. While she does not refuse to take male students, she has none. While there is no overt friction between her and male students, they seem to feel uncomfortable with the all-female environment that has come to characterize her group of students. Professor Reynolds has always made a special attempt to nurture and care for women graduate students. She has a regular luncheon for them and often has them over to her home. She does not do this for male students. Female students gravitate to her because she is kind and sympathetic as well as competent.

> *Discussion:* In **Case 4** on page 160 we criticized Professor Warren for discriminating against Kim because he did not make the same opportunities available to her as he did for his male students. Should we likewise criticize Professor Reynolds? There are two features of this case that may distinguish it from the Warren case. First, none of the male students who are not invited to the social occasions are her students. Hence, unlike Professor Warren, she is not providing unequal opportunities to students for whom she has accepted responsibility. Moreover, there is no indication that Professor Reynolds refuses to accept male students as her advisees or that, having taken them, would provide differential opportunities to them.

Second, women as a group have been discriminated against in higher education and remain under-represented in many areas of scholarship, including some areas of educational research. Thus it may be reasonable for female faculty to take a special interest in nurturing other women. If so, there are some cautions that should be exercised. Professor Reynolds should be careful that she is not advising women out of her field of expertise and that she is not substituting for other faculty who are more appropriate advisors for some of her students. Similarly, she should be attentive to whether or not male students who would be appropriate for her to advise feel unwelcome. If either of these situations is true, she might consider whether there is something she can do to alleviate these difficulties.

QUESTIONS

1. Is this a case of affirmative action?

2. Might Professor Reynolds claim that her social affairs are private matters and that she has a right to socialize with whomever she pleases for whatever reasons?

3. Suppose that the number of women graduate students and professors in Professor Reynold's department was over 50 percent. Would the female exclusivity of her group of students be more of an issue?

4. If students feel more comfortable with or identify more strongly with mentors of their own race or gender, is this a reason why they should work with them? Are there circumstances where acting on such reasons might become discriminatory?

ISSUE

Standard 5 requires fairness in evaluations and openness in communicating appraisals of competence. A number of issues are raised, including what counts as fairness or what ensures confidentiality of evaluations.

Case 4

Gene was excited when he read the announcement about the faculty position. His excellent graduate record, impressive dissertation, and his early success in getting papers published all made him a superb candidate for the position. Since graduation, Gene had been working in state-level policy analysis, but he was eager to land the kind of faculty position advertised. The position announcement indicated that three letters of recommendation should be submitted along with the application. Gene knew that he could count on two good letters—one from his advisor and one from another member of his thesis committee. He asked his advisor whether he should get the third letter from another faculty member or from his current supervisor at the state agency, who was very well-known and admired in education-policy circles. His advisor suggested that he should request a letter from his supervisor, since his involvement with the state agency would be seen as an advantage to his candidacy.

A few months after Gene learned that he did not get the job, his advisor had dinner with a friend who had served on the faculty search committee. The friend told him that in the tight competition for the job, the letter from Gene's agency supervisor had proven to be a liability. It seems that his letter mentioned the many problems that his state project had encountered, ostensibly to indicate Gene's skill in solving them, but effectively leaving the narrative open to the interpretation that Gene had contributed to the problems. The supervisor, moreover, had always considered Gene a talented but very junior staff member in an agency whose pecking order was determined largely by seniority and politics, and this bias could be inferred from his language. The overall impression that the letter gave was that Gene had spent time working under a big name in the policy field, but hadn't quite lived up to expectations.

> *Discussion:* Whether Gene's supervisor has been unfair in his recommendation is not entirely clear. Despite Gene's impressive academic qualifications, he may not have been outstanding in his work for the agency and his supervisor may have honestly and justly stated his contributions. It is also possible that the supervisor intended the letter to be complimentary and was simply unaware of how his statements might be interpreted in an academic environment. Sometimes the position that a student or other novice is applying for does not fall within the personal experience of the recommender. Standards and criteria sometimes differ across research arenas, and what may be clearly understood in one context may be misinterpreted in another. The agency supervisor may have written a letter that one of his counterparts would quite readily understand to be highly complimentary but that someone in a different setting could easily misinterpret. Writing a fair evaluation that communicates what one intends to evaluators in a different field requires careful consideration of all the candidate's experiences and qualifications in light of the expectations of the search committee. Perhaps Gene could have provided the supervisor with detailed background about the position and its context so that he would better understand what the committee was seeking. The responsibility for a fair evaluation, however, rests with the writer of the recommendation.

QUESTIONS

1. Fairness in hiring depends on fairness in reading evaluations as well as writing them. The tendency of some to "read between the lines" can distort the entire recommendation process, creating negative judgments where positive ones were intended. Should someone from the committee have contacted the supervisor to clarify his comments about Gene?

2. If the supervisor did not believe that he could write Gene a strong recommendation, should he have told him so and urged him to ask someone else? Consider that the evaluation process is not well served if only those having positive views of the candidate write letters of support.

3. Finally, it appears that a member of the search committee violated the promise of confidentiality typically given to recommendation writers in such cases. If Gene's supervisor was promised confidentiality, did the committee member behave unethically in letting Gene's advisor know what had happened? The code is not sufficiently detailed to provide guidance here. (See also **Part I, Case 18** and **Hard Case 8**).

ISSUE

Standard 6 requires that researchers not permit their personal animosities or intellectual differences to prevent access to other colleagues and that students should not be placed in untenable relationships with other colleagues. This is not always easy to achieve. Typically, as in a previous case (**Case 9**) dealing with this topic, the issue concerns telling one's students that they may not take a class with some disfavored colleague. However, when two colleagues have sharply differing views or intellectual standards, they may also place students at risk by subjecting them to conflicting standards and expectations that students cannot simultaneously meet. Furthermore, as the next case illustrates, there are other complexities.

Case 5

It occurred to Satoshi that someday he would be able to laugh about it all, but at the moment it wasn't very funny. His faculty committee was not originally a problem. For his preliminary oral exam, he had five committee members, three from his program and two from other departments as the Graduate School required. But then his advisor was seriously injured in a car accident and took a medical leave, and one of the other committee members from his program went on sabbatical abroad. The remaining faculty member from his program agreed to step in as advisor to help him finish his degree, but Satoshi still had to recruit two faculty replacements from his own program to serve on the dissertation defense committee.

Satoshi could choose among four professors. Professor Jansen flatly refused to serve on the final defense committee of any student whom she had never had in class, and Satoshi unfortunately fell in that category. Professor Kostner was very reluctant to step in since, as he put it, he did not feel that he could fairly evaluate Satoshi's dissertation because its subject was so far from his area of expertise. When Professor Kostner found out, moreover, that Satoshi was going to try to recruit Professor Lane for his committee, he frowned and said, "I'm not sure you realize what it means to bring her into the process at this point. She generally wants to be part of students' projects from the start. She'll probably keep you in revisions for a year. I think that for your own good you should find someone else. And, under the circumstances, I don't think I care to get involved if she's going to hold the whole thing up." That left Professor Moynahan. She expressed deep doubts about her ability to contribute to a project supervised by Satoshi's new advisor. She indicated that her perspective was in such conflict with his that it was not in Satoshi's interest to try to have both of them on his committee.

Satoshi went home wondering just how he was supposed to get a committee together.

> ***Discussion:*** **Standard 6** states that *educational researchers should not permit personal animosities or intellectual differences vis-a-vis colleagues to foreclose student and student researcher access to those colleagues, or to place the student or student researcher in an untenable position with those colleagues.* It appears that Satoshi's ability to put together a doctoral committee has been compromised by various faculty members' attitudes toward each other. It is conceivable that Professors Jansen, Kostner, Lane, and Moynahan have defensible reasons for their behavior in this case. They may even feel that they are maintaining high standards for the good of the students and the graduate program or that they are giving Satoshi good advice.

But reasons for not serving that might be reasonable under ordinary conditions, such as not working with students who have not been in one's classes, appear less reasonable given the background to Satoshi's problem—the withdrawal of two of the original members of his committee. The professors should consider setting aside their preferences and their personal differences in the interest of helping Satoshi complete his degree. In this way, they would show their commitment to his *welfare and progress* and honor their obligation to encourage and support him in his academic work.

QUESTIONS

1. We have argued that implicit in the standards' view of the expert/novice relationship is the obligation not to supervise students when one is not competent to judge their work. Thus Professor Kostner has a valid point in questioning whether he should serve on Satoshi's committee if his own expertise is so unrelated to Satoshi's dissertation research that it would make fair evaluation difficult. Should he make an exception given the exigencies of this case?

2. If Satoshi's new advisor and Professor Moynahan have fundamental disagreements about research frameworks and standards, can they be asked to work together on a common project? Frequently students are left on their own to put together a committee and negotiate differences among committee members. How can expert researchers best honor the obligation to nurture students while not compromising their own integrity?

3. Could it be argued that these researchers have inadequate respect for methodological pluralism? If so, is their refusal to serve unethical?

4. Does Satoshi's institution or academic program have a responsibility to see to it that he has a committee? Is so, how should the institution seek to provide one?

PROFESSIONAL CODES, MORALITY, AND THE LAW

Martha McCarthy and Barry Bull

*In this essay, we deal with several issues concerning the use and interpretation of the **Ethical Standards of the American Educational Research Association** (the AERA Code) and the cases included in this volume, the AERA Code's relationship to established law, and the use of this volume for instruction about the AERA Code specifically and about the ethics of education research more generally. On the whole, we are concerned about the status, application, and use of the code and its accompanying materials.*

AERA is explicit about its intention to promulgate the code: "The **Ethical Standards of the American Educational Research Association** were developed and, in June 1992, adopted by AERA to be an educational document, to stimulate collegial debate, and to evoke voluntary compliance by moral persuasion. Accordingly, it is not the intention of the Association to monitor adherence to the **Standards** or to investigate allegations of violations to the code." Thus the AERA Code is intended to be exclusively aspirational or advisory. It shares this intention with ethical codes of many other professional organizations. Such codes have become "a sine qua non of every profession as well as every occupation aspiring to professional status" (Constantinides, 1991, p. 1327). They are designed to persuade the members of the profession to adopt common values and to convince the public that the profession holds these values (Kultgen, 1998).

However, some professional codes not only lay down moral expectations about professional actions but also levy sanctions for their violation, sometimes including termination of membership in the organization. These sanctions may lead to two further consequences, often intentionally. First, they may persuade the public to grant full professional status to members of the association— to allow the organization to exercise the public's right to regulate members of the profession.

Second, in the absence of such full professional autonomy, these codes often become the basis for the public's regulation of practitioners by, for example, defining malpractice. Here the sanctions of the organization do not replace those levied by the public, but the code does define, at least in part, the criteria for levying public sanctions. Because AERA does not intend its code to have such legal status, it is important to distinguish between the moral standards implicit in the code and the legal obligations that follow from existing law.

Before that, we will clarify the ethical status of the AERA Code, since it is in that arena that the code has its intended meaning and use. In particular, we will treat an apparent ambiguity about the source of moral authority of AERA's ethical standards that is created by the publication of this volume of cases.

The Relationship Between Principles and Cases

This volume includes cases intended to explicate the meaning of the AERA Code. These cases can be understood as descriptions of particular contexts in which ethical decisions are made. The code then can be viewed as providing general principles of ethical guidance for making those decisions.

Aristotle's practical syllogism provides one account of the relationship between principles and cases when it is understood in this way. The major premise of this syllogism is a principle that specifies the general rule for acting morally. The minor premise specifies a particular context for action. The conclusion of the argument tells how one should act in this particular situation. A simplified argument based on the code might be:

- *Major Premise:* Education researchers must not fabricate, falsify, or misrepresent evidence, data, findings, or conclusions.
- *Minor Premise:* A particular research project demonstrates a correlation between social class and intelligence.
- *Practical Conclusion:* The report of this research project must not claim that it shows no relationship between social class and intelligence.

There are a number of questions not resolved by this argument. How well was the minor premise supported by the research project? For example, were all plausible correlates with intelligence tested? Exactly what should the report say about this correlation? Is the researcher free to remain silent about the relationship between social class and intelligence, or must the researcher reveal all such results with appropriate qualifications about the quality of the evidence?

Despite its failure to tell us everything we want to know about how we should act in this situation, this argument evinces a particular account of reasoning about morality. The major premise supplies the ethical principle, or the moral content, of the argument. The minor premise supplies the relevant facts, or empirical content, of the situation. The conclusion supplies practical guidance about what is required, allowed, or forbidden in this situation. From this perspective, the principle captures the essence of morality. All the case does is describe a context in which the moral principle is applied. And the conclusion determines the correct application of the principle in this context. Of course, any conclusion we reach about a particular case might be subject to amendment because we might have misunderstood the meaning of the principle or we might have failed to describe the case fully and accurately.

But this is not the only way in which the connection between codes and cases can be understood. Rather, one can seek certain cases in which our intuitions or conventions about moral actions are clear. These cases, rather than principles, can be considered the bedrock of morality. Of course, one might attempt to figure out what accounts for our intuitions or conventions in these specific cases, such as the presence or absence of features that seem to lead us to a clear moral conviction about the case. Then one might try to infer from these features a general principle for action in similar cases about which we have no clear conviction.

Nevertheless, the principle is always derivative of the case, and it might provide erroneous guidance in other cases if, for example, we have made a mistake about the morally relevant features of the original case. Or, worse, it might be inappropriate to generalize to a principle if the moral action in the original case simply reflects a convention.

To illustrate, we might unanimously agree that under particular circumstances, it would be wrong to make a false claim about a research project. From this case, we might reason to the general principle that it is wrong to make false claims about the results of research. This principle might allow us to think that it is permissible to omit certain findings from our reports of research if we make no claim one way or the other. However, in some situations, we might anticipate that the readers of the research report are likely to reach a false belief unless we explicitly state our finding to the contrary. In such cases, would it be right to fail to make any claim at all? According to the principle derived from the original case, such an action is permissible because no false claim has been made. Yet, that principle is based on a particular construction of the original case. It may not be the making of false claims, but rather the inducing of false belief that was responsible for our conviction that the researcher's action in the original case was morally wrong. We may have reasoned to the wrong principle based on the original case. Here, the case—rather than any putative principle based upon it—reflects our fundamental moral convictions. Furthermore, any moral principle derived from the case is subject to critique and correction upon further reflection.

How, then, should the relationship between cases and principles be construed? Do principles or cases reflect our fundamental convictions about morality? Are conclusions about cases or principles best understood as subject to revision? If the principles have a regulatory purpose, there might be good reason to hold that they supersede any reasoning we might do about their adequacy in certain cases. After all, in the context of regulation or law, practitioners rely upon the principles articulated in a code as defining the specific expectations of good professional practice. Practitioners assume that, in complying with these principles, they are protected against sanctions that might be levied by the professional organization or the public. In other words, it would be unfair to practitioners to hold them to revised principles after they have acted in good faith to comply with the principles originally promulgated.

This line of argument does not really answer the question that we have asked about the priority of principles or cases. First, the principles of the AERA Code do not purport to have a regulatory or legal function, and particular sanctions against practitioners are not involved. Our conclusion about the priority of principles in a regulatory context does not apply.

Second, even when principles do have a regulatory purpose, they also have moral content; indeed, the legitimacy of their regulatory use depends in part upon the adequacy of that moral content in the eyes of practitioners and the public. When that adequacy is challenged, the professional association has a moral and practical obligation to consider a revision of the principles, even if it does not judge practitioners' past actions by any revised principles it may adopt. In making such a change, should an association consider challenges that derive from cases, or should it simply focus on general considerations that arise at the level of the principles themselves?

We are still faced with our original question about the priority of principles or cases in moral reasoning. One way of answering this question might be to consider whether the justification of ethics is on more solid ground if it proceeds from principles or cases. One of the standard objections to basing morality on our settled convictions about cases is that such convictions are likely to reflect our habits, prejudices, or cultural conventions, rather than any inherent moral quality of the actions. In other words, any agreement, no matter how broadly based, about how a particular case is resolved is no more than a widely held opinion about what is ethical. And the simple fact that most or all accept a particular opinion does not necessarily make it right. Therefore, we should seek some other basis than mere agreement for justifying a particular ethical claim. Perhaps principles can provide this basis.

Principles can be held to be correct for the same reason as convictions about cases—namely, that such principles are widely accepted. But, we obviously need a better justification for principles than this if they are to prove a better source of morality than cases. The search for this independent source of justification for principles has been a consistent theme of Western philosophy since the time of the ancient Greeks.

For example, the eighteenth century German philosopher Immanuel Kant thought that the consistency of principles when generalized to all provides such a justification. He posited that the basic formula for morality is: Act in such a way that you can at the same time will the maxim (or principle) of your action to be a universal law (Kant, 1785/1985). Based on this formulation, he maintained that lying is immoral because the act of lying assumes that what a person says will be taken for the truth, but if lying is taken as a general principle, this assumption will be mistaken. In other words, Kant asserted that certain acts are inherently self-contradictory and therefore immoral when their principle is generalized.

As appealing as this account of the justification of principles may be, it still faces difficulties. For example, how can we tell which particular description of an act is authoritative or correct? In some circumstances, a person can lie in order to spare others the suffering that knowing the truth would inevitably cause. In these cases, why is the correct description of the act "telling a lie" rather than "preventing suffering"? Because the principle "prevent suffering whenever possible" can be generalized consistently, it appears that, under this description, the act would be moral. Since most acts are subject to alternative descriptions, we are left with an apparent dilemma: either such acts are both moral and immoral, or we must rely upon our intuitions or conventions to determine which description is correct in any particular case. The first conclusion is unacceptable because we wish principles to provide us with moral guidance in specific situations. However, the second conclusion leaves the morality of particular acts subject to the very prejudices, habits, and conventions that principles are supposed to allow us to avoid.

Kant's formulation of morality, which he called the Categorical Imperative, is only one of dozens of philosophers' efforts to find a justification for principles of morality independent of our experience, but its failure is very instructive. For unlike some similar efforts, Kant's attempted justification appeals to precepts of reasoning, such as the avoidance of self-contradiction, that are ostensibly accessible to everyone whatever their experience may be.

In this way, he hoped to justify morality without appealing to particular theological doctrines, modes of argument, or metaphysical assumptions that some people find controversial. It may be doubted whether these precepts have the universal acceptability that Kant asserted, but, even assuming that they do, the application of Kant's principles to specific cases still apparently requires our intuitions or conventions about such cases to come into play. In other words, our judgments and interpretations of individual cases, which may be affected by our upbringing and culture, seem to have an unavoidable role in the application of principles. This suggests, but does not prove conclusively, that the general considerations we might apply in formulating and judging principles of morality seem to need to be informed by our contextual insights about particular cases.

In light of considerations of this kind, John Rawls proposed a way of thinking about the justification of morality in which both principles and cases play a role but neither is given absolute priority (Rawls, 1972). He suggested that these two ethical judgments are in creative tension with one another and that we can reach a temporary resolution of moral questions through a process he called reflective equilibrium. Schematically, this process might be represented thus:

Judgments	$\rightarrow$	Judgments
about	$\leftarrow$	About Cases
Principles		

$\uparrow\downarrow$ $\qquad\qquad\qquad\qquad\qquad\qquad\qquad$ $\uparrow\downarrow$

General $\qquad\qquad\qquad\qquad\qquad\qquad$ Contextual
Considerations $\qquad\qquad\qquad\qquad\qquad$ Considerations

This scheme recognizes that we apply general considerations to our judgments of principles (e.g., whether they are impartial or generalizable), and contextual considerations to our judgments about particular cases (e.g., whether they take account of the full range of facts about a specific situation or of the interests of all affected parties). It also recognizes that we can apply principles to cases and also can infer principles from our judgments about those cases. But beyond this, it recognizes that our judgments about principles can cause us to change our judgments about individual cases and therefore the contextual considerations we think appropriate in reaching them. Equally important, our settled convictions about cases can cause us to change what principles we think are justified and therefore what general considerations we apply to those principles. In other words, the method of reflective equilibrium does not suppose that our judgments of either principles or cases are beyond criticism, or that the considerations we currently deem relevant in devising those judgments are beyond revision.

As we go through this reflection, we may reach a state in which our judgments of principles and cases are fully consistent with one another, or a state of equilibrium in our judgments. In these circumstances, we are confident about the moral assertions we make. However, as we encounter new situations or explore new theoretical territory, any equilibrium we may have reached may be disrupted. Here, new general or contextual considerations may cause us to revise our judgments and justifications until we reach a subsequent and different state of equilibrium.

Rawls's suggestion certainly does not solve the problem of the justification of morality that we have found: It does not provide us with an assurance that our judgments are in some way independent of our experience, and free of the bias that such experience may reflect. In fact, Rawls may have given up on the goal of ensuring that our judgments can be free of the prejudices induced by our cultures. However, the method of reflective equilibrium provides us with a way of continuously subjecting such prejudices about either our moral principles or our settled convictions in particular cases to the criticism that may arise from experience or analysis, and of injecting new experiences and fresh deliberations into our judgments. This may be all that we can ask of ourselves in justifying morality.

This way of thinking about morality helps us see the AERA Code and this volume of cases in a new light. The cases are not mere illustrations of the meaning and application of the code. While they function in this way, the cases can also help us to refine and even to criticize the principles contained in the code. Although the code may represent its drafters' best thinking about the ethics of education research at a given time, it should not be taken to be either final or complete.

Cases can be the source of insights into, or considerations about, the ethics of research that simply did not occur to the drafters. At the same time, the principles of the AERA Code can help us to reconsider the conventional practices of the education research enterprise. Those principles and the thinking behind them can give us reasons to reject or have doubts about our standard ways of designing, conducting, analyzing, and communicating about our research endeavors.

In this way, the AERA Code and this volume are part of an ongoing conversation about the ethics of education research. Neither should be understood as intending to preempt debate or reflection about our conduct as inquirers into educational phenomena or institutions. Nor should they necessarily be seen as independent from broader debate about the ethics of education or even ethics more generally.

It is tempting to suppose that decisions about our obligations as professional researchers can be disconnected from those we have as educators, citizens, or human beings. There is a grain of truth in this supposition in that the contexts in which we pursue research are special. Universities and other research venues do involve us in distinctive relationships with our colleagues, students, and the subjects of our research, and it is extremely important for us to be sensitive to the special obligations and prerogatives that such relationships imply. For example, because we are granted extraordinary authority in our society, we may have to be more cautious about the truthfulness of our statements than we are in our other roles. However, any such qualifications to commonly accepted principles of ethics must be carefully justified on the basis of general and contextual considerations that withstand the test of the process of reflective equilibrium. Inevitably, this process will involve the consideration of cases and principles that do not refer explicitly or exclusively to education research.

In other words, the simple fact that a decision takes place in a particular professional context does not automatically absolve us of the responsibility to take into account judgments about principles and cases that concern other contexts. At the very least, the specifics of the professional context must be arguably different enough in kind or degree from the considerations that lead us to the commonly justified position in other situations to suggest that an exception or qualification is warranted. Although principles and contextual judgments that emerge from nonresearch and even noneducational contexts are not dispositive of the ethics of education research, neither should their relevance be unreflectively dismissed. As a result, we may often think about general ethical questions or cases in which research is not involved when we are clarifying our professional obligations as education researchers. The method of reflective equilibrium implies that the debate over the ethics of education research will inevitably and justifiably stray into other professional and nonprofessional territory.

Legal Considerations

A professional association can seek compliance with a code of ethics through various strategies, including personal persuasion, educational activities, professional sanctions, and legal penalties. As discussed previously, AERA has chosen the first two approaches. The AERA Code is designed to stimulate dialogue that will persuade education researchers and future researchers to maintain the integrity of their research and to protect others affected by it. AERA envisions voluntary compliance with the code, and the **Preface** of this book also recognizes that it is *both impossible and inappropriate* for the organization to attempt to enforce its ethical standards.

Nonetheless, the AERA Code has legal dimensions and raises some potential legal concerns that deserve attention. For example, several of the provisions are grounded in or analogous to constitutional or statutory requirements in contrast to being framed purely on ethical principles or appropriate professional practice. Accordingly, there may be sanctions for noncompliance based on legal grounds. In addition, there is the potential for ethical standards to be incorporated into policies of education institutions or into state regulations or laws and to assume a legal status beyond that originally intended by AERA.

Provisions Grounded in Law

Several provisions of the AERA Code correspond to legal mandates that apply to U.S. citizens generally, not only to AERA members. It is important for education researchers to understand that they might comply with ethical standards couched in general terms and still not fulfill all their legal obligations. In short, compliance with the AERA Code does not necessarily ensure compliance with the law. Therefore, researchers need to be familiar with legal mandates that parallel the AERA Code, and to realize that these legal requirements are not discretionary. A few illustrations are provided below.

CIVIL RIGHTS MANDATES

These legal obligations are more comprehensive than their treatment in the AERA Code. For example, the code provides general guidance to researchers in connection with their obligation to avoid sexual harassment of their employees, research subjects, or students. Regulations accompanying Title VII of the Civil Rights Act of 1964 and Title IX of the Education Amendments of 1972, as well as constitutional guarantees and judicial rulings interpreting such mandates, are far more explicit as to what behaviors are legally permissible, and the circumstances under which employees and students can secure damages for sexual harassment (see *Burlington v. Ellerth,* 1998; *Davis v. Monroe County,* 1999; *Gebser v. Lago Vista,* 1998). In addition to understanding the ethical issues surrounding sexual harassment, it is essential for education researchers to be familiar with federal and state mandates and institutional policies pertaining to grievance procedures for employees and students who have allegedly been subjected to harassment.

Employers, including researchers who hire assistants, are also expected to avoid discrimination in hiring personnel and to know what constitutes unlawful discrimination based on various characteristics such as race, gender, religion, age, and disabilities. A number of federal civil rights laws, such as the Americans With Disabilities Act of 1990, the Age Discrimination in Employment Act of 1967, Title VII of the Civil Rights Act of 1964, as well as state laws, impose detailed obligations on employers. Ignorance of the law is no excuse for noncompliance, and employers can be liable for damages for violating clearly established federal rights (see *Wood v. Strickland,* 1975).

The AERA Code actually is more explicit than federal civil rights laws and the U.S. Constitution in prohibiting discrimination based on sexual orientation. Also, the code places a duty on researchers to avoid *all forms of harassment, not merely those overt actions or threats that are due cause for legal action* (**Standard 11** in **Part I**). As discussed in the **Introduction** of this volume, AERA members are expected to comply with the more stringent requirements in the code. Conversely, where the AERA Code imposes a lesser duty than legally required, individuals must comply with the law.

PROTECTION OF HUMAN SUBJECTS

Some ethical standards in the AERA Code are similar also to legal requirements that protect public school students involved in research projects and experimental treatment programs. Congress and state legislatures have been active during the past few decades in enacting measures to safeguard students' privacy in connection with these activities. Under the federal Protection of Human Subjects law, individuals are protected in research projects supported by federal grants and contracts in any private or public institution or agency. Informed consent must be obtained before placing subjects at risk of being exposed to physical, psychological, or social injury as a result of participating in research, development, or related activities. Most states have enacted parallel legal requirements, and all education agencies are required to establish review committees to ensure that the rights and welfare of subjects are adequately protected. Thus, regardless of how this topic is approached in ethics codes, researchers must comply with the federal and state legal mandates.

Two 1974 amendments to the General Education Provisions Act require that all instructional materials in federally assisted research or experimentation projects designed to explore new or unproven teaching methods or techniques be made available for inspection by parents of participating students. The amendments also stipulate that children cannot be required to participate in such research or experimentation projects if their parents object in writing.

In 1978, Congress enacted the Hatch Amendment, retaining the protection of parents' rights to examine instructional materials in experimental programs. This Act also requires parental consent before students could participate in federally supported programs involving psychiatric or psychological examination, testing, or treatment designed to reveal information in specified sensitive areas pertaining to personal beliefs, behaviors, and family relationships. The U.S. Department of Education is charged with reviewing complaints under this law, and federal funds can be withheld from educational institutions not in compliance. This law generated substantial controversy, with conservative citizen groups asserting that the law entitled parents to broad control in all curricular matters. In response, a group of professional education associations and other interested organizations developed guidelines to clarify the limited scope of the amendment (see Hatch Amendment Coalition & AERA, 1985; Lewis, 1985).

Extending the Hatch Amendment, the 1994 Grassley Amendment to the General Education Provisions Act stipulates that parents must be allowed to review in advance all instructional materials that will be used in connection with any survey, analysis, or evaluation as part of programs administered by the Department of Education. The amendment further specifies that students cannot be required to submit to a federally funded survey, analysis, or evaluation that reveals information in areas covered by the Hatch Amendment without written parental consent. These requirements pertaining to the protection of human subjects go beyond the AERA Code, and researchers working in schools are expected to understand and abide by these provisions. If not, researchers can jeopardize a school district or a university obtaining federal funds.

PRIVACY OF RECORDS

Education researchers also have legal obligations beyond the AERA Code in connection with the privacy of students' records. The Family Educational Rights and Privacy Act (FERPA), enacted in 1974, stipulates that federal funds may be withdrawn from any educational agency or institution failing to provide parents access to their child's educational records or disseminating such information, with some exceptions, to third parties without parental permission. Private notes become education records and are subject to legal specifications if they are shared, even among educators who have a legitimate need for access to such information (see *Parents Against Abuse v. Williamsport*, 1991). Individuals can file complaints with the U.S. Department of Education if they believe a school district is not complying with the provisions of FERPA. The remedy for FERPA violations is the withdrawal of federal funds, and the Department of Education has enforcement authority (see *Girardier v. Webster College*, 1977; *Rothman v. Emory University*, 1993).

Other federal laws, such as the Individuals with Disabilities Education Act of 1990, include additional protections regarding the confidentiality and accessibility of student records. Many states also have enacted legislation addressing the privacy of student records. Indiana law stipulates that school boards must maintain a list of all persons or agencies having access to personal files. In addition, they must furnish prior notice before files are disclosed to a third party, and inform individuals of their rights to access and to contest the accuracy or appropriateness of the material in such files (Ind. Code Ann. 4-1-6-2 to 4-1-6-5). These laws have implications for education researchers, because data must be collected and disseminated to prevent the disclosure of personally identifiable information about students (see *Bowie v. Evanston*, 1989; *Human Rights v. Miller*, 1984). Composite information on pupil achievement can be released to the public as long as individual students are not personally identified (see *Laplante v. Stewart*, 1985; *Western Services v. Sargent School District*, 1988).

Unfortunately, fears of legal sanctions under FERPA and similar provisions have resulted in actions that have not always been in the best interests of students (Bull & McCarthy, 1995). While school personnel should ensure that irrelevant or damaging materials are eliminated from students' records, they should not overreact to the legal requirements. For example, fears that materials in students' files will be questioned have caused student records to be purged of some useful information that could help educators in designing appropriate instructional programs for a given child. When educators do not understand the rationale for legal requirements, they are more likely to misinterpret the mandates and possibly overreact in ways that place unwarranted constraints on professional decisions. This can lead to conflicts between perceived legal duties and what is considered educationally and morally sound.

REPORTING CHILD ABUSE

Education researchers need to know their responsibilities in reporting child abuse to the designated social service agency or law enforcement unit. All states have adopted legal mandates that require professionals dealing with children to inform appropriate welfare agencies of their suspicions of child abuse. In most states, the statutes impose sanctions (like fines, prison terms) for failure to report these suspicions. Proof of such abuse is not necessary to trigger this legal duty, and all states grant immunity from liability to individuals who report their suspicions in good faith.

In addition to state laws that place obligations on educators to report suspected abuse, the Fourteenth Amendment to the U.S. Constitution affords individuals a liberty right to bodily security, which has been interpreted as including the right to be free from abuse. School districts and school authorities may be vulnerable to liability if they maintain policies or practices reflecting deliberate indifference to this right (see *Doe v. Taylor,* 1994; *Stoneking v. Bradford Area School District,* 1989). As noted previously, school districts also can be liable under Title IX of the Education Amendments of 1972 if school personnel with the authority to curtail sex discrimination in the form of abuse or harassment have actual knowledge of the behavior and are deliberately indifferent toward the victim (see *Franklin v. Gwinnett County,* 1992; *Davis v. Monroe County,* 1999; *Gebser v. Lago Vista,* 1998). Education researchers need to know their legal responsibilities as well as their ethical obligations to protect children from abuse.

Similar to overreactions to FERPA that may have negative results, fears that school personnel may be charged with child abuse have resulted in the adoption of policies that impose unnecessary restrictions on educators' activities. For example, some school districts prohibit all physical contact between staff members and children, which precludes physical contact to comfort a child who has fallen on the playground or to pat a student on the back for a job well done. This is unfortunate, as some physical contact between staff members and students is appropriate and desirable. Researchers working in schools need to be attentive to each school district's policies in this regard. Even though researchers may question the efficacy of some of these policies, all adults working in the school environment are expected to comply with school board directives.

COPYRIGHT INFRINGEMENTS

Education researchers must adhere to provisions of the federal copyright law, which extend beyond the ethical considerations stated in the AERA Code. The copyright law has been amended in part to address copyright issues in connection with electronic communications like the Internet and computer programs. The amended law retains the fair use doctrine that provides some flexibility to teachers, librarians, and education researchers in using copyrighted materials, but it does not make them exempt from copyright infringements (Digital Millennium Copyright Act, 1998).

In determining whether use of specific materials constitutes fair use, courts will assess the purpose and character of the use, the nature of the copyrighted work, the amount used in relation to the work as a whole, and the effect of the use on the market for or value of the copyrighted work. Education researchers need to fully understand what activities are legally proscribed, such as copying software or taping television programs at home to show students in the classroom.

Related to, but distinct from, copyright infringements are legal sanctions for plagiarism. Plagiarism involves the unauthorized use of someone's ideas without giving appropriate credit. One commentator has asserted that copyright infringements focus on "creative results," whereas plagiarism focuses on "the creative process" (Stearns, 1992). Plagiarism can, but does not always, constitute a copyright violation.

Part III of the AERA Code focuses on intellectual ownership that extends beyond copyright infringements, and many universities and other institutions have developed detailed regulations pertaining to ownership of intellectual property. Education researchers need to be familiar with these institutional policies, as disciplinary sanctions can be imposed for violations. Education researchers are also expected to adhere to the standards in the code where the AERA Code is more explicit than such policies in connection with intellectual property.

Conflicts Between Ethical and Legal Considerations

Some unethical behaviors do not violate civil rights or criminal laws or any other legal provisions. As discussed previously, a code of ethics can place far more stringent requirements on researchers than required by law. There is obvious overlap between unethical and unlawful behaviors, but not an absolute match between the two. Over time, some laws have been challenged as immoral (e.g., laws requiring school segregation), which is the essence of civil disobedience (McCarthy, Bull, Quantz, & Sorenson, 1994). And there are many examples of potentially unethical behaviors that do not implicate *any* legal provisions, including administering assessment techniques without adequate training, failing to supervise research assistants adequately, or engaging in research activities without competence.

Most troublesome are the relatively few instances where ethics and law may appear to be in conflict. For example, in a situation where a government agency has the legal control over findings from a given research project and decides to withhold the findings from the public for political reasons, the researcher involved is faced with an ethical dilemma. If the researcher is silent while policymakers distribute statements that are not supported by the data gathered, the researcher has not fulfilled ethical obligations of the profession. But if the researcher speaks out, contractual agreements with the agency may be breached. There are other instances where the researcher might believe that the sponsoring agency's policies are not morally appropriate and must decide whether to be a whistle blower to the media.

Also, researchers, and more commonly journalists, must occasionally deal with conflicts over confidentiality issues. They may be faced with a choice between being in contempt of court for refusing to testify when subpoenaed or violating their profession's ethics, for example, revealing confidential information about clients, subjects, or informants (see *Ruzicka v. Conde Nast,* 1991). In 1998, the First Circuit Court of Appeals equated researchers with reporters. The Court's reasoning was that if researchers were required to disclose all transcripts and other materials from their research, this "would sharply curtail the information available to academic researchers and thus would restrict their output" (In re Cusumano, 1998). However, most courts have required disclosure of information that is relevant in legal proceedings, noting the extensive judicial discretion to ensure the broadest possible discovery (Wright, 1998). Also, federal law requires those involved in federal research grants to waive any research privilege that would shield their research from subpoenas (Freedom of Information Act, 1998).

In some instances, there may be a clash not only between legal and ethical concerns but also between competing ethical considerations. For example, revealing information from a student may breach confidentiality, but not making the revelation may jeopardize the safety of the individual or someone else. If such information is not revealed, there may also be legal consequences (see *Eisel v. Board of Education,* 1991).

The *Ethical Principles of Psychologists and Code of Conduct* (1992) of the American Psychological Association (APA) has a section dealing with the sensitive relationship between ethics and law (1.02). The APA Code stipulates that in instances of conflicts between the code and institutional rules and expectations, psychologists must inform proper institutional authorities regarding the ethical issues involved and regarding their commitment to the code (7.06). Without such action, the individual may be subject to professional sanctions for a code violation. When a court orders release of records in violation of the APA Code's stipulation that psychologists must obtain consent, they may avoid a conflict between legal requirements and the code by negotiating a judge's review of the materials instead of their public release.

The AERA Code does not have a comparable section dealing with possible conflicts with legal provisions. As noted previously, however, the code indicates that AERA members are expected to adhere to legal requirements, and cases in this book can assist researchers in identifying potential friction between legal and ethical responsibilities. Moreover, the cases can be useful in exploring possible resolutions of such conflicts.

Legal Sanctions for Violations of Ethics Codes

Whereas use of collegiality to influence others is at one end of the enforcement continuum, incorporation of a code of ethics that imposes legal penalties for noncompliance in state law is at the opposite end. Despite the asserted intent of the AERA Code to persuade education researchers to comply voluntarily, sometimes other enforcement strategies evolve. The code itself hints at such possibilities. For instance, the AERA standard that education researchers should not *agree to undue or questionable influence by government or other funding agencies* (**Standard 4** in **Part V**) includes the specification that instances of such inappropriate influence should be reported to AERA. This suggests that some action by the association might be taken to expose such agencies, or perhaps to impose sanctions. Conceivably, AERA could name an ethics committee to assess these claims or other ethical violations. Such a committee could be empowered to censure individuals or agencies for infractions to exert professional pressure on education researchers and sponsoring groups to comply with the code. Also, independent of AERA's intentions, the code could be adopted by a university or school district and used to impose sanctions on researchers who do not comply. And as discussed below, other applications of the code in legal proceedings are possible, especially in light of the use of some organizations' ethical codes, such as APA's.

There is a tension in most codes between vagueness and specificity, which is not easily resolved (Constantinides, 1991). If a code is written in very general terms, it appears aspirational only and provides insufficient direction to practitioners. However, if it is quite detailed and prescriptive, the likelihood that it will be used to establish a legally enforceable standard of care is increased. No profession wants to "expose its members to increased liability by encouraging use of its ethics code in court" (Constantinides, 1991, p. 1327), but a code is meaningless if it does not provide useful guidance. Most professions want their respective ethics codes to be taken seriously, which may mean that they will be used in legal proceedings. This has happened with several professional codes of ethics that have been given legal status by being incorporated in state laws or regulations of state licensing boards.

If decided that a given ethics code will serve more than a moral purpose because it will be used to establish a legally enforceable standard of care (Constantinides, 1991), then the disciplinary sanctions must be precise. Lawyers, for example, can face disbarment for failure to comply with the American Bar Association (ABA) *Model Code of Professional Responsibility and Code of Judicial Conduct* (1990). Initially, the ABA *Canons of Ethics* were considered advisory. These subsequently were replaced by the *Model Code* that contains ethical prescriptions as well as a comprehensive code of disciplinary rules. The *Model Code* now is adopted by courts in the District of Columbia and almost all states as a basis for disciplinary action against noncomplying lawyers.

Violations of the ABA ethical rules have generated more litigation than most codes because state courts have explicitly adopted them to govern attorney conduct. Attorneys are held to be officers of the court, and judges are particularly qualified to evaluate attorney conduct (Constantinides, 1991). However, the ABA *Model Code* indicates that although violations can be the basis for disciplinary action against attorneys, a violation of the rules should not give rise to a civil suit, such as a malpractice claim (ABA, 1990; Constantinides, 1991). Some courts, nevertheless, have allowed ethical standards to be admitted as evidence to establish or prove a breach of a duty or standard of care (Wolfram, 1979).

Unlike the ABA *Model Code,* the American Medical Association (AMA) *Code of Medical Ethics* (1996) does not specifically disclaim using the principles in legal proceedings pertaining to malpractice or other matters. The preamble notes that the principles "are living, dynamic precepts" that constitute a "potent, vigorous contract of caring between physicians and patients" (AMA, 1996, p. 1). The AMA Code further states that a physician must "strive to expose those physicians deficient in character or competence, or who engage in fraud or deception" (AMA, 1996, principle II). Thus, the AMA not only expects its members to adhere to ethical standards but also to identify for the profession those who do not.

The APA Code (1992) has also generated a fairly large body of litigation. Almost six years of work went into the 1992 version of the APA Code, which is substantially different from earlier versions.[1] The code clearly distinguishes "ideal ethical goals toward which all psychologists should aspire and minimal standards of professional conduct, with which every psychologist must comply" (Canter, Bennett, Jones, & Nagy, 1994, p. 20).

The 1992 APA Code entails a preamble, six general principles, and ethical standards in eight areas ranging from advertising to confidentiality, and the 102 standards have been recognized in statutes of many states. The "standards are mandatory in nature . . . listing specific enforceable rules of conduct" for psychologists (Canter et al., 1994, p. 21).

To illustrate, under North Carolina's Psychology Practice Act, the licensing board has authority to discipline any psychologist found guilty of unprofessional or unethical conduct as defined by the APA Code (North Carolina General Statutes 90-270.15(a)(10); *Elliott v. North Carolina Psychology Board,* 1997). In Alabama, the state board charged with certification of professional psychologists is required to apply the APA Code in assessing charges of malpractice or misbehavior (Acts of Alabama, 34-26-3; Ex parte Givens, 1991).

A number of court cases deal with patient confidences where state licensing boards have adopted the APA Code as a basis for suspending licenses (see *Mississippi State Board v. Hosford,* 1987). Under the code, only two exceptions to the principle of patient confidentiality are found—the patient consents to the release of information or the circumstances portend that maintaining confidentiality would result in danger to the patient or to others. Where psychologists have breached confidentiality beyond these two exceptions, disciplinary action, including loss of license, has been imposed.[2]

It is unlikely that the AERA Code will be adopted in state laws or administrative regulations as has been the case with the APA Code. There is a crucial difference because psychologists, subject to the APA Code, are licensed by the state, whereas education researchers are not. Also, the APA Code is far more detailed on the ethical duties of psychologists.

Nonetheless, some ethical expectations are similar in the two codes. For example, an APA standard requires psychologists to represent accurately their competence, education, training, experience, and credentials (APA, 1992, 3.03). The AERA Code similarly stipulates that *educational re-*

searchers should honestly and fully disclose their qualifications and limitations when providing professional opinions (**Standard 4** in **Part I**). Conceivably, legal sanctions could evolve for some AERA provisions as they have for the APA Code. Researchers undoubtedly would take compliance more seriously if faced with threats of legal liability.

It is also imaginable that professional standards boards for teachers and administrators that are currently operating in a number of states might incorporate some features of the AERA Code into state standards and assessments being developed for education professionals. National efforts to establish standards for teachers and school leaders, such as the Interstate School Leaders Licensure Consortium for school administrators (Council of Chief State School Officers, 1998; Murphy & Shipman, 1998), also might draw on ethics codes of various professional organizations, including AERA, to design standards and indicators that the standards have been satisfied.

The AERA Code might also be used in litigation where an individual is arguing that his or her action was reasonable based on professionally accepted standards of conduct. In short, the AERA Code might be used to assert that an individual has or has not exhibited a standard of care in a specific situation that would be supported by the community of education researchers.

Other professional education associations also have ethics codes, such as the American Association of School Administrators (AASA), the Association for Supervision and Curriculum Development, and the National Education Association. In addition, many of the organizations that focus on particular subject areas, such as the National Council for Social Studies (NCSS), have established ethical standards to guide their membership. These ethical codes vary as to length and specificity. For example, the AASA *Standards of Ethics for School Administrators* (1981) are ten general statements to guide school leaders. Illustrative of the level of generality in the AASA document is the first standard that calls for education administrators to make "the well-being of students the fundamental value of all decision-making and actions" (p. 1). The NCSS *Revised Code of Ethics for the Social Studies Profession* (1990) contains six principles with three to six subpoints under each. Although more detailed than either of these, the AERA Code resembles codes of most education associations in being less specific than the APA Code and ethical standards of other professions, such as law and medicine.

A number of professional associations whose members are involved only in part in education research and/or practice also have ethics codes. Although the APA Code is probably the most pertinent to education researchers, other associations with ethics codes that apply to some school practices are: the National Federation of Societies for Clinical Social Work, the American Counseling Association, the American Association for Counseling and Development, the National Association of Social Workers, the National Federation of Societies for Clinical Social Work, and the American Counseling Association. Codes of several of these organizations have evolved beyond their original aspirational statements and are used to represent the standards of the profession in legal proceedings (*Jaffee v. Lu Redmond*, 1996).

Using the AERA Code in Graduate Instruction

Individuals preparing to become education researchers, and educators in general, should have regular exposure to ethical deliberations throughout their university courses. The AERA Code in conjunction with this volume can be useful as a launching pad for a broader investigation of ethics for education researchers and the relationship between law and ethics. If students develop habits of criticism by discussing and debating ethical concerns throughout their graduate programs, the next generation of education researchers should be better informed about these critical issues and appreciate the centrality of ethical considerations in their work.

Currently, too many people hold misperceptions regarding the ethical responsibilities of education researchers and practitioners. There are commonly held erroneous assumptions about the nature of ethics—it is not strict moralizing or a list of correct behaviors to be learned (Bull & McCarthy, 1995; Keith-Spiegel & Koocher, 1985). These misunderstandings lead people to view ethical considerations as more definitive than they actually are. Graduate students need to grasp that ethical concepts are continually contested not only within specific disciplines, but also in the broader society. If individuals gain a robust understanding of ethical discourse, perhaps they will abandon the restrictive view of ethics as confining rather than facilitating professional decisions.

Exposure to the AERA Code and ethics codes from other professional associations is particularly important during graduate school so students can learn to appreciate how such codes might direct their actions. Studies have indicated that graduate students and practitioners often view codes of ethics as irrelevant to the dilemmas they face daily; they do not see the codes as a guide to making ethical decisions (Nash, 1996; Stefkovich & Shapiro, 1999). The cases in this book that interpret the AERA Code can serve as a bridge to assist students in making connections between ethical principles and situations they confront in conducting research and engaging in other activities in school settings. Scenarios in this book can be used to stimulate discussions in university classes about ethical dilemmas, and students can develop their own scenarios based on various aspects of the AERA Code. Moreover, graduate students should be encouraged to develop their own ethics codes and to explore similarities and differences between their personal platforms and the AERA Code. Also instructive would be comparative analyses of the AERA Code and codes of other professional organizations.

In addition, there are relationships between law and ethics that would be meaningful for future education researchers to explore during their graduate studies. For example, as mentioned previously, some professional codes of ethics have assumed the force of law over time. The APA Code has been incorporated in a number of state statutes and administrative regulations for licensing boards. Investigating how codes of ethics have evolved into legal documents and how the level of specificity in such codes differs from that of the AERA Code should be enlightening to future education researchers.

Thus far, we have addressed the circumstances and occasions for teaching about the ethics of education research. Because ethical considerations generally are interwoven throughout the process of conducting education research, so should formal and informal consideration of ethical issues be a part of every aspect of students' learning process about the research enterprise from coming to understand what others have done to planning and carrying out individual research. The conduct of education research simply cannot be neatly divided into technical and ethical tasks, which can be considered cogently in isolation from one another. These intertwining dimensions of the research enterprise do call on distinctive content and skills that require focused study and practice. As a result, the learning process must at times emphasize a particular dimension of the research enterprise without encouraging the student to lose track of the other.

The distinctive content of the technical dimension of research is familiar in graduate programs; separate courses in statistical techniques or ethnographic methods are standard fixtures in these programs. The problem with such courses lies not so much in their emphasis on distinctive content as the impression they leave that such content is neutral to or even immune from ethical considerations. This impression must be consciously counteracted by at least occasional attention to the ethical problems raised by the application of such methods in particular contexts. Although it has received less attention in graduate programs, the ethical dimension of research has its own distinctive content. On the one hand, such content includes the conventions represented in explicit ethical codes, laws, and authoritative interpretations of cases, both moral and legal. On the other, such content also includes analysis of, deliberation about, and criticism of these conventions.

The mastery of this distinctive content may well justify courses or units within courses that emphasize such subject matter. But, like courses that focus on distinctive technical content, such courses or units in the ethics of research should not be taught to leave the impression that ethical problems can be resolved independently of technical considerations. In fact, resolving ethical issues in education research almost always depends upon a clear and even imaginative understanding of the technical meaning and limitations of specific research methodologies.

Keeping in mind the caveat that technical and ethical considerations go hand in hand, in the remainder of this section, we analyze and elaborate upon this distinctive ethical content. As we have suggested, the general goal of teaching the ethics of the education research enterprise is to enable students to participate in the ongoing conversation about the moral responsibilities of those who use and conduct research for and about the various purposes, processes, and institutions of teaching and learning.

First, joining this conversation implies familiarity with and facility in the conventions by which the conversation is currently conducted—the terminology, precepts, rules of interpretation and argument, and other ideas that inform the conversation. In other words, one of the instructional purposes that must be fulfilled in meeting this general goal is the induction of students into the current practice of education research ethics. These conventions stem in part from the official statements of organizations to which education researchers belong. As noted, formal exposure to the AERA Code, and the cases and their interpretations included in this volume, plays an obvious role in the achievement of this instructional purpose. But these conventions also include the legal codes, case law, and institutional regulations governing the status, prerogatives, and actions of education researchers, which are not necessarily identical in their intention, scope, or application with professional codes or case interpretations.

Thus, there is a considerable body of content to be mastered in the process of induction into the conventions of education research ethics, content that speaks both to what students know and understand and what they are able to do. For these conventions speak not only to principles and rules that students are expected to follow but also to the styles of analysis and argument that are acceptable in interpreting and implementing them. Graduate programs are obviously only the beginning of the induction process for education researchers. The objective of such graduate instruction cannot be the acquisition of all the knowledge and skills relevant to the wide variety of ethical problems that education researchers may encounter in the course of their careers, even those that the conventions explicitly address. Rather, such instruction must enable students to recognize the problems of greatest concern in the profession, particularly those that arise in the student's specific field of inquiry, and to gain access to the professional and legal literature in which those problems are considered. It is difficult to see how even this more limited objective can be accomplished without focused and explicit attention on the conventions and their related texts, but the specifics of this attention may vary considerably with the phenomena of interest and the research techniques of the students' programs.

Just as critical to induction as mastery of the content of the conventions is the attitude that students learn to bring to the research enterprise. Students must come to see themselves as members of the education research professions, with obligations to the organizations and laws that define and embody them. For without the motivation that this developed attitude implies—the willingness to refer and defer to the ethical standards of their research enterprise—any command of the conventions that students gain will seem irrelevant to them. The habits that students form in assessing others' research and in devising their own, including the habits of considering the relationship between the construction of particular research studies and the dicta of the relevant professional organizations and laws, are vital to developing a respect for ethical standards of their research enterprise. Only sustained attention to the ethics of research as articulated in the professional and legal literature can develop these habits.

Second, the goal of enabling students to join the conversation about the ethics of education research implies not just an education in the conventions of that conversation but also in how the adequacy of those conventions can be assessed. Here, the instructional purpose is to enable students to engage in the constructive criticism of the professional and legal conventions that govern the ethics of education research. The intention is to enable students to contribute to the development of those conventions and to propose alternatives to them when necessary and appropriate.

These conventions sometimes explicitly acknowledge that the current state of their precepts and reasoning is imperfect and include an invitation to render them more adequate and complete. For example, this volume includes both easy cases, through which the meaning of the principles of the AERA Code can be explained and their application can be exemplified, and hard cases, in which those principles seem to conflict or that appear to raise issues not covered by the principles in their current form.

Similarly, the law includes both authoritative interpretations and applications, in cases where its meaning has been settled by the courts, and also instances of indeterminate or controversial significance, in cases that are still in litigation or have not yet been brought to the courts. In these latter cases, the law includes both procedures for resolving the issues and general strategies of legal argument, such as the determination of legislative intent, in accordance with which the resolution is to be framed. One objective of an education in criticism of the conventions is to enable students to participate in the clarification and extension of the conventions in ways anticipated by professional and legal authorities themselves. To this end, students need to become acquainted with the cases that those authorities judge to be difficult or indeterminate, and with the generally accepted argumentative strategies, if any, for dealing with them.

An education for criticism of the conventions cannot be limited to instances in which professional and legal authorities already foresee the need for elaboration or correction of the prevailing conventions. After all, these authorities' expectations of change are likely to be infused with the interests and prejudices of their established professional and legal stations. Thus, students must go beyond these authorities in constructing criticisms of the conventions of education research ethics. And the construction of principles and cases that represent alternatives to the judgments of these authorities is an important additional instructional objective of an education in criticism.

Now finding a standpoint that avoids all such interests and prejudices is likely to represent an impossible aspiration. Thus, at most a graduate education in criticism can seek to broaden the basis from which the shortcomings of the conventions can be viewed and expressed. There are at least two sources for the expansion of student perspectives on the conventions of education research ethics. The first is a familiarity with the meaning and application of what we have called general considerations that apply to ethical principles, such as whether they are impartial or generalizable. The second is the construction or interpretation of cases from the perspective of various parties—children, women, ethnic minorities, and others. Such cases seek to expand the range of contextual considerations brought to bear on the ethics of education research.

Just as the attitude to be developed in the induction of students into the conventions of ethics is their identification with the profession, the attitude to be developed in the criticism of those conventions is ideally the identification with humanity more broadly. These general and expanded contextual considerations represent an effort to become more inclusive in the sources of students' criticism of the conventions. Of course, there is an inevitable tension between these two attitudes. But progress in the understanding and resolution of ethical concerns depends profoundly upon students' appreciation of this tension and their attempts to achieve reflective equilibrium in the face of such tension.

The content of an education for participation in the ongoing conversation about the ethics of education research can be summarized in a deceptively simple table:

		INSTRUCTIONAL PURPOSE	
		Induction	*Criticism*
STUDENT LEARNING	*Instructional Objectives*	Recognition and Access	Participation and Construction
	Attitudes	Identification with the Profession	Identification with Humanity

Of course, we have spoken in general terms to the occasions for and content of graduate education in the ethics of research in education; the details of carrying out such an education effectively depend on the imagination and inventiveness of instructors and students.

References

Age Discrimination in Employment Act of 1967, 42 U.S.C. § 621 *et seq.*

American Association of School Administrators. (1981). *Standards of ethics for school administrators.* Washington, DC: AASA.

American Bar Association. (1990). *Model code of professional responsibility and code of judicial conduct.* Chicago, IL: ABA.

American Educational Research Association. (1992). *Ethical standards of the American Educational Research Association.* Washington, DC: AERA.

Americans With Disabilities Act of 1990, 42 U.S.C. § 12101 *et seq.*

American Medical Association. (1996). *Code of medical ethics: Current opinions with annotations.* Chicago: AMA.

American Psychological Association. (1992). *Ethical principles of psychologists and code of conduct.* Washington, DC: APA.

Bowie v. Evanston Community Consolidated District, Dist 65, 538 N.E.2d 557 (Ill. 1989).

Bull, B., & McCarthy, M. (1995). Reflections on the knowledge base in law and ethics for educational leaders. *Educational Administration Quarterly 31,* 613–631.

Burlington Industries v. Ellerth, 524 U.S. 742 (1998).

Canter, M., Bennett, B., Jones, S., & Nagy, T. (1994). *Ethics for psychologists: A commentary on the APA ethics code.* Washington, DC: APA.

Constantinides, C. A. (1991). Professional ethics codes in court: Redefining the social contract between the public and the professions. *Georgia Law Review, 25,* 1327–1373.

Council of Chief State School Officers. (1998, August). *The interstate school leaders licensure consortium's collaborative professional development process for school leaders.* Washington, DC: CCSSO.

Davis v. Monroe County, 526 U.S. 629 (1999).

Digital Millenium Copyright Act of 1998, 17 U.S.C. § 117.

Doe v. Taylor Independent School District, 15 F.3d 443 (5th Cir. 1994), *cert. denied,* 513 U.S. 815 (1995).

Eisel v. Board of Education, 597 A.2d 447 (Md. 1991).

Elliott v. North Carolina Psychology Board, 485 S.E.2d 882 (N.C. App. 1997).

Ex parte Givens, 576 So. 2d 1277 (Ala. 1991).

Family Educational Rights and Privacy Act of 1974, 20 U.S.C. § 1232g *et seq.*

Franklin v. Gwinnett County Public Schools, 503 U.S. 60 (1992).

Freedom of Information Act, Shelby Amendment, 5 U.S.C.A. § 552 (1998).

Gebser v. Lago Vista Independent School District, 524 U.S. 274 (1998).

Girardier v. Webster College, 563 F.2d 1267 (8th Cir. 1977).

Grassley Amendment to the General Education Provisions Act, 20 U.S.C. § 1232g(c) (1994).

Hatch Amendment to the General Education Provisions Act, 20 U.S.C § 1232h (1978).

Hatch Amendment Coalition and American Educational Research Association. (1985). *The Hatch Amendment regulations: A guidelines document.* Washington, DC: AERA.

Human Rights Authority of State Guardianship Commission v. Miller, 464 N.E.2d 833 (Ill. App. Ct. 1984).

Individuals With Disabilities Education Act of 1990, 20 U.S.C. § 1401 *et seq.*

In re Cusumano, 162 F.3d 708 (1st Cir. 1998).

Jaffee v. Lu Redmond, 518 U.S. 1 (1996).

Kant, Immanuel (1785/1985). *Foundations of the metaphysics of morals.* Translation by L. W. Beck. New York: Macmillan Publishing Company.

Keith-Spiegel, P., & Koocher, G. P. (1985). *Ethics in psychology: Professional standards and cases.* New York: Random House.

Kultgen, J. (1988). *Ethics and professionalism.* Philadelphia: University of Pennsylvania Press.

Laplante v. Stewart, 470 So. 2d 1018 (La. Ct. App. 1985), *cert. denied,* 476 So. 2d 352 (La. 1985).

Lewis, A. (1985). Little-used amendment becomes divisive, disruptive issue. *Phi Delta Kappan, 66,* 668.

McCarthy, M., Bull, B., Quantz, R., & Sorenson, G. (1994). *Legal and ethical dimensions of schooling: Taxonomy and overview.* New York: McGraw-Hill Primis.

Mississippi State Board of Psychological Examiners v. Hosford, 508 So. 2d 1049 (Miss. 1987).

Murphy, J., & Shipman, N. (1999, April). *The interstate school leaders licensure consortium: A standards-based approach to strengthening educational leadership.* Paper presented at the annual meeting of the American Educational Research Association, Montreal.

Nash, R. J. (1996). *"Real world" ethics: Frameworks for educators and human service professionals.* New York: Teachers College Press.

National Council for Social Studies. (1990). *Revised code of ethics for the social studies profession.* Washington, DC: NCSS.

Parents Against Abuse in Schools v. Williamsport Area School District, 594 A.2d 796 (Pa. Commnw. Ct., 1991).

Protection of Human Subjects, 42 U.S.C. § 201 *et seq.*

Rawls, J. (1972). *A theory of justice.* Cambridge, MA: Harvard University Press.

Rothman v. Emory University, 828 F. Supp. 537 (N.D. Ill. 1993).

Ruzicka v. Conde Nast Publications, 939 F.2d 578 (8th Cir. 1991).

Stearns, L. (1992). Copy wrong: Plagiarism, process, property, and the law. *California Law Review, 80,* 513–553.

Stefkovich, J. A., & Shapiro, J. P. (1999, April). *The ethic of the profession: A paradigm for the preparation of ethical educational leaders for the 21st century.* Paper presented at the annual meeting of the American Educational Research Association, Montreal.

Stoneking v. Bradford Area School District, 882 F.2d 720 (3d Cir. 1989), *cert. denied,* 493 U.S. 1044 (1990).

Title IX of the Education Amendments of 1972, 20 U.S.C. § 1681 *et seq.*

Title VII of the Civil Rights Act of 1964, 42 U.S.C. § 2000e *et seq.*

Western Services, Inc. v. Sargent School District No. RE-33J, 719 P.2d 355 (Colo. Ct. App. 1986), *rev'd en banc,* 751 P.2d 56 (Colo. 1988).

Wolfram, C. (1979). The code of professional responsibility as a measure of attorney liability in civil litigation. *South Carolina Law Review, 30,* 281–319.

Wood v. Strickland, 420 U.S. 308 (1975).

Wright, C. A. (1998). *Federal practice and procedure,* 3d ed. (Civil Section), St. Paul: West.

NOTES

PART I

1. Kuhn, T. (1970). *The Structure of Scientific Revolutions.* Chicago : University of Chicago Press.

2. AERA has endorsed a statement issued by the American Council on Education titled "On the Importance of Diversity in Higher Education." This statement was published in the February 12, 1999, issue of the *Chronicle of Higher Education* and is available on the AERA Web site.

PART II

1. *The Belmont Report: Ethical Principles and Guidelines for the Protection of Human Subjects of Research*, The National Commission for the Protection of Human Subjects of Biomedical and Behavioral Research. Washington, DC: U.S. Government Printing Office, 1978. DHEW Publication No. (OS) 78-0012. Reprinted in Federal Register 44 (April 18, 1979): 23192.

PART IV

1. *Publication Manual of the American Psychological Association,* 4th ed. (Washington, DC: American Psychological Association, 1994), pp. 50–59.

McCARTHY AND BULL ESSAY

1. A revision of the 1992 version is now under consideration and is scheduled to be acted upon in 2002.

2. In addition to provisions of professional ethics codes that address confidentiality, all states by statute recognize psychotherapist privilege. For a list of these laws by state, see footnote 11 in *Jaffee v. Lu Redmond* (1996).